THE GROWTH OF GOVERNMENT

By the same author
Statesmen in Disguise

The Growth of Government

The Development of Ideas about the Role
of the State and the Machinery and Functions
of Government in Britain since 1780

GEOFFREY K FRY

FRANK CASS

First published 1979 in Great Britain by
FRANK CASS AND COMPANY LIMITED
Gainsborough House, Gainsborough Road,
London, E11 1RS, England

and in the United States of America by
FRANK CASS AND COMPANY LIMITED
c/o Biblio Distribution Centre
81 Adams Drive, P.O. Box 327, Totowa, N.J. 07511

British Library Cataloguing in Publication Data

Fry, Geoffrey Kingdon
    The growth of government.
    1. Great Britain — Politics and government — 1760–1820
    2. Great Britain — Politics and government — 19th century
    3. Great Britain — Politics and government — 20th century
    354'.41'0009   JN210

ISBN 0–7146–3116–7

Printed in Great Britain by
The Bourne Press, 3–11 Spring Road, Bournemouth

To My Wife

Contents

Preface

This is an historical study of the growth of government in Britain. It was begun in 1970, and that is the point down to which the study is really taken. The most recent developments in government necessarily receive only limited attention, and the author hopes to publish separately a fuller study of administrative change in Britain since the 1950s. God willing, I hope to follow the present book with another historical study, this time about why the role of government changed, a convincing explanation of which requires more comparative work to be done.

The present book is derived from a much larger manuscript. The original manuscript covered the period from 1485 and included material about the machinery of government down to 1780, and a detailed history of the changing functions of the State in the economy and in social provision. To keep the book within the bounds of economic viability the above-mentioned material has been discarded.

Multi-disciplinary work of the kind that this book is based on is difficult to sustain without help and encouragement from others. Almost all of this support has come from serving or former members of the staff of the University of Leeds: Maurice Beresford, Forrest Capie, Doreen Collins, Christie Davies, Alan Deacon, Heather Fry, Justin Grossman, Harry Hanson, Owen Hartley, Harold Hillman, Maurice Kirk, James Macdonald, Peter Sedgwick, Harold Seidman, and Dennis Warwick. I am indebted also to Jindrich Veverka and Nevil Johnson. When I say that none of these scholars can bear any responsibility for what appears in this book I am not being merely formal. Their views are not my views. I am responsible for the contents of this book.

The staff of the Brotherton Library at Leeds, and particularly of its Inter-Library Loan Service, were very helpful in locating the literature for this book. I am especially grateful to Jenny Cooksey, Yvonne Fennell, Tim Hargreave, Anne Reed, Hugh Wellesley-Smith and Ruth Taylor. To the extent that the literature was from government sources, I am grateful to the Controller of Her Majesty's Stationery Office for general permission to quote from its published material.

The Select Bibliography means what it says. It contains a selection of the works that I have found most useful in writing this book. I have largely left out the material contained in the extensive bibliography of my earlier book, *Statesmen in Disguise*, including government paper.

I take this opportunity too of thanking Alex Robson for her excellent typing of the manuscript, and Janet Brown for her meticulous proof reading.

This book is dedicated to my wife, Heather Fry, whose idea it was, and without whom it would never have been completed.

March 1978   G K FRY

Chapter 1

The Growth of Government

What should government do? Few would dispute governmental responsibility for such functions as the maintenance of internal law and order, and also of external defence and the conduct of foreign policy. Controversy over the role of the State is chiefly concerned with its functions in relation to the economy and social welfare. Should government abstain from interference in the economy as much as possible? Should it control the economy? Should it manage the economy, whilst leaving most of it in private ownership? Should the State leave social provision mainly to individuals and groups, or should it dominate such provision itself?

Since the time of Adam Smith, liberalism has provided most of the British answers to these questions. Liberalism was for long the British ideology.[1] Liberal theorists from Smith to John Stuart Mill provided a rationale for *laissez-faire*. Thomas Hill Green turned liberalism towards the Welfare State, as did the economics of Alfred Marshall. Liberal politicians such as Asquith and Lloyd George played a major practical part in extending the State's role in social welfare. The liberal economist, John Maynard Keynes provided the managing theory for the Managed Economy. Sir William Beveridge, the author of the Report that remains the core of the Welfare State, was not always intellectually loyal to liberalism. Nevertheless, he stood as a Liberal in the 1945 Election.[2] The Labour victory in that

Election seemed to confirm a new order. The Positive State or
the Managed Economy Welfare State, which was mainly constructed in the period during and immediately after the Second
World War, was the creation of Conservative and Fabian as
well as liberal ideas and action. Yet, the Fabians claimed it for
themselves. There was rough justice in this. The Fabians, after
all, had come nearest to predicting what the general outlines of
the new dispensation would be. They approved of its mass
bureaucracies. They were the most enthusiastic for going farther,
as was done in the extension of public ownership in the economy
and in State social provision. By the middle of the twentieth
century, the Positive State had been established with a massively
extended range of economic and social welfare functions compared with those performed by government in the nineteenth
century.

This book is an historical study of the growth of government
which has taken place in Britain during the last two hundred
years.

There is not much doubt about the general scale of governmental growth over that period, even though it is difficult to
establish in detail. From the statistics which are available, it can
be seen that between 1790 and 1910 – when the respective
figures were both 12 per cent – the proportion of the Gross
National Product accounted for by public expenditure averaged
about 13 per cent, and never went above 23 per cent. Since 1920,
the proportion of the Gross National Product accounted for by
government expenditure has never been below 24 per cent in any
year. Indeed, since 1946, it has never been below 36 per cent in
any year. To take another measure, the cumulative rate of increase per annum in government expenditure was 3·7 per cent
during the period 1890–1961, compared with 1·9 per cent during
the years 1790–1890, and 2·7 per cent over the whole period
1790–1961. This was despite the fact that the rate of population
increase and the growth of the Gross National Product was
slower in the period 1890–1961 than in the other periods. To
take a further measure, the numbers in government employment
probably more than doubled between 1850 and 1890 at a time
when the labour force generally increased by 40 per cent.
Between 1890 and 1950, while the working population rose by
57 per cent, the numbers of public employees increased by almost

1,000 per cent. The proportion of the working population accounted for by government employment increased from 2·4 per cent in 1850 to 3·6 per cent in 1890 to 24·3 per cent in 1950. Moreover, not only has the extent of State activity changed considerably, so has the range of governmental functions. Although the nineteenth century was one in which Britain was not involved in a major war after 1815, war related expenditure represented 44·9 per cent of all government spending in 1890. In 1950, halfway through a century in which there had already been two World Wars, war related expenditure represented 11·6 per cent of the Gross National Product compared with 4 per cent sixty years before. However, it only accounted for 29·7 per cent of all government expenditure. By 1950, the most important area of public expenditure had become the social services (meaning mainly public provision for education, child care, health services, national insurance, national assistance, family allowances, and housing). Between 1890 and 1950, public spending on the social services increased from 1·9 per cent of the Gross National Product to 18 per cent; and from 20·9 per cent to 46·1 per cent of government expenditure.[3]

This study of the growth of government in Britain since 1780 relates changing ideas about what the State should do to what government has come to do, and relates them all to the machinery available.

Part I of this book considers changing ideas about the role of government during the last two hundred years. The ideas of economists and political philosophers have been an important influence in helping to create the climate of opinion about what the role of the State should be. There is no published work which covers the period from Adam Smith to Keynes as a whole, and which studies it from this perspective. A study of such ideas is essential to a book on the growth of government. Keynes went too far when he said that the ideas of economists and political philosophers are the decisive influence in changing society. Keynes's own intellectual triumph seems evidence for his case, at least in relation to Britain. Yet, he himself conceded that the contemporary mood in the 1930s was a particularly favourable one for the kind of fundamental diagnosis of the working of the economy which he felt that his *General Theory* represented. More often, as Keynes said, it was 'the gradual encroachment of ideas' which took place.[4] The swift victory that fell to Keynes had tended to be denied to his intellectual predecessors. There was a time lag before the ideas of Adam Smith triumphed over those which he attributed to the mercantile system. Similarly, the undermining of the dominance of the Classical Economists by later liberals, and also by the eclectic Fabians, took time. Even then, the intellectual breaks were not usually complete. Keynes certainly remained a prisoner of his intellectual past, although he did not recognize this. What he did see was that his 'new theory' would be changed when it was 'mixed with politics and feelings and passions'.[5] The translation of theory into practice is unlikely to be a straightforward process. Ideas may not work in the manner expected either by their advocates or their opponents. Moreover, there are few theories about the role of government which are not capable of differing interpretations. Even when it seems to be clear what prevailing opinion says that the State should do, the machinery of government may not be able to perform the preferred role.

Part II of this book examines the developments of the machinery of government in Britain since 1780 in relation to its 'traditional' as well as economic and social welfare functions, and against the background of the preceding examination of changing ideas about the role of government. There is no other published work which does this. Most attention is given to the machinery and functions of government in relation to the economy and social provision, because these are the main areas of controversy about the role of the State and where the changes in that role have been most marked. Sole consideration has not been given to such functions because, for much of the period, the 'traditional' functions of government – law and order, defence, conduct of foreign policy, imperial management – dominated State activity, and, with the exception of imperial management, remain important. Moreover, as they are not contentious, in the sense that few would dispute that if such functions are to be performed they should be the responsibility of government, then 'traditional' functions can be taken as representing a base line from which to measure change.

The normal pattern which emerges from this study of the development of the machinery and functions of government in Britain is one of continuity and slow change. During some periods, of course, the pace of change has been faster than in others. This is particularly, and predictably, true of periods of war, especially total war, and their aftermath. The portrayal of periods of British administrative development – such as the middle quarters of the nineteenth century – in revolutionary terms may make for greater excitement on the part of both writers and readers;[6] but incremental growth is what actually characterized that particular period and most others. The increments are not necessarily closely related to changes in ideas about the role of the State.

As one should expect, there is a gap between the aspirations of government action and their realization. For example, in the supposed age of mercantilism, there was a widespread belief in the virtues of government regulation of the economy. What was lacking was effective machinery to do the regulation. Similarly, in the nineteenth century, when, even with *laissez-faire* as the dominant ideology, governments wished to closely regulate public health, the lack of efficient machinery was a factor limiting the effectiveness of intervention. The ambitions of the twentieth century Managed Economy Welfare State are immodest. Previous inhibitions about public expenditure were undermined by the popularized lessons of Keynes and the experience of total war. Nevertheless, contrary to contemporary expectations, recent experience has been that the State cannot at one and the same time increase real incomes, achieve price stability, sustain full employment, and constantly expand the social services. Modern British government is not generally short of machinery, but the successful pursuit of all these aims has proved beyond its capacity.

The historical evidence in this book does not provide us with a full explanation of the growth of government in Britain since 1780. It does provide a partial explanation in the sense that it explores the interplay between prevailing ideas on the role of government, the State's formal responsibilities, and actual practice. This book begins with an analysis of the ideas of the Classical Economists on the role of government.

PART ONE

CHANGING IDEAS ABOUT THE ROLE OF GOVERNMENT SINCE 1780

Chapter 2

The Classical Economists and Government

If government closely regulated the economy, then a country prospered. That was the dominant view in British political economy as Adam Smith found it in 1776, when he published the *Wealth of Nations*. It was a view that he forcefully dissented from. The existing system, he said, did not benefit either Britain or the world. Only his preferred liberal system of economics could do that. The beneficiaries of the existing system were manufacturers and, particularly, merchants. The system was thus well called the mercantile system. It rested on two principles. One was the belief that wealth consisted in gold and silver. The other was that these metals could be brought into a country which had no mines only by the balance of trade, or by a country exporting a greater value of goods than it imported. The system's two great engines for enriching the country, therefore, were restraints on imports and encouragements to export.

The various means that were employed included high protective duties; various export subsidies; bounties to encourage favoured industries; and the acquisition of privileges or monopolies for British goods and merchants abroad by treaties or by the establishment of colonies.[1] The balance of trade and the other ideas that Smith associated with the mercantile system, he subjected to relentless criticism in the course of promoting his own preferred free market system. A necessary casualty of this assault was belief in the virtues of State control of the economy.

Whether pre-Smithian writers actually or only believed in the mercantile system as depicted by its sworn adversary can be doubted. As a description of the active arrangements for economic regulation in his time, Smith's picture of the mercantilist system had an unrealistic coherence. Did Smith similarly mis-represent mercantilist theory? Taking the period between 1500 and Smith's time as a whole, there were sufficient theorists for this to be a risk. The belief in the need to accumulate bullion seems to have been less pronounced after the trade crisis of the 1620s. Against this, the balance of trade was certainly a continuing and distinctive feature of mercantilist thought. The overriding concern of the mercantilists seemed to be to try to secure full employment. The accumulation of bullion and a favourable balance of trade were means of achieving this goal. Smith seems to have overlooked the concern of some of his intellectual predecessors with contemporary problems of under-employment and the resulting poverty. The mercantilist writers' policy recommendations and proposed institutional instrumentalities were not based upon any highly unified body of economic thought.[2] What they did was to accord government a more positive role in economic affairs than that generally favoured by their immediate intellectual successors, Smith and the other Classical Economists.

Although their ideas were challenged by Tories such as Carlyle, the Lake Poets, and Shaftesbury, the Classical Economists were the dominant force in British political economy between the publication of the *Wealth of Nations* and the 1870s, and influential long after that. Among the Classical Economists can be counted David Hume, Adam Smith, David Ricardo, Jeremy Bentham, Thomas Robert Malthus, James Mill, Robert Torrens, John Ramsay McCulloch, Nassau William Senior, John Stuart Mill, and John Elliott Cairnes.[3] Generalizations are difficult about a School characterized by the longevity of its existence and by so many members. The experience, talents and relative influence of those members differed considerably. There were divisions between members, notably between Ricardo and Malthus; a division which Keynes saw as crucial to the subsequent development of economics. Even J S Mill had his difficulties in constructing a Classical synthesis in successive editions of his *Principles of Political Economy* from 1848 onwards. Yet, the general role that the Classical Economists assigned to the State was clear enough. It was a limited role. They were advocates of the free market system with its connotation of the minimization of government economic activity. They relied on market forces to resolve the basic economic problems such as resource allocation and income distribution. They emphasized private property and free enterprise with private participation as buyers, sellers, consumers and investors. In other words, they favoured just such ideas as the term *laissez-faire* signifies.[4] The Classical Economists provided the theory for the Gold Standard. They provided the theory for Free Trade. That they did not always support even the latter without qualification is an indication of the pragmatism which normally characterized their work, as the following summaries of that work show.

I. ADAM SMITH

The economic philosophy of Adam Smith was subtler than the most quotable parts of the *Wealth of Nations* led some of his later interpreters to believe. Despite the vigour of his advocacy of the virtues of *laissez-faire* in principle, Smith was not dogmatic about its application.

This is not to say that he pulled many punches in his onslaught on what he saw as the existing system of governmental regulation of the economy in the interests of merchants and manufacturers. Those interests, he said, were never the same as those of the public. The system was characterized by price fixing, and by monopoly of one kind or another. Whereas consumption should be the sole end and purpose of all production, the interest of the consumer was almost constantly being sacrificed to that of the producer. Smith wanted the apprenticeship regulations, the Settlement Laws, the Corn Laws, the privileges of the overseas trading companies, the costly colonial system, and the rest of what he saw as the paraphernalia of mercantilism to be swept away. This paraphernalia was obstructing the maximization of the annual produce of the land and labour of the country, or real wealth.[5]

What Smith fervently believed would maximize real wealth was a free, competitive domestic market combined with external Free Trade. The extension of the market that would result would encourage an increased division of labour. This would make possible, among other things, greater mechanization and, therefore, greater productivity. The capital accumulation necessary for sustaining the system would take place because the desire to save was 'with us from the womb and never leaves us till we go into the grave'. Moreover, every individual was 'constantly exerting himself to find the most advantageous employment for whatever capital he can command. It is his own advantage indeed, and not that of the society, which he has in view. But the study of his own advantage naturally, or rather necessarily leads him to prefer that employment which is most advantageous to the society'.

Smith believed that an individual by directing an industry 'in such a manner as its produce may be of greatest value' necessarily labours 'to render the annual revenue of the society as great as he can'. For, although 'he intends only his own gain', he was in this, as in many other cases, led by an invisible hand to promote an end which was no part of his intention. Nor was it 'always the worse for the society that it was no part of it', because, by pursuing his own interest, the individual 'frequently promotes that of the society more effectively than when he really intends to promote it'.[6]

If the swiftest way for a society to increase wealth was to adopt Smith's 'obvious and simple system of natural liberty', what was the role of the State to be? Under such a system, 'the sovereign is completely discharged from a duty, in the attempting to perform which he must always be exposed to innumerable delusions, and for the proper performance of which no human wisdom or knowledge could ever be sufficient; the duty of superintending the industry of private people, and of directing it towards the employments most suitable to the interest of the society'. The sovereign had only three duties under Smith's preferred system. Together with the power to raise the revenue to meet the expense involved, these duties were defence, the administration of justice, and the erection and maintenance of certain public works and institutions.[7]

The first duty of the sovereign was that of 'protecting the

society from the violence and invasion of other independent societies'. This was a duty which could be performed only by means of a military force. Smith in fact described defence as being of much more importance than opulence. This led him to acknowledge that defence needs might make it prudent for Britain to subsidize certain domestic manufactures rather than place reliance on foreign suppliers. It also led him, whilst still generally critical of them, to describe the Navigation Acts as 'perhaps the wisest of all the commercial regulations of England'. This was because they promoted English shipping, and, therefore, naval strength, the main essential for defence.[8]

The second duty of the sovereign was that of 'protecting, as far as possible, every member of the society from the injustice or oppression of every other member of it, or the duty of establishing an exact administration of justice'. Smith recognized the need for some sort of police or city guard for the execution of justice in the sense of crime prevention. He believed that 'commerce and manufactures can seldom flourish long in any state which does not enjoy a regular administration of justice'. People needed to feel secure in the possession of their property. Contracts had to be supported by law. The authority of the State had to be used to enforce the payments of debts from all those able to pay. It can be noted that Smith in fact favoured governmental regulation of the banking system on the same principles as building party walls in order to prevent the spread of fire. Otherwise, he feared, the security of the whole society might be threatened.[9]

The third and last duty of the sovereign was that of 'erecting and maintaining those public institutions and those public works, which, though they may be in the highest degree advantageous to a great society are, however, of such a nature, that the profit could never repay the expense to any individual or small number of individuals, and which it therefore cannot be expected that any individual or small number of individuals should erect or maintain'. For Smith, this meant not only the public works and institutions connected with defence and the administration of justice. It also meant, among others, those connected with education, and those which facilitated commerce such as good roads, bridges, navigable canals and harbours. Smith thought that private persons could not be trusted to maintain highways adequately; but he generally seemed to prefer them, rather than government commissioners, to run canals. He believed that the Post Office was perhaps the only mercantile project which had been successfully managed by every sort of government.

As regards education of the young, he considered that the education of the common people needed more public attention in a civilized and commercial society than that of rank and fortune. He thought that the most essential parts of education – the ability to 'read, write, and account' – could be encouraged for a very small expense. It could be done, as in Scotland, by establishing in every parish or district a little school where children could be educated at a cost so moderate that even a common labourer could afford it; the master being partly, but not wholly, paid for by the public. Smith envisaged people of all ages receiving formal religious instruction. He saw education as encouraging a respect for public order among 'the inferior ranks of the people'. He saw it too as a possible corrective to the deleterious effects that he feared that the division of labour had on the intellectual, social and martial virtues of such people. Other governmental duties that Smith indicated were 'the maintenance of cleanliness', including 'carrying dirt from the streets', and responsibilities for the containment of infectious diseases. He also recognized that, since the Tudor Poor Law, the relief of the poor had come to be at least partly a communal responsibility, financed by a parish rate.[10]

How these various governmental activities were to be financed was given careful attention by Smith. His maxims for taxation were equality, certainty, convenience of payment and economy in collection. He believed that the rich should contribute more than proportionately to public revenue. His test for financing governmental functions from general taxes was whether or not they were for the general benefit. Such taxes should finance defence and the sovereign's public duties and maintenance of dignity, because society derived such benefit from them. In other cases, whether it was the administration of justice or the maintenance of public works and institutions, he thought that they ought to be financed as much as possible by those that used them. He did envisage them being subsidized from general taxation, if absolutely necessary. Local and provincial expenses, if their benefits were obtained at those levels, should be met by local and provincial taxes. Smith viewed public debts with disfavour. He believed that financing them caused resources to be diverted from productive private uses to unproductive public ones with a resulting net loss to society.[11]

The moderation of Smith's approach to the practical application of his theories contrasted with the forcefulness with which he condemned the mercantile system, and the forthrightness with which he had advocated his own preferred theories. Even if Free Trade was established, he believed that to be fair to employers it would have to be introduced 'slowly, gradually and after a very long warning'. He envisaged the continuance of moderate taxes of foreign imports, and the retention of a small tax on imported wool for revenue purposes. He was also prepared to recognize circumstances in which export restrictions on corn could be justified. Despite his distaste for trading companies, he thought that those who established 'a new trade with some remote and barbarous nation' should receive a 'temporary monopoly'. He justified this on the same principle that authors retained their copyright and inventors their patents. As Smith believed that the establishment of freedom of trade in his own country was as unlikely as that of Oceania or Utopia, his moderation was not tactical. He was a man prepared to examine his own prejudices and, as over the Navigation Acts, to modify them if this was needed to meet practical objections. He avoided outright inconsistency in his work, except in arguing for the retention of the Usury Laws on the grounds that investors could not be trusted to put their funds into productive activities.[12]

The *Wealth of Nations* was both a tract for the time and a contribution to the development of economic theory. For all the eventual moderation with which it was presented, Smith's message was clear enough. It was that the role of government in economic affairs was to be important, but subordinate. The State was to provide a framework within which competitive capitalism, the most efficient means of increasing wealth, could safely operate.

II. JEREMY BENTHAM

There seem to be almost as many interpretations of what

Jeremy Bentham believed the role of government should be as there are interpreters. That role is negative rather than positive for one interpreter, and positive rather than negative for another. There are even confusions within the work of interpreters. The same author that roundly condemned Dicey and Halévy for portraying Bentham as one of the fathers of *laissez-faire*, said that for his own time Bentham considered that the State had best practise *laissez-faire*. Bentham's writings are themselves confusing. Until relatively recently, many of them were not easily available. Even when they were made so, one commentator suggested, Bentham's views can be seen to have been constantly changing, sometimes according to a steady long term trend, sometimes simply fluctuating around the trend, or according to no discernible trend. Nonetheless, the commentator concerned felt able to suggest that Bentham was more the prophet of the Welfare State than of the Gladstonian Budget.[13] Bentham certainly anticipated some later developments in State social provision, particularly in his posthumously published *Constitutional Code*. His utilitarian creed, though, is best seen as a pragmatic one. For his own time, that creed certainly pointed to a role for the State in economic affairs of *laissez-faire*.

Under Bentham's principle of utility, the 'all embracing end' of a community was 'the greatest happiness of the greatest number of the individuals belonging to the community in question'. The means of achieving that end, themselves subordinate ends, were security, equality, subsistence, and abundance (or opulence as he also called it). That the uncoerced and unenlightened propensities and powers of individuals were inadequate to attain the greatest happiness without government intervention was 'a matter of fact of which the evidence of history, the nature of man, and the very existence of political society are so many proofs'. Of the four subordinate ends of political action, security was more especially and essentially the work of the legislator than subsistence, opulence and equality, where his interference was comparatively unnecessary.[14]

Bentham left to the spontaneous actions of individuals 'practically all the operations by which increase of wealth is produced in a direct way'. As for the *agenda* of government, the 'general rule' should be that 'nothing ought to be done or attempted by government for the purpose of causing an augmentation to take place in the national mass of wealth, with a view to increase of the means of either subsistence or enjoyment, without some special reason. *Be quiet* ought on those occasions to be the motto, or watchword, of government'. Government intervention to promote wealth was needless. 'The wealth of the whole community is composed of the wealth of the several individuals belonging to it taken together', and 'to increase his particular portion' was 'generally speaking, among the constant objects of each individual's exertions and care'. There was 'no one who knows what it is for your interest to do as you yourself: no one who is disposed with so much ardour and constancy to pursue it'.

Government intervention was likely to be unconducive, even obstructive, to the promotion of wealth because 'each individual, bestowing more time and attention upon the means of preserving and increasing his portion of wealth than is or can be bestowed by government, is likely to take a more effectual course than what in his instance and on his behalf could be taken by government'. The inter-position of government was pernicious because it meant constraints being imposed on the free agency of the individual. Bentham declared that 'coercion, the inseparable accompaniment, precedent, concomitant, or subsequent, of every act of government, is in itself an evil: to be anything better than a pure evil, it requires to be followed by some more than equivalent good. Spontaneous action excludes it: action, on the part of government, and by impulse from government supposes it'.[15]

Where Bentham did think it was 'necessary or expedient' for the State 'to interfere for the purpose of regulating the exertions of individuals' was primarily with regard to 'security in respect of subsistence and security in respect of defence'. Nevertheless, his position on defence was a complex one. In arguing against colonies because they increased the chances of war, he said it was not in Britain's interest to have a naval force beyond that sufficient to defend its commerce against pirates. So, he condemned the Navigation Acts. However, he also said that if it was generally desired to make provision for defence, then measures such as the Navigation Acts were necessary, because they encouraged maritime skills and provided naval reserves.

Regarding what he called 'national security in respect of subsistence' he thought that 'what an individual is glad to give to
insure himself against loss by fire, governments need not scruple
to give to insure its subjects in this way against loss and distress
by scarcity'. For example, the State ought to maintain stocks of
grain as a safeguard against famine.[16]

Bentham did envisage government intervention to ensure 'the
removal of obstructions to *sponte acta*'. Among other things,
this would enable individuals 'spontaneously associated for the
purpose to give a more effectual combination to their exertions
in the pursuit of a common end'. For instance, where 'corporate
powers are requisite for the management of a common stock'.
Bentham believed in the local provision of public works in
times of a temporary stagnation of trade. If necessary, they
could be subsidised from national funds. Examples of such
works he gave included the digging of canals, the deepening of
harbours and road construction. He indicated approval of
government supported education, because of the public benefit
to be gained by the diffusion of knowledge which would not
otherwise take place. He advocated a public system of social
insurance on a voluntary basis, including contributory old age
pensions to be paid out through the medium of the Post Office.
He envisaged government supported hospitals for the incurable
sick and helpless, the curable sick and hurt among the poor, and
for the prevention or mitigation of contagious diseases. He also
thought that the State should provide 'establishments for the
occasional maintenance and employment of the able bodied
among the poor'. Bentham seriously drew up plans for a
Panopticon or Inspection House, which would be applicable
'without exception to all establishments whatsoever'. He
believed that morals would be reformed, health would be preserved, public opinion would be enlightened, economy would
be 'seated . . . upon a rock', and 'the gordian knot of the Poor
Laws not cut, but untied – all by a simple idea in architecture!'
The government of the day was less enthusiastic about Bentham's
scheme, a fact he resentfully attributed to the personal opposition of the monarch.[17]

While his more grandiose schemes were not implemented –
such as another one that he had for a joint stock National
Charity Company – Bentham's views on retaining, but reform-

ing, the Poor Law were important. He was, for instance, an advocate of the principle of less eligibility. For all his distaste for abstract rights, Bentham came closer than most of his contemporaries to consistently asserting the right of the poor to relief through a legal provision. Bentham wrote that 'in his endeavour to provide a remedy against deficiency, in regard to subsistence, the legislator finds himself all along under the pressure of this dilemma – forbear to provide supply, and death ensues, and it has you for its author; provide supply, you establish a bounty upon idleness, and you give increase to the deficiency it is your endeavour to exclude. Under the pressure of this dilemma, how to act is a problem, the solution of which will in a great degree, be dependent upon local circumstances: nor can anything like a complete solution be so much as attempted without continual reference to them. One leading observation applies to all places and all times. So long as any particle of the matter of abundance remains in any one hand, it will rest with those, to whom it appears that they are able to assign a sufficient reason, to show why the requisite supply to any deficiency in the means of subsistence should be refused'.[18]

An Indigence Relief Minister, an Education Minister, and a Health Minister were among the posts provided for in the ministerial structure Bentham proposed in his *Constitutional Code*. This structure was an elaborate one for his time. It was headed by a Prime Minister. It also included a Justice Minister, an Election Minister, a Legislation Minister, an Army Minister, a Navy Minister, a Preventive Service Minister, an Interior Communication Minister, a Domain Minister, a Foreign Relation Minister, a Trade Minister, and a Finance Minister. As for the duties of, for instance, the Prevention Service Minister, examples of 'the principal calamities to which prevention is capable of being applied under the care of government' included 'disease and mortality, the results of unhealthy and unmedicated situations'.

They included also 'unhealthy employments, the unhealthiness of which is capable of being removed or lessened by appropriate arrangements'; natural disasters; contagious diseases; and dearth and famine. The Preventive Service Minister had responsibility for police and fire services. The Domain Minister had responsibility for subjects not assigned to others. The Health Minister had responsibility for 'the preservation of the national health'. Bentham said that it would be preferable if both Ministers and their various subordinates had specialised knowledge of the most relevant subject matters, where this was practicable. He thought that not just administrative staff, but also judges and legislators should be selected by public examination, although mainly to save money he did make provision for this principle to be modified in practice.[19]

Bentham considered that the system under which the utilitarian aim of the 'greatest happiness' was most likely to be realised was representative democracy. One of the features of the ideal system that he outlined in his *Code* was a supreme and omnicompetent legislature. This was to be elected on the basis of equal electoral districts by means of a secret ballot on a universal male franchise. The executive was to be directly answerable to this legislature. Bentham emphasized the individual responsibility of Ministers, and he compared administrative boards not under direct parliamentary surveillance with screens. He also envisaged a system of elected local authorities with, where relevant, similar fields of activity to those practised at the centre, but with some scope for experiments in legislation. Among other functions, there was to be local provision for the collection of data about births, deaths and marriages. Indeed, throughout the *Code*, Bentham emphasized the need for the government to take seriously the collection of statistics, just as he did the 'inspective function' of government.[20] He wanted government to take informed decisions, and to see that they were being carried out.

There was little doubt about Bentham's radical intent in drawing up his *Constitutional Code*. He said at the outset that 'in whatever political community' it was adopted, 'it would, to a greater or less extent, probably to a very large extent, involve the abolition of the existing institutions'. In Britain, for example, he envisaged the abolition of the monarchy and of the House of Lords. His radicalism, however, had limits. One writer associated him with beliefs in proportional representation, a national high wages policy, and the redistribution of corporate profits largely as wage increases. In fact, Bentham's attitude towards taxation was that it was needed to finance government activity, given that the money would not be otherwise forthcoming from the spontaneous actions of individuals. He believed that indirect taxes were preferable to direct taxes. He wrote in terms that anticipated the Iron Law of Wages, and which expounded Wage Fund theory. He also recognised the importance of the profit motive, and criticized the 'mischievous prejudice' against it.

Bentham's belief in the free market was such at one time that he severely criticized Smith's remarks about retaining the Usury Laws, and pleaded with him to recant. Bentham's radicalism did not extend to socialism. He did not envisage fundamentally altering the system of private property, although he did propose the imposition of moderate death duties. He did favour measures which 'gently' led to the acquisition of wealth; but he did say that by equality he meant 'not the utmost conceivable equality but only practicable equality'. Although he believed that all men have been placed 'under the governance of two sovereign masters, pain and pleasure', he recognized that 'sum for sum, the enjoyment from gain is never an equivalent for the suffering from loss. If it were, the reason for the creation and preservation of property would cease'.[21] He was clear enough that what men principally wanted from government was security.

Bentham's views on the role of the State were grounded in pragmatism. He wrote: 'The imposition of government may be desirable or not, according to the state of the account: according as the inconveniences attached to the measures in which the interposition of government consists, preponderate or fail of preponderating over the advantage resulting from the effect which it is proposed should be produced'. The role that he ascribed to government in economic matters was neither positive nor negative, but dependent on the circumstances. In much the same way, for example, his advocacy of Free Trade was modified by his recognition of the possible need to protect infant industries. It will be recalled that his attitude to provision for defence was similarly pragmatic.

In proposing that the machinery of government should be remodelled, Bentham may have been pointing to the collectivism of the future, particularly as he made it clear that the machinery was to be actively employed. On the other hand, his eventual attitude to public expenditure had more in common with the

Gladstonian Budget than the Welfare State. Bentham was no dogmatic advocate of *laissez-faire*. Nonetheless, he did seem to believe that the more highly developed a nation was economically, the more activites fell under the head of *sponte acta*. The more backward a country was, the more activities were *agenda* for government.[22] That contemporaries, and many who followed, equated Benthamism with a belief in a restricted role for the State in the economy is understandable.

III. DAVID RICARDO

'If only Malthus, instead of Ricardo, had been the parent stem from which nineteenth century economics proceeded, what a much wiser and richer place the world would be today'.[7] Keynes's famous remark[23] overrated the coherence of Malthus's economic theorizing and misjudged its content. Nonetheless, David Ricardo's importance was considerable. He literally invented the technique of economists when he published his *Principles of Political Economy* in 1817. He also made clear his preferred economic policies.[24] For instance, he was both an author of the theory of comparative costs, and an advocate of Free Trade. It was Ricardo's theoretical position on effective demand, and the policy attitudes that followed from it, that caused Keynes to regret Malthus's relative unimportance in economics.

Ricardo accepted Say's Law that 'supply creates its own demand'. Ricardo's economic model assumed that economies tended towards a full employment equilibrium. He assumed government activity to be either unproductive, or, at best diversionary. When in the situation of mass unemployment and distress that followed the Napoleonic Wars, public works were proposed by Malthus among others to alleviate it, he told Parliament that the capital that would be used 'in the formation of roads and canals' would be 'withdrawn from another quarter'. In a letter to Malthus, he wrote: 'I am not one of those who think that the raising of funds for the purpose of employing the poor is a very efficacious mode of relief, as it diverts those funds from other employments which would be equally if not more productive to the community. That part of the capital which employs the poor on the roads, for example, cannot fail to employ men somewhere and I believe every interference is prejudicial'.[25]

Whereas Ricardo believed that 'to save is to spend', Malthus thought that above a certain level saving could result in the labouring classes being thrown out of work because of the diminution of 'the effectual demand for produce'. He believed that 'it is obvious that the adoption of parsimonious habits beyond a certain point may be accompanied by the most distressing effects at first, and by a marked depression of wealth and population afterwards'. Malthus, however, was doomed to lose in his subsequent dispute with Ricardo over economic theory. As he tended to argue that no new investment could be profitable unless preceded by extra consumption, it followed that expenditure on public works, which he favoured, would worsen any tendency to excess supply operative in the economy. In fact, in reply to Ricardo, Malthus actually agreed with him that 'the funds for the support of the poor (though perhaps necessary at the moment) essentially interfere with other employments'. Keynes found 'the completeness of the Ricardian victory' over Malthus's ideas on effective demand 'something of a curiosity and a mystery'. He suggested one reason himself when he said that, apart from an appeal to the facts of common observation, Malthus was unable to explain his position clearly.[26] Whereas Malthus lacked a coherent economic theory, Ricardo was able to present one that seemed to have the virtues of both elegance and logic.

Ironically, Ricardo's theoretical models tended to have so many assumptions built into them, that their practical utility was often minimal. This did not deter their author from applying them, and making what he saw as appropriate policy recommendations. This has been called the Ricardian Vice.[27] More ironically still, Keynes was to be a later victim of this Vice.

Ricardo's attitude towards the role of the State was not entirely a restrictive one. He did say that such were the advantages of 'liberty of trade' that there were only 'a few exceptions to it where the interference of government may be beneficially exerted'. He associated himself with the view that government intervention was 'justifiable in only two cases; first, to prevent a fraud, and secondly, to certify a fact'. This, however, included coinage, and in fact led him to advocate State regulation of the banking system. He went on to propose the establishment of a national bank. Indeed, Ricardo came into public prominence as a result of his involvement in banking controversies. He was instrumental in carrying Britain back to the Gold Standard at the old parity in 1819. His ideas on banking made him the father of the Bank Charter Act of 1844.[28] Ricardo's thinking was not thus consistently inimical to State economic activity, but *laissez-faire* was the broad message of his work.

IV. THOMAS MALTHUS

Malthus's theory of population established him as a leading figure among the Classical Economists. This theory influenced the School's attitudes, notably towards poverty in general and the State's responsibilities for alleviating it. Malthus himself advocated the abolition of the Poor Law.

The nub of Malthusian population theory, at least in its first version, was that 'the power of population is indefinitely greater than the power in the earth to produce subsistence for man. Population when unchecked, increases in a geometrical ratio. Subsistence increases only in an arithmetical ratio. A slight acquaintance with numbers will show the immensity of the first power in comparison with the second. By that Law of our nature which makes food necessary to the life of man, the effects of these two unequal powers must be kept equal. This implies a strong and constantly operating check on population from the difficulty of subsistence. This difficulty must fall somewhere and must necessarily be severely felt by a large portion of mankind'.[29] The statistics were simply not available at the time (1798) that Malthus first advanced his thesis for it to be examined on any serious factual basis. He elaborated it in the end to such an extent that it was tautological.[30] Whatever its intellectual limitations, Malthusian population theory was influential in supporting the view that poverty was beyond alleviation.

Fatalism ran through Malthus's policy prescriptions that followed from his beliefs about population growth. 'It has appeared from the inevitable laws of our nature some human beings must suffer from want' he wrote: 'these are the unhappy persons who, in the great lottery of life, have drawn a blank'. The 'pressure of distress' on 'the lower classes of society' was 'an evil so deeply seated that no human ingenuity can reach it'.

So, the various provisions of the existing Poor Law, for instance, were designed to achieve something that could not be done. Indeed, in Malthus's opinion, 'the parish laws of England have contributed to impoverish that class of people whose only possession is their labour'.

This was partly because they diminished 'the power and the will to save among the common people', who knew that they could rely upon the parish to support them in the event of accidents, and so they spent all their money on 'drunkenness and dissipation'. It was also the result of the labour market being disrupted by the obstructions of the Settlement Laws which, he thought, were in themselves 'utterly contradictory to all ideas of freedom'. As the prevention of poverty was 'beyond the power of man', it followed that 'in the vain endeavour to attain what in the nature of things is impossible, we now sacrifice not only possible but certain benefits. We tell the common people that if they submit to a code of tyrannical regulations, they shall never be in want. They do submit to these regulations. They perform their part of the contract, but we do not, nay cannot perform ours and thus the poor sacrifice the valuable blessings of liberty and receive nothing that can be called an equivalent in return'.[31]

Palliative action was all that was possible in dealing with poverty, Malthus believed. Nevertheless, 'the total abolition of all the present parish laws' would 'at any rate give liberty and freedom of action to the peasantry of England, which they can hardly be said to possess at present. They would then be able to settle without interruption wherever there was a prospect of a greater plenty of work and a higher price for labour. The market for labour would then be free, and those obstacles removed which, as things are now, often for a considerable time prevent the price from rising according to demand'. He envisaged the labourer 'being now in better circumstances, and seeing no prospect of parish assistance' as being 'more able as well as more inclined to enter into associations for providing against the sickness of himself or family'. He thought that 'for cases of extreme distress county workhouses might be established, supported by rates upon the whole kingdom, and free for persons of all counties, and indeed of all nations. The fare should be hard, and those that are able, obliged to work. It would be desirable that they should not be considered as comfortable asylums in all difficulties, but merely as places where severe distress might find some alleviation'.[32]

In his writings on the Poor Law, Malthus combined a readily comprehensible theory with a simple, straightforward policy. As will be seen, it was not a policy that commanded lasting support from other economists, except, in a qualified manner, Ricardo. Malthus's population theory, however, assured him a central position among the Classical Economists, from which he influenced their ideas on the causes of poverty and also their attitudes on wages. For his part, he generally shared their faith in the free market, although his opinion that essays in Free Trade would be unlikely to be reciprocated made him sceptical about the benefits to be gained from the repeal of the Corn Laws. In fact he echoed Smith's doubt that 'a perfect freedom of trade' was 'a vision which it is feared can never be realized'. However, he had no doubt that freedom of trade was the ideal to be aimed for, writing that 'it should be our object to make as near approaches as we can. It should always be considered as the great general rule. And when any deviations from it are proposed, those who propose them are bound clearly to make out the exception'.[33] Malthus's inclination was to minimize the role of government.

V. NASSAU SENIOR

Like Malthus, with whom he differed over population theory, Nassau Senior had a public reputation as well as a professional one as an economist. He was an architect of the Poor Law reform of 1834 and a prominent opponent of both trade unionism and factory legislation, so it is small wonder that he was portrayed as an extreme advocate of *laissez-faire* by contemporaries and historians alike. Yet, on taking up an Oxford Chair in 1826, Senior had made it clear that he regarded the explanation and cure of the poverty of the bulk of the working classes as the main task and justification of the study of economics,[34] and from time to time he associated himself with proposals that involved governmental intervention in pursuit of that object.

Senior's views on the role of government in fact modified over time. In 1830, for instance, he wrote to Lord Melbourne saying that 'the duty of the government is simply to keep the peace, to protect all of its subjects from the violence and fraud of one another and, having done so, to leave them to pursue what they believe to be their interests in the way which they deem advisable'. Twenty years later, Senior's outlook was a less limited one, for he said that 'the only rational foundation of government, the only foundation of a right to govern and of a correlative duty to obey, is expediency – the general benefit of the community. It is the duty of a government to do whatever is conducive to the welfare of the governed. The only limit to this duty is its power. And as the supreme government of an independent state is necessarily absolute, the only limit to its power is physical or moral inability. And whatever it is its duty to do it must necessarily have a right to do'. Senior said that 'the expediency of the exercise of some of the powers of government is more obvious than that of the exercise of some others. It is obviously expedient that a government should protect the persons and the property of its subjects.

'But if it can also be shown to be expedient that a government should perform any other functions, it must also be its duty and its right to perform them. The expediency may be more difficult of proof, and until that proof has been given, the duty and the right do not arise. But as soon as the proof has been given they are perfect. It is true that in such matters a government may make mistakes. It may believe its interference to be useful when it is really mischievous. There is no government which does not make such mistakes; and the more it interferes the more liable it must be to them. On the other hand, its refusal or neglect to interfere may also be founded on error. It may be passively wrong as well as actively wrong. The advance of political knowledge must diminish both these errors; but it appears to me that the most fatal of all errors would be the general admission of the proposition that a government has no right to interfere for any purpose except for that of affording protection, for such an admission would prevent our profiting by experience, and even from acquiring it'.[35]

Senior certainly thought that the State should intervene in Ireland to try to raise that country's productive capacity by building roads, railways, harbours, docks and canals, draining bogs and reclaiming waste land, as well as by subsidizing emigration and encouraging large scale farming. He also advocated or supported proposals which meant government expenditure on the extension and improvement of medical services in Ireland. For Britain too he proposed at various times State intervention in the spheres of health and housing (mostly in the form of building regulations). He was also an advocate of government provision of free compulsory elementary education. There, however, Senior's reformism largely stopped, mainly because his view of personal freedom involved the recognition of personal responsibility for self support, and the support of the family, in ordinary contingencies of life, such as old age and sickness, as well as for the other actions for which responsibility was recognized by the civil and criminal law.

With this outlook, he at first wanted the Poor Law to be abolished, because it was wrongly based on the assumption that the labouring classes were peculiarly unfitted to look after themselves. Later, he assisted in the Poor Law's amendment, trying to have it financed so that it hindered what he saw as the emancipation of the labouring classes as little as possible. His distaste for the Poor Law was founded on adherence to the ideal of individual self determination rather than on any crude dislike of State interference of any sort. His view that the ordinary adult was the best judge of his own interests and so did not need official protection was what mainly lay behind his opposition to factory legislation; although he also feared that it would undermine both the owner's profits and national competitiveness.[36]

Senior was an inconsistent advocate of *laissez-faire*. His position, even in theory, was often complex. He did not treat government expenditure as being essentially unproductive. On the other hand, he believed that 'the infinite variety of men's wants' ensured that there could not be an overall insufficiency of demand.[37] However, the leading authority on Senior's work went too far, when she suggested that his proposals for alleviating poverty in Ireland were such as would have made a serious believer in *laissez-faire* disown professional acquaintance with him.[38] The Classical Economists' general attitude towards less developed countries like Ireland was to use, if necessary, State action to create the conditions in which free enterprise could work.[39] Senior did not envisage substantial government intervention in the British economy, so a serious believer in *laissez-faire* could easily associate with him, even if his ideas on public health, for instance, would make it difficult for a dogmatic believer to do so.

VI. JOHN STUART MILL

J S Mill was the last major figure among the Classical Economists. He was also the intellectual spokesman for liberal democracy in the third quarter of the nineteenth century. Mill was the synthesizer and expounder of the views of the Classical Economists, from the quantity theory of money down to the Gold Standard. In his economics, he remained faithful to the Ricardian doctrines as he understood them; and, to some extent, improved on them in the process of interpreting them. In the fields of law and politics, his departures from Bentham's views were mainly methodological rather than substantive ones,[40] with important differences over the centralization of government activity. As regards the State's role in economic affairs, Mill, like Bentham, was a moderate advocate of *laissez-faire* for his own time.

Mill believed that 'the ground of the practical principle of non-interference' on the part of government was that 'most persons take a juster and more intelligent view of their own interest, and of the means of promoting it, than can either be prescribed to them by a general enactment of the legislature, or pointed out in the particular case by a public functionary'. He was, therefore, 'in favour of restricting to the narrowest compass the intervention of a public authority in the business of a community'. He said that 'in every instance the burthen of making out a strong case' for such intervention should be thrown 'not on those who resist, but on those who recommend, government interference. *Laissez-faire*, in short, should be the general practice: every departure from it unless required by some great good, is a certain evil'.[41]

Mill did not consider that this meant that the role of government should be restricted to 'the protection of person and property against force and fraud'. While the maxim of *laissez-faire* was 'unquestionably sound as a general rule', there was no difficulty in perceiving 'some very large and conspicuous exceptions to it'. For example, 'the individual who is presumed to be the best judge of his own interests may be incapable of judging or acting for himself; may be a lunatic, an idiot, an infant; or though not wholly incapable, may be of immature years and judgment. In this case the foundation of the *laissez-faire* principle breaks down entirely. The person most interested is not the best judge of the matter, not a competent judge at all'. On this basis, Mill supported factory legislation which protected children.[42]

In the sphere of education, Mill thought that it was undesirable that the State should have a monopoly of educational provision 'either in the lower or in the higher branches'. Nevertheless, he believed that government intervention was justifiable because the case was not one in which the interest and judgment of the consumer are a sufficient security for the goodness of the commodity. He said that 'there are certain primary elements and means of knowledge which it is in the highest degree desirable that all human beings born into the community should acquire during childhood.

'If their parents, or those on whom they depend, have the power of obtaining for them this instruction, and fail to do it, they commit a double breach of duty towards the children themselves, and towards the members of the community generally, who are all liable to suffer seriously from the consequences of ignorance and want of education in their fellow citizens. It is therefore an allowable exercise of the powers of government to impose on parents the legal obligation of giving elementary instruction to children'. On this basis, he supported government financial aid to elementary schools of a level that was 'such as to render them accessible to all the children of the poor, either freely, or for a payment too inconsiderable to be sensibly felt'.[43]

Mill thought it to be highly desirable, too, that 'the certainty of subsistence should be held out by law to the destitute able-bodied rather than that relief should depend on voluntary charity'. Provided that, as under the post-1834 Poor Law, 'consistently with guaranteeing all persons against absolute want, the condition of those who are supported by legal charity can be kept considerably less than the condition of those who find support for themselves'. Otherwise, the system would strike at 'the root of all individual industry and self government'. Mill wrote of private charity that 'in the first place' it 'almost always does too much or too little: it lavishes its bounty in one place, and leaves people to starve in another.

'Secondly, since the State must necessarily provide subsistence for the criminal poor while undergoing punishment, not to do the same for the poor who have not offended is to give a premium on crime. And lastly, if the poor are left to individual charity, a vast amount of mendicity is inevitable. What the State may and should abandon to private charity is the task of distinguishing between one case of real necessity and another. Private charity can give more to the more deserving. The State must act by general rules. It cannot undertake to discriminate between the deserving and the undeserving indigent. It owes no more than subsistence to the first and can give no less to the last'.[44]

In addition, Mill said that there were 'a multitude of cases in which governments, with general approbation, assume powers and execute functions for which no reason can be assigned except the simple one that they conduce to general convenience. We may take as an example the function (which is a monopoly too) of coining money. This is assumed for no more recondite purpose than that of saving to individuals the trouble, delay, and expense of weighing and assaying. No one, however, even of those most jealous of State interference, has objected to this as an improper exercise of the powers of government. Prescribing a set of standard weight and measures is another instance. Paving, lighting, and cleaning the streets and thoroughfares is another; whether done by the general government, or, as is more usual, and generally more advisable, by a municipal authority. Making or improving harbours, building lighthouses, making surveys in order to have accurate maps and charts, raising dykes to keep the sea out, and embankments to keep rivers in, are cases in point'. He thought that there were also a variety of instances in which important public services had to be performed, and only the government was likely to perform them, such as supporting voyages of geographical or scientific exploration, scientific research, and the maintenance of a learned class. He also thought that colonization was a matter in which the State had responsibilities.[45]

Mill's position was that 'anything which it is desirable should be done for the general interests of mankind or of future generations, or for the present interests of those members of the community who require external aid, but which is not of a nature to remunerate individuals or associations for undertaking it, is in itself a suitable thing to be undertaken by government: though, before making the work their own, governments ought always to consider if there be any rational probability of its being done on what is called the voluntary principle, and if so, whether it is likely to be done in a better or more effectual manner by government agency, than by zeal and liberality of individuals'.[46]

Mill believed that 'most things which are likely to be even tolerably done by voluntary associations should, generally speaking, be left to them'. He countenanced limited liability joint stock organizations, provided that their activities were adequately publicized, and that they operated in competitive conditions. He did not, however, think that private monopolies should be entirely free from government control, because their market position made their charges the same in effect as taxes. He said that on the same principle that patents were awarded for inventions, the companies that ran railways and canals, for instance, should be allowed a limited time in which to secure rewards for their initial enterprise. After that, he considered, 'the State should either reserve to itself a revisionary property in such public works, or should retain, and freely exercise, the right of fixing a maximum of fares and charges and from time to time varying that maximum'. He envisaged that it would be preferable if local authorities actually ran gas and water undertakings, but he felt it necessary to emphasize that 'the State may be the proprietor of canals or railways without itself working them; and that they will almost always be better worked by means of a company renting the railway or canal for a limited period from the State'.[47]

The role of government, then, was not seen as a minimal one by Mill. As to how government itself was to be organized, despite some important waverings over the virtues of democracy, he believed that the 'supreme controlling power in the last resort' should be 'vested in the entire aggregate of the community'. Since 'in a community exceeding a single small town' no more than a few could actively participate in public business, 'the ideal type of a perfect government must be representative'. He favoured what he called a 'universal, but graduated suffrage' (including votes for women) in which there would also have to be 'some mode of plural voting which may assign to education as such, the degree of superior influence due to it, and sufficient as a counterpoise to the numerical weight of the least educated class'. He believed that 'the assembly which votes the taxes, either general or local, should be elected exclusively by those who pay something towards the taxes imposed.

'Those who pay no taxes, disposing by their votes of other people's money, have every motive to be lavish and none to economise'. He thought that 'taxation in a visible shape, should descend to the poorest class'. He hoped that this class would come to identify their interest with 'a low scale of public expenditure'. He advocated that 'a direct tax, in the simple form of capitation, should be levied on every grown person in the community'. He also considered that the receipt of parish relief within the five years immediately before registration should be 'a peremptory disqualification for the franchise. He who cannot by his labour suffice for his own support has no claim to the privilege of helping himself to the money of others. By becoming dependent on the remaining members of the community for actual subsistence, he abdicates his claim to equal rights with them in other respects. Those to whom he is indebted for the continuance of his very existence may justly claim the exclusive management of these common concerns, to which he now brings nothing, or less than he takes away'.[48]

'The first needs, and the primary ends, of government', for Mill were 'security of person and property, and equal justice between individuals'. He said that 'if these things can be left to any responsibility below the highest, there is nothing, except war and treaties, which require a general government at all. Whatever are the best arrangements for securing these primary objects should be made universally obligatory, and, to secure their enforcement, should be placed under central superintendence'. He believed that 'it is but a small portion of the public business of a country which can be well done, or safely attempted, by the central authorities; and even in our own government, the least centralized in Europe, the legislative portion at least of the governing body busies itself far too much with local affairs'. He said that 'all business purely local – all which concerns only a single locality – should devolve upon the local authorities. The paving, lighting and cleaning of the streets of a town, and in ordinary circumstances the draining of its houses, are of little consequence to any but its inhabitants'. He thought that 'the administration of the Poor Laws, sanitary regulation, and others, which, while really interesting to the whole country, cannot consistently with the very purpose of local administration be managed otherwise than by the localities'. He also considered, however, that 'if the administration of justice, police and gaols included, is both so universal a concern, and so much a matter of general science independent of local peculiarities, that it may be, and ought to be, uniformly regulated throughout the country, and its regulation enforced by more trained and skilful hands than those of purely local authorities'. He said that 'if the local authorities and public are inferior to the central ones in knowledge of the principles of administration, they have the compensating advantage of a far more direct interest in the result'.[49]

Mill's 'practical conclusion' from his analysis was that 'the authority which is most conversant with principle should be supreme over principles, while that which is most competent in details should have the details left to it. The principal business of the central authority should be to give instruction, of the local authority to apply it. Power may be localized, but knowledge, to be most useful, must be centralized; there must be somewhere a focus at which all its scattered rays are collected, that the broken and coloured lights which exist elsewhere may find there what is necessary to complete and purify them. To every branch of local administration which affects the general interest there should be a corresponding central organ, either a Minister, or some specially appointed functionary under him; even if that functionary does no more than collect information from all quarters, and bring the experience acquired in one locality to the knowledge of another where it is wanted.

'But there is also something more than this for the central authority to do. It ought to keep open a perpetual communication with the localities: informing itself by their experience, and them by its own; giving advice freely when asked, volunteering it when seen to be required; compelling publicity and recordation of proceedings, and enforcing obedience to every general law which the legislature has laid down on the subject of local management'. He believed that 'experience is daily forcing upon the public a conviction of the necessity of having at least inspectors appointed by the general government to see that the local officers do their duty'. This was Benthamite sentiment in an analysis which placed less emphasis on centralization than Bentham had done.[50]

Mill wrote a great deal and his views were subject to change or modification over time, so that even if one confined oneself to his major published works, it is sometimes difficult to establish his position firmly on several matters with which he concerned himself during his intellectual career. The attraction of utilitarianism for him was its flexibility; where the line was to be drawn between liberty and authority was to be decided by the facts. Government intervention was not dismissed in principle by Mill, even in economic matters. On Free Trade, for instance, which he thought had moral and intellectual benefits as well as economic ones, Mill nevertheless envisaged the retention of revenue tariffs if other countries would not act reciprocally. He also conceded the possible need to protect domestic infant industries. Mill, in fact, displayed more rigidity in defending what he saw as central tenets of Classical doctrine, such as Say's Law and Malthusian population theory, than he sometimes did over what was actually to be the practice. Indeed, as is well known, he became interested in socialistic experiments, most markedly towards the end of his life. He came to believe that co-operative profit sharing associations would eventually become the main basis of industrial organization.[51]

For his own time, though, despite the modifications that often adorned his proposals, Mill's beliefs about his preferred social order were fairly clear. Competitive capitalism was to be the driving force of the economy. The competition of life could be made fairer by inheritance taxes to reduce unearned financial advantages; but progressive direct taxation could not be favoured because it would be inimical to industry and economy. He wrote that 'speaking generally, there is no one so fit to conduct any business, or to determine how or by whom it shall be conducted as those who are personally interested in it'. Moreover, he believed that even where private initiative was less efficient than government action it was better for society that wherever possible individuals should do things rather than the State; because the development of the individual was encouraged and the opportunities of creative social experimentation were greater.

Mill thought that 'the most cogent reason for restricting the interference of government is the great evil of adding unnecessarily to its power'. He observed, 'If the roads, the railways, the banks, the insurance offices, the great joint stock companies, the universities, and the public charities, were all of them branches of the government; if, in addition, the municipal corporations and local boards, with all that now devolves on them, became departments of the central administration; if the employees of all these different enterprises were appointed and paid by the government, and looked to the government for every rise in life; not all the freedom of the Press and the popular constitution of the legislature would make this or any other country free otherwise than in name. And the evil would be greater, the more efficiently and scientifically the administrative machinery was constructed – the more skilful the arrangements for obtaining the best qualified hands and heads with which to work it'. Mill said that there had to be 'a circle around every individual human being' within which 'the individuality of that person ought to reign uncontrolled either by any other individual or by the public collectively'; and that 'even in those portions of conduct which do affect the interest of others, the onus of making out a case always lies on the defenders of legal prohibitions'. [52] His clear preference in contemporary circumstances was for an emphasis on individual rights and voluntary action rather than communal rights and governmental action. For his own time, Mill was an adherent of the principle of *laissez-faire* and of its moderate practice.

VII. THE CLASSICAL ECONOMISTS AND LAISSEZ-FAIRE

The Classical Economists were not, as a group, extreme advocates of *laissez-faire*. Such extreme advocacy was mainly confined in Britain to popularizers such as Jane Marcet and Harriet Martineau; *The Economist* newspaper, at least under its founder and first editor, James Wilson; and Herbert Spencer. [53] On Free

Trade, the Manchester School was similarly extreme. Nevertheless, the ideas that were popularized and simplified for such advocacy were to be found in the work of the Classical Economists. Modern writers who have said that none of the Classical Economists favoured laissez-faire[54] are wrong. They all favoured laissez-faire, certainly for their own time. What they did not all favour was its dogmatic application. So, the intellectual position of the Classical School on laissez-faire in practice was often complex, even if popularizers rendered it simply.

The complexity of the Classical Economists' position can be seen in their attitudes to State social provision. They supported a variety of public health measures, and the State subsidization of education. Bentham anticipated several later social welfare measures, some of which were only introduced in the twentieth century. J S Mill pronounced private charity to be unreliable. Smith favoured progressive taxation, but McCulloch believed that redistribution of income was no part of the role of government.[55] The Classical Economists were divided over the Poor Law. Malthus pronounced its abolition. This policy at one time attracted the support of Ricardo and James Mill. Ricardo, however, always had a gradualist attitude. He envisaged the retention of the Poor Law, if it was limited to 'relieving only the aged and infirm and, under some circumstances, children'.[56] McCulloch, initially an abolitionist, eventually became one of Malthus's main opponents.[57] Indeed, he was a leading adversary of the Poor Law Amendment Act of 1834, in which Bentham's ideas, Malthus's theories, and Senior's involvement were all evident.

The Classical School's view of adults as free agents made it a major obstacle to factory legislation.[58] J S Mill's case for treating women factory workers the same as men, and thereby placing them beyond legislative protection, was based on the best liberal sentiments.[59] This may not have been a consolation to the individuals concerned. Malthusian population theory, which many Classical Economists accepted, was based on humane intentions. Nevertheless, this theory was open to the interpretation that measures to alleviate poverty could only be temporarily ameliorative at best in the face of the ever rising tide of numbers. Similarly, the benefits of the reformed Poor

Law of 1834 were most obvious to those groups who were concerned about the cost of the previous arrangements. The benefits were less obvious either to the paupers it was intended to make 'less eligible', or to those members of the community who had real cause to fear that they would at some time come to be dependent on the changed, and formally harsher system. The Classical Economists were not indefatigable opponents of social reform.[60] They were the opponents of some reforms, and the authors and anticipators of others. They did provide some ideas that, interpreted in particular ways, supported arguments against State social provision.

The Classical Economists were neither uncritical advocates of the free market, nor defenders of subsistence wages indifferent to the well being of the working classes.[61] That they were seen as such is not surprising, given, for instance, Senior's opposition to trade unionism[62] and the School's association with Wages Fund theory. J S Mill specifically recanted this association in order to align himself with what he saw as the aspirations of the working classes. Nevertheless, his revised view on wages still impressed upon trade unions that the price for pressing their claims beyond certain narrow limits would be to keep 'a part of their number permanently out of employment'.[63]

The Classical Economists could not be fairly said to be unconcerned about the needs of the working classes; but their concern was qualified by their faith in the virtues of the competitive market economy. Not that the régime that the Classical Economists designed for capitalism was necessarily that which capitalists desired for themselves. Smith's severe comments on merchants and manufacturers as willing monopolists were hardly deferential to such groups. What Smith preached was a competitive individualism that, for example, was opposed to joint stock organisation, except in very restricted instances.[64] McCulloch was still making Smithian noises on the subject in the 1850s, objecting, for instance, to limited liability legislation.[65] The Classical Economists were not unquestioning admirers of industrialization. Malthus, for example, was worried about the effects on the community of rapid technological progress.[66] McCulloch feared that such development was socially divisive.[67] Despite all these important qualifications, that the Classical

Economists were linked with the capitalist interest is only to be expected, because theirs was a theory of economic growth and that interest was to provide the dynamic element.

The policy prescriptions of the Classical School were, of course, comprehended at different levels. The popular view of what they said and that of the popularizer was unlikely to be the same as that present in full in their texts. The student of those texts has little difficulty in dismissing views that the Classical School favoured 'a night watchman State', or that their preferred system of government was 'anarchy plus the constable'.[68] The less informed, the politicians and the interested public of the time included, were unlikely to be aware of the reservations with which Smith, for example, usually hedged his policy proposals. His elegant sloganizing was more likely to catch the attention. If Smith said that it was 'the highest impertinence and presumption in Kings and Ministers to pretend to watch over the economy of private people':[69] then, *laissez-faire*. To interpret the Classical theory of economic policy in terms of minimum or minimum necessary role for government, other than for its propaganda value as a formula, doubtless is a distortion and a caricature.[70] The point is that the Classical Economists were engaged in trying to influence policy. The ifs and buts of their theorizing was bound to be sacrificed not just by their opponents but by their converts too.

Economic Man did not crudely stalk the pages of the Classical Economists' writings. Their attitude towards State economic activity was rarely dogmatic, often pragmatic, but not neutral. Their policy for economic progress, and a way out of the economic stagnation that until the latter part of J S Mill's life they thought was threatening, was not one that assigned a generally purposive role to the State in the productive process. The Classical School recognized the need for the State to provide social capital, but adherence to Say's Law and a tendency to regard government expenditure as unproductive was present in most of their work.[71] Sentiments of the kind that Ricardo expressed in denying that, for instance, public works could ameliorate unemployment were to pass down to later generations as conclusive arguments against such measures. Even the interpreter of the Classical School most anxious to sever the link between it and *laissez-faire* did not attribute the

School's bias against State activity to the relative inefficiency of contemporary governmental machinery. He saw J S Mill's attitude as being much more ambiguous than that of the other Classical Economists.[72] This could be said of Bentham too. The utilitarian test required an assessment of the facts before making pronouncements. For their own time, in both cases, the facts pointed to *laissez-faire*.

The Classical Economists clearly considered that a developed economy was a free enterprise one, and that the State's role in such an economy was primarily to ensure that the private system worked properly and flourished. The less developed an economy, the readier the Classical Economists were to countenance direct government economic activity, as in Ireland. Aside from strident voices such as James Mill, the Classical Economists tended towards moderate policies.

The last of their number, J E Cairnes generally summarized the Classical School's view on the choice between government and private economic activity when he wrote in 1873, 'as a practical rule, I hold *laissez-faire* to be incomparably the safer guide. Only let us remember that it is a practical rule, and not a doctrine of science; a rule in the main sound, but like most other sound practical rules, liable to numerous exceptions; above all, a rule which must never for a moment be allowed to stand in the way of a candid consideration of any promising proposal of social or industrial reform'.[73] The Classical Economists required that what was significantly called government interference had to be argued for; but they showed even on such a central matter as Free Trade that they were by no means always ready to reject State intervention where it could be shown to be needed.[74] In short, as a group, the Classical Economists were either advocates of *laissez-faire* in principle or on the basis of contemporary facts: but, also as a group, they were too sophisticated always to insist on *laissez-faire* in practice.

Chapter 3

Who Killed *Laissez-Faire?*

Who killed *laissez-faire* as the dominant intellectual belief about the role of the State? Conservatives had long sniped at the liberalism of the Classical Economists, but they had not been able to do more than inflict minor wounds on the dominant creed. There was a long tradition, too, of socialist thought. Some of this was inspired by particular interpretations of Bentham's and Ricardo's work. More of it was inspired by Christianity than by the teachings of Marx, whose main influence came later. The Fabians provided intellectual ammunition against *laissez-faire*. The crucial change, however, came within liberalism. The Marshallian School at Cambridge turned economics away from *laissez-faire*. The School intellectually fathered Keynes. Its ideas and his will be considered in the next chapter. The leading figure in this chapter is the man who in Britain decisively undermined the position of *laissez-faire* in political philosophy: T H Green. A note about Conservative ideas on the role of the State precedes an analysis of Green's views, and a consideration of Fabian ideas follows it.

Green's contribution was the critical one in changing the British outlook. At Oxford, he preached a positive liberalism that was heard by a generation and more of politicians and civil servants trained there. Asquith was a student and a colleague of Green's before going on to head the reformist Liberal Government of the early twentieth century.[1] Green's philosophy was passed on to William Beveridge when he studied at Balliol.[2] Toynbee Hall, a settlement founded in the East End of London in memory of Green's most famous disciple, was to be a training ground for Beveridge and others who helped to construct the Welfare State. After Green, the onus of proof about State intervention was no longer automatically placed on those advocating government activity.

I. THE CONSERVATIVES

The Conservatives provided important dissenting voices during the dominance of the Classical Economists, and their Party then went on to establish its own ascendancy.

The dissident voices were not all saying the same thing in their contempt for the Classical School, except to tend to revere the pre-industrial past as against the present. This was most marked in Thomas Carlyle's work. He saw *laissez-faire* as an abdication on the part of the governors not least in their responsibilities towards the working classes.[3] His solution to the condition of England question, however, was authoritarian government. Such a solution was not one that recommended itself to the Lake Poets: Samuel Taylor Coleridge, William Wordsworth and Robert Southey. Converted to conservatism after youthful flirtations with radicalism, they viewed *laissez-faire* and industrialization with distaste. They stressed nationalism and, to a lesser extent, empire. The latter did not necessarily bring them into conflict with Liberals because the final position of the Classical Economists was unclear.[4]

The emphasis on national self sufficiency to be found, for example, in Coleridge's writings was certainly in contrast with at least the cruder advocacy of *laissez-faire*. Coleridge was the most formidable political philosopher of the Lake Poets. He was ranked by J S Mill with Bentham as one of the two great seminal minds of his time. Coleridge was a great Christian philosopher in an age in which at least formal allegiance to Christianity was strong, and so was that to the Anglican Church in particular. There were always groups in the Church who rejected the arguments of the Classical Economists, and who concerned themselves with the condition of England problem. Some of the more forceful advocates of social legislation were the Evangelicals, most notably Lord Shaftesbury. Inheriting, probably from Southey, a distaste for manufacturers, as men who did not respect traditional values, Shaftesbury devoted his life to seeking legislative protection for those employed in mines and factories, particularly children. He was a Tory, although, of course, he shared his Evangelicalism with Liberals. He wanted to win the working classes not so much for the Tory Party as for Heaven.[5]

There was no coherent or distinct Tory or Conservative attitude to the role of the State. Certainly, Edmund Burke did not hand one down. He regretted the passing of what he called 'the age of chivalry' and its supersession by the age of 'sophisters, economists and calculators'. This did not mean that he viewed *laissez-faire* with disfavour. An advocate of Economical Reform in government expenditure, Burke was 'against the overdoing of any sort of administration, and more especially against this most momentous of all meddling on the part of authority: the meddling with the subsistence of the people.' Burke said that if he had to draw any line it would leave to the State that which was 'truly and properly public': namely, the basic governmental functions of his day.

Coleridge on the other hand, did not think that the role of the State should be limited to defence and the protection of people and property. He saw the duties of government as extending to being a 'hinderer of hindrances' to freedom, and as a provider of the minimum conditions of a civilized life for the citizen. Even if the more sympathetic political philosophers did not always advocate *laissez-faire*, the Tory Governments of the younger Pitt and Lord Liverpool tended to practise it. The need to protect the landed interest, the electoral base of the Tories, ensured that it was a modified *laissez-faire*. When Peel removed the main element of protection, the Corn Laws, he sentenced the Conservatives to the political wilderness. Protection was not only dead but damned, and so the Conservatives seemed to be until the electorate expanded after 1867. Benjamin Disraeli then developed a programme of nationalism, imperialism and social reform (mainly public health) that was presented as an alternative philosophy to that of the 'two nations' of rich and poor the Liberals were said to have created.[6]

Despite the elegance of Disraeli's style, there was never much that was distinctive in Conservative attitudes even as to social policy. The Conservatives were perhaps slightly more influenced by paternalism and slightly less by economic orthodoxy than the Liberals. They had a bias against the extension of central intervention and control, and an emphasis on individualism and freedom, that was similar to that of the Liberals.[7] The Conservatives lacked an economic policy of their own after 1846, and they split when Joseph Chamberlain provided one in the form of a renewal of protection, this time plus imperial unity. That proved less electorally popular than a combination of scepticism about ideas, particularly new ones, and a mild reformism. The Conservatives took on broad Liberal ideas, and socialistic ones too as the twentieth century progressed.[8] The Conservative Party's main function was to provide alternative politicians, and sometimes policies, to those of the Liberal and Labour Parties. Conservatism constituted an important political tradition. What it lacked was original views about the role of the State.

II. T H GREEN

Few, even those critical of it, doubt the importance of T H Green's influence on British thought and public policy between 1880 and 1914.[9] The socialist Laski credited Green and his fellow Oxford Idealists and disciples with achieving 'something akin to revolution in the English theory of the State'. Writing in 1911, L T Hobhouse credited them with 'setting liberalism free from the shackles of an individualist conception of liberty and paving the way for the legislation of our own time'. Laski further commented in 1940 that 'under the philosophic auspices of Green, not least as his doctrine was given both a deeper and wider social content by Hobhouse, the main gains in the legislation of the last fifty years are to be recorded'.[10]

Such views have since been interpreted as paying too little attention to the systematic ambiguity and mediating quality said to be inherent in Green's style of thought. These views are said to exaggerate the role he assigned to the State. They play down his allegiance to the ideas of the Manchester School. They minimize his distinctly mid-Victorian assumptions about the nature of British political life.[11] This latter interpretation, critical of Laski and Hobhouse, is wrong. When one takes into account Green's theory of rights, his theory of positive freedom, his theory of property, and the extent to which he built on utilitarianism, Green can be seen as an intellectual progenitor of the Welfare State.

Green's theory of rights was at the heart of his attack on *laissez-faire* doctrines because it challenged the logic of the Lockean idea of rights as inalienable and personal: and because it saw rights as arising out of social relations in general and out of the capacity to contribute to the common good in particular.

For Green, 'a right against society, in distinction from a right to be treated as a member of society, is a contradiction in terms', because 'it is on the relation to a society, to other men recognizing a common good, that the individual's rights depend, as much as the gravity of a body depends on relations to other bodies'. The State presupposed rights, and rights of individuals.[8] It was a form which society took in order to maintain them. It was his belief that 'no exercise of a power, however abstractedly desirable for the promotion of human good it might be, can be claimed as a right unless there is some common consciousness of utility shared by the person making the claim and those on whom it is made'.[12]

This was a potentially radical doctrine, which supplemented the utilitarian critique of the older doctrine of pre-social, personal rights, which neither governments nor society could rightfully interfere with. Green said that they not only could, but that where the common interest demanded, they must intervene.

The capacity for rights, Green wrote, was 'a capacity for spontaneous action regulated by a conception of a common good, either so regulated through an interest which flows directly from that conception, or through hopes and fears which are affected by it through more complex channels of habit and association'. It was, he said, 'a capacity which cannot be generated – which on the contrary is neutralized – by any influences that interfere with the spontaneous action of social interests. Now any direct enforcement of the outward conduct, which ought to flow from social interests, by means of threatened penalties – and a law requiring such conduct necessarily implies penalties for disobedience to it – does interfere with the spontaneous action of those interests, and consequently checks the growth of the capacity which is the condition of the beneficial exercise of rights.

'For this reason the effectual action of the State, i.e. the community as acting through law, for the promotion of habits of true citizenship, seems necessarily to be confined to the removal of obstacles. Under this head, however, there may and should be included much that at first sight may have the appearance of an enforcement of moral duties, e.g. the requirement that parents have their children taught the elementary arts. To educate one's children is no doubt a moral duty, and it is not one of those duties, like that of paying debts, of which the neglect directly interferes with the rights of someone else. It might seem, therefore, to be a duty with which positive law should have nothing to do, any more than with the duty of striving after a noble life. On the other hand, the neglect of it does tend to prevent the growth of the capacity for beneficially exercising rights on the part of those whose education is neglected, and it is on this account, not as a purely moral duty on the part of a parent, but as the prevention of a hindrance to the capacity for rights on the part of children, that education should be enforced by the State.

'It may be objected, indeed, that in enforcing it we are departing in regard to the parents from the principles above laid down; that we are interfering with the spontaneous action of social interests, though we are doing so with a view to promoting this spontaneous action in another generation. But the answer to this objection is, that a law of compulsory education, if the preferences, ecclesiastical or otherwise, of those parents who show any practical sense of their responsibility are duly respected, is from the beginning only felt as compulsion by those in whom, so far as this social function is concerned, there is no spontaneity to be interfered with; and that in the second generation, though the law with its penal sanctions still continues, it is not felt as a law, as an enforcement of action by penalties, at all'.[13]

'On the same principle the freedom of contract ought probably to be more restricted in certain directions than is at present the case', Green wrote. He believed that 'the freedom to do as they like on the part of one set of men may involve the ultimate disqualification of many others, or of a succeeding generation, for the exercise of rights. This applies most obviously to such

kinds of contract or traffic as affect the health and housing of
the people, the growth of population relatively to the means of
subsistence, and the accumulation or distribution of landed
property. In the hurry of removing those restraints on free
dealing between man and man, which have arisen partly perhaps
from some confused idea of maintaining morality, but much
more from the power of class interests, we have been apt to take
too narrow a view of the range of persons – not one generation
merely, but succeeding generations – whose freedom ought to be
taken into account, and of the conditions necessary to their
freedom ("freedom" here meaning their qualification for the
exercise of rights).

'Hence the massing of population without regard to conditions of health; unrestrained traffic in deleterious commodities;
unlimited upgrowth of the class of hired labourers in particular
industries which circumstances have suddenly stimulated without any provision against the danger of an impoverished pro-
letariat in following generations. Meanwhile, under pretence of
allowing freedom of bequest and settlement, a system has grown
up which prevents the landlords of each generation from being
free either in the government of their families or in the disposal
of their land, and aggravates the tendency to crowd into towns,
as well as the difficulties of providing healthy house rooms, by
keeping land in a few hands. It would be out of place here to
consider in detail the remedies for these evils, or to discuss the
question how far it is well to trust to the initiative of the State
or of individuals in dealing with them. It is enough to point out
the directions in which the State may remove obstacles to the
realization of the capacity for beneficial exercise of rights,
without defeating its own object of vitiating the spontaneous
character of that capacity'.[14]

'Advancing civilization brings with it more and more interference with the liberty of the individual', Green believed. At one
time, he said, the theory that the State 'goes beyond its province
when it seeks to do more than secure the individual from violent
interference by other individuals' had led to 'real reforms'. By
1880, in his view, this theory had become obstructive because
it afforded 'a reason for resisting all positive reforms, all reforms
which involve an action of the State in the way of promoting
conditions favourable to moral life'. He considered that 'it is one

thing to say that the State in promoting these conditions must take care not to defeat its true end by narrowing the region within which the spontaneity and disinterestedness of true morality can have play; another thing to say that it has no moral end to serve at all'. Morality, he said, consisted of 'the disinterested performance of self imposed duties', and in his opinion 'the true ground of objection to paternal government is not that it violates the *laissez-faire* principle and conceives that its office is to make people good, to promote morality, but that it rests on a misconception of morality. The real function of government being to maintain conditions of life in which morality shall be possible'.[15]

There was undoubtedly 'a work of moral liberation which society through its various agencies is constantly carrying on for the individual', Green wrote. The State was one such agency: indeed, it was the supreme one, and it provided an essential mechanism through which the individual could realize his full potentialities. As he put it, 'the actual powers of the noblest savage do not admit of comparison with those of the humblest citizen of a law abiding state'. This did not mean, however, that, as things stood, 'an untaught and underfed denizen of a London yard with gin shop on the right hand and on the left' was much freer than an Athenian slave subject to his master's whim had been.

For freedom, he said, did not merely mean freedom from restraint or compulsion: it meant 'a positive power or capacity of doing or enjoying something worth doing or enjoying, and that, too, something that we do or enjoy in common with others. We mean by it a power which each man exercises through the help or security given him by his fellow men, and which he in turn helps to secure for them. When we measure the progress of a society by its growth in freedom, we measure it by the increasing development and exercise on the whole of those powers of contributing to social good with which we believe the members of the society to be endowed; in short, by the greater power on the part of the citizens as a body, to make the most and best of themselves'.[16]

'Freedom in all forms of doing what one will with one's own', Green believed to be 'valuable only as a means to an end. That end is what I call freedom in the positive sense: in other words, the liberation of the powers of all men equally for contributions to a common good. No one has a right to do what he will with his own in such a way as to contravene this end. It is only through the guarantee which society gives him that he has property at all, or, strictly speaking, any right to his possessions. This guarantee is founded on a sense of common interest. Everyone has an interest in securing to every one else the free use and enjoyment and disposal of his possessions, so long as that freedom on the part of one does not interfere with a like freedom on the part of others, because such freedom contributes to that equal development of the faculties of all which is the highest good for all. This is the true and the only justification of rights of property'.[17]

'It is the business of the State', Green said, 'not indeed directly to promote moral goodness, for that, from the very nature of moral goodness, it cannot do, but to maintain the conditions without which a free exercise of the human faculties is impossible'. By 1880, in several fields 'a sense of the facts and necessities of the case had got the better of the delusive cry of liberty', he wrote, 'and Act after Act had been passed preventing master and workman, parent and child, house builder and house-holder from doing as they pleased, with the result of a great addition to the real freedom of society. The spirit of self reliance and independence was not weakened by those Acts. Rather it received a new development. The dead weight of ignorance and unhealthy surroundings with which it would otherwise have had to struggle, being partially removed by law, it was more free to exert itself for higher objects'. Green believed that 'a society in which the public health was duly protected, and necessary education duly provided for, by the spontaneous action of individuals' was one 'in a higher condition than one in which the compulsion of law was needed to secure these ends. But we must take men as we find them. Until a condition of society is reached, it is the business of the State to take the best security it can for the young citizens growing up in such health and with so much knowledge as is necessary for their real freedom'.[18]

Educational reforms and public health measures, indeed, were prominent in Green's political programme. He thought that 'without a command of certain elementary arts and knowledge, the individual in modern society is as effectually crippled as by the loss of a limb or a broken constitution. He is not free to develop his faculties. With a view to securing such freedom among its members it is as certainly within the province of the State to prevent children from growing up in that kind of ignorance, which practically excludes them from a free career in life, as it is within its province to require the sort of building and drainage necessary for public health'.

In his views on education, Green displayed a distaste for the distinctions of social class that he had learnt to abhor at public school and then at Oxford: he wanted the State to ensure that 'something else than the accidents of birth and wealth should regulate the intellectual development of the people'. He said that 'in every nation, perhaps, there must be a certain separation between those who live solely by the labour of their hands and those who live rather by the labour of their heads or by the profits of capital, between members of the learned professions and those engaged constantly in buying and selling, between those who are earning their money and those who are living on the income of large accumulated capital; but in England these separations have been fixed and deepened by the fact that there has been no fusion of class with class in school or at the universities'.

He believed that 'common education is the true social leveller. Men and women who have been at school together, or who have been at schools of the same sort, will always understand each other, will always be at their ease together, will be free from social jealousies and animosities however different their circumstances in life may be'. He thought that 'a properly organized system of schools would level up without levelling down', and with provision for scholarships and exhibitions 'a "ladder of learning" could be provided stretching from the humblest well disciplined home to the universities'.[19]

That the State needed to do so much for the working classes was not blamed by Green upon the capitalist system, but rather ascribed by him to the serf-like attitudes that the landowning classes had inculcated into their workers over generations. He viewed capitalism favourably, and he wrote of the lot of the workers under it that 'there is nothing in the fact that their labour is hired in great masses by great capitalists to prevent them from

being on a small scale capitalists themselves', and 'their combination in work gives them every opportunity, if they have the
needful education and self discipline, for forming societies for
the investment of savings. In fact, as we know, in the well paid
industries of England the better sort of labourers do become
capitalists, to the extent often of owning their houses and a good
deal of furniture, of having an interest in stores, and of belonging to benefit societies through which they make provision for
the future'.[20]

It was sentiments of the above kind, presumably, which have
led to the association of Green with mid-Victorian attitudes, and
the alignment of him with the Manchester School. Certainly,
Green was a personal admirer of John Bright. He shared the
antipathy of both Bright and Richard Cobden for the landed
interest. He had similar pacific attitudes on international
relations. What did allegiance to the Manchester School really
mean? It remains one of the more evocative terms in the history
of economic policy, being associated with a policy that relies
on the market as much as it can and, even to today's classical
liberals, more than it ought.

In fact, the School was singular in aim, which was to make a
change in policy: namely, to place Britain on the course of
Free Trade. After 1846, what the Manchester School had in
common was little more than a broad personal loyalty to
Cobden and Bright.[21] Green had such a loyalty to Bright, and on
such a basis he could be associated with Manchester liberalism.
The association cannot be pressed much farther as one interpreter who tried to do so seemed to find.[22] Green's political
programme differed from Bright's both in its Idealist mode of
thought, and in the admission that there was an intolerable
degree of inequality in British society. Green taught a theory of
community drastically different from individualism. In the name
of community, he called upon those who had privileges to
sacrifice them to their duty as citizens.

Green was not an opponent of either trade unions or of
factory legislation. These are fairly important qualifications to
an association with Manchesterism. Cobden and Bright were
antipathetic to the trade union movement. They generally
opposed legislation restricting adult hours of factory work.
Bright maintained such opposition to the end of his political

career, and he was a notable opponent of the Ten Hours movement. Cobden was a strong advocate of State intervention in
education, but Bright, though he subsequently relented, was a
critic of the Education Act of 1870. On public health, Cobden
disliked the strong centralizing tendencies of Chadwick's 1848
Public Health Act, but he was prepared to envisage a locally
controlled public health organization.

Bright, who was much more prominent in the public debate
on the matter, has been described by a biographer as attempting
to follow a *laissez-faire* line in relation to public health regulation. In general, both Cobden and Bright placed great emphasis
upon retrenchment in government expenditure. They seem to
have been fairly described as being 'not far seeing in economic
and social questions', expecting Free Trade to bring general
prosperity 'without the need for much positive social and
economic legislation'.[23] Green's definite commitment to education and public health measures marked him off from some of
the attitudes that Bright in particular seemed to have. Green's
allegiance to the ideas of the Manchester School was not, then,
a firm one.

Green's reputation as the first British philosopher to justify
collectivism and the Welfare State has been subject to challenge.
His Idealism has been said to have pointed in different directions.
His disciples were split on the question of choosing among the
Majority and Minority Reports of the Poor Law Commission
of 1905–9. Some Idealists such as Bernard Bosanquet, when
confronted with proposed improvements in social services, felt
able to stress the possible adverse effects on individual initiative
of such measures. Yet, they considered themselves to be followers of Green. The social morals of the Charity Organization
Society, of which Bosanquet and his wife were leading figures,
were described by Hobhouse as being such as to mean 'a State
which cannot actively promote the well-being of its members,
but can only remove obstructions and leave them a fair field in
which to run the race'. On the other hand, Hobhouse, who
said that from Green 'we get most of the cream of Idealism and
least of its sour milk', clearly treated Green as a precursor of
what he himself called 'Liberal Socialism'.[24]

Green's specific commitments to reforming measures, aside
from contemporary matters such as temperance and Irish land

reform, were largely confined to education and public health. In the economic sphere, he did not appear to favour government intervention beyond regulatory functions such as factory legislation. For all his dislike of the landed interest, Green's views on private property and on incentives inhibited him from supporting land taxes.[25] His adherence to the mid-Victorian notions of self help and thrift that were prominent in political circles in his formative years may well have had a limiting effect on his vision about contemporary extensions of State activity. To go on from this and write in terms of a profound ambivalence in Green's work, which led to conflicting interpretations of his work by men taking it as their model,[26] is to go too far.

Green's conception was of a community state, whose justification rested upon a notion of an identifiable common good, and which made possible a society of individuals self consciously interested in each other's well-being and recognizing their interdependence, their mutuality. The connection of this with later Welfare State and even socialist thought is obvious, especially when it is contrasted with the older Lockean and more modern Spencerian theory of the limited State serving individuals, each seeking independently his own good, and being the sole judge of what he owed to others. When Green wrote about 'the removal of obstacles' he was not advocating a theory of the negative State, but only warning that the State could not do more than affect the material conditions of morality and not morality itself.

As to the material conditions, he placed no *a priori* limits on their regulation, except, of course, the most general and obvious: for example, each man must have enough personal property to moralize him. Both Green's theory of positive freedom and his theory of rights, derived from Hegel and Kant, meant, for instance, that he could never give more than qualified support for any property system, including capitalism: the test was its actual contribution to morality and social well-being. This test made it possible for him to consider drastic State regulation of landed property, and in principle to extend this to include other types of property because one would merely have to find that the additional regulation was necessary on the criteria stated. That is, it is a matter of what the facts are to be, and that is a contingent matter. So that different interpretations of the facts by other Idealists such as Bosanquet did not necessarily point to any systematic ambiguity in Green's theory any more than they would in the case of any political or social theory open to empirical testing.

Green's emphasis on morality often masked the degree to which actual welfare was his constant concern. It is a largely unnoticed aspect of his critique of utilitarian ethics that Green's theory subsumes much of Bentham's. He wrote 'it is impossible that an action should be done for the sake of its goodness, unless it has been previously contemplated as good for some other reason than that which consists in its being done for the sake of its goodness. In other words, a prior morality, founded upon interests . . . is the condition of there coming to be a character governed by . . . an ideal of goodness'.[27]

Green built on utilitarianism, both theoretically and practically. The Fabians added little that was new in the way of theory. They merely attended more closely to the facts and their consequences, and developed some new remedial ideas. Other liberals such as Hobhouse may have elaborated similar views and attempted to integrate them with socialist ideas, but Green, for all the limitations of his work, was the main intellectual agent in turning liberalism in the direction of a more purposive role for the State in society. He was an intellectual precursor of the Welfare State.

III. THE FABIAN SOCIALISTS

What separated radicals of the type that followed Green from socialists was clear to his most ardent disciple, Arnold Toynbee. Tory acts of socialism were rejected because what was wanted was not paternal but fraternal government. Continental socialism was rejected because of the materialism of socialists, the radicals' adherence to the principle of private property and their repudiation of confiscation and violence. Toynbee said that radicals had not abandoned 'our old belief in liberty, justice, and self help, but we say that under certain conditions the people cannot help themselves, and that they should be helped by the State representing directly the whole people. In giving this State help, we make three conditions: first, the matter must be one of primary social importance; next, it must be proved to be practicable; thirdly, the State interference must not diminish self reliance. Even if the chance should arise of removing a great social evil, nothing must be done to weaken those habits of self reliance and voluntary association which have built up the greatness of the English people'.[28]

These sentiments, indeed, had little in common with the views of Karl Marx, who wished for the overthrow of the capitalist system. Continental socialism, however, was not British socialism. This had disparate origins and traditions. They included the idealism of Robert Owen and the pragmatism of the Co-operative Movement his ideas helped to found.[29] A Christian Socialist tradition can be traced from the antagonists of Victorian capitalism down to R H Tawney. From the 1880s onwards, the Fabians led by Sidney and Beatrice Webb came to straddle this position and British socialism too. The Webbs had little taste for the individualism and emphasis on voluntary action that Toynbee had talked of. They were advocates of an extended role for the State. They did reject foreign excesses, until in later life they were converted to Soviet Communism. Their earliest aims were for their socialistic ideas to permeate both the Conservative and Liberal Parties. Their main avenue for influence, and the main avenue for British socialism, was the Labour Party, which they helped to found with other Socialists and with and upon the trade union movement. The Fabian contribution was a practical one. They added little in the way of theory to that they inherited from Green and borrowed from Marx.

The intellectual frontal attack on capitalism that Marx led did not attract much attention in Britain until after his death in 1883. The Social Democratic Federation led by H M Hyndman was the main early outlet for Marxist views, and an ineffectual one. Even during the labour troubles of the first two decades of the twentieth century, it seems doubtful if there was anything which amounted to a revolutionary movement in Britain. The formation of a British Communist Party in 1920 was not to lead to electoral success,[30] although there was success in penetration of the trade union movement. Marxist ideas permeated the Labour Party. Few, even among those who called themselves Marxists, faced the rigours of actually reading *Capital*. The brief, sloganizing *Communist Manifesto* carried the essence of Marx's message and that of Engels too. The capitalist system of production exploited the working class, whose labour was the source of wealth. The system had to be forcibly over-thrown by those it oppressed, and would be. Marx and Engels said that the theory of the Communists could be summed up in a single sentence: abolition of private property.

How the socialist system that was to follow was to work was not explained in detail. There was to be 'a common plan' involving agriculture and the extension of factories and instruments of production owned by the State. Credit was to be centralized in the hands of the State, by means of a national bank with State capital and an exclusive monopoly. The means of com-munication and transport were to be centralized in the hands of the State. Industrial conscription was envisaged, especially for agriculture. The State was to provide free education for all children. A heavy progressive or graduated income tax would provide finance.

Marx's view of the role of the State has been described by a leading disciple as being pervaded by a powerful anti-authoritarian and anti-bureaucratic bias, not only in relation to a distant communist society but also to the period of transition which preceded it. Nevertheless, Russia, the first country to be ruled in the name of Marx, proceeded to be both authoritarian and bureaucratic. The Russian Revolution perhaps did leave British socialism as the insular, traditional, empirical movement it professed to be,[31] but it was not without influence even on the relentlessly conservative Labour Party. Marx had changed the world, and by 1917 Britain's position in that world was no longer such that outside influences could be treated with disdain. Marxism not only gave confidence to the working classes that they were the real producers, it also became with Christianity and Liberalism one of the few all embracing systems of thought in Western political philosophy. That Marxism was a negative creed, which savagely criticized capitalism without clearly indicating how the proposed socialist alternative would work, mattered little. The savage criticism attracted those who felt the need to be armed with it. The vagueness about what social-ism entailed encouraged all sorts of visions in the faithful. The vision was not always what was likely to be the authoritarian and bureaucratic reality. The consolation for idealists, and the hard headed expectation of others, was that they would hold the key places in the bureaucracy, that they would wield authority.

'Christian socialism is but the holy water with which the priest consecrates the heart burnings of the aristocrat'. Thus Marx and Engels tried to dismiss a rival socialist creed. The first Christian Socialist movement in Britain was short lived, lasting really only between 1848 and 1854. Differences of view between its main leaders – F D Maurice and J M Ludlow – contributed to the movement's demise. Its influence lived on through the novels of Charles Kingsley, one of its devotees, and through a Working Men's College that it founded in London. The movement played the main part in securing the passage in 1852 of the Act which gave the Co-operative Movement legal standing.

The Christian Socialists of the 1850s stood for co-operation rather than for collectivism or State intervention, for profit sharing and copartnership rather than for public ownership. The movement expressed a Broad Church theology which emphasized rationality and tolerance, and it introduced to Britain the French socialist ideas of the 1830s and 1840s. Without the breakthrough of the 1850s, it would have been much harder for the Christian Socialists of a later vintage to establish themselves in the 1880s. The Christian Socialist revival that took place then owed something to the laying bare of urban problems in the forceful Congregationalist pamphlet, *The Bitter Cry of Outcast London* (1883) and the work of Charles Booth. Its chief intellectual catalyst, like that of the socialist revival of the 1880s in general, was probably the work of the American, Henry George, whose *Progress and Poverty* was published in Britain in 1880. This book, combining as it did, a plausible economic argument with powerful emotional and even religious appeal, was particularly attractive to many Christians who were unhappy with the social conditions of late Victorian Britain but uncertain about the causes of unemployment and distress.

In George many of them found an answer, and the influence of his best selling book was reinforced by the lecture tours he gave in the 1880s. George saw himself, and was seen, as sweeping away the fatalistic Wages Fund Theory and Malthusianism. He emphasized that God could not be blamed for misdeeds that were essentially man's. His advocacy of a Single Tax, a steadily increasing toll on the increment of land values appealed to

Christian Socialists looking for radical but not violent change.[32]
The Christian Socialists of the period from the 1880s onwards
were a motley collection, divided by sectarianism as well as by
definitions of socialism, and a minority among Christians
generally. Nevertheless, they played an important part in
pressing for collectivist measures in general, and in the development of the Fabian Society and the Independent Labour Party
in particular.

Christian Socialism did bequeath to the Labour movement
its finest writer, R H Tawney. From Balliol and then to Toynbee
Hall, and eventually into academic life at the Webbsian
foundation, the London School of Economics, Tawney progressed to become the leading serious British socialist thinker.
Through *The Acquisitive Society* (1921) and *Equality* (1931),
Tawney preached an egalitarian message based on Christian
principles. From his Christian point of view, capitalism was
ungodly, both for its irreverence towards nature, and because
like its totalitarian rival miscalled Communism it had the
characteristics of a counter religion. Instead of encouraging in
man a creaturely attitude to the divine creation, capitalism put
a premium on a Promethean lust for limitless, almost blasphem-
ous, exploitation of nature and dominion over nature. It put
productivity and associated materialistic values on an altar
where Tawney felt no economic or political value should be put.
Tawney's historical studies, such as *Religion and the Rise of
Capitalism*, were partly designed to show how capitalism had
thrust aside Christian values, and also that capitalism had not
necessarily any more permanence than feudalism before it.

In demonstrating the historical mortality of capitalism, it
could be suggested that Tawney strengthened the resolve of
those who did not like capitalism, but had no conviction of the
possibility of replacing it. Capitalism, Tawney held, erected
production and the making of profit, which should be a means
to certain ends, into ends in themselves. The ultimate confusion
of means and ends lay in labour (people) being seen by capitalism
as of use as an instrument by capital (things). It followed from
this, and from Tawney's Christian view of man's nature, that
capitalism encouraged the wrong instincts in man (acquisitive-
ness), and went against the grain of the instinct of service and
solidarity which he thought existed in man and which could be

drawn out by different social arrangements. Those different arrangements were to be characterized by fellowship, which was central to Tawney's socialism. This rested, firstly, on a dispersion of power, which meant preventing one man or group 'lording it over the others'. It made people more accessible to each other than a system in which power is highly centralized and where society is a tapestry of authoritarian links. Secondly, fellowship and equality were directly connected.

Tawney was concerned not only with how to treat individuals, but also with the consequences for society of the way individuals are treated. Thirdly, there was the idea of function. Tawney reached the idea of a social purpose common to the whole society by means of the high value he put on fellowship. Fourthly, Tawney's notion of citizenship centred upon a certain quality of human and social communication. Equality and dispersion of power were its preconditions. It was the lubricant of good government. It was also valuable in itself, for the rich quality of relationships it represented, not only between the citizen and the State but among the citizenry.[33] Tawney drew a picture of a new society based on different tenets to those he ascribed to liberal capitalist society. He led the moral assault on capitalism in Britain.

The Fabian Society, which was later to include Tawney in its ranks, was a disparate group from its beginnings in the 1880s. Sidney Webb, Sydney Olivier, and Graham Wallas were the Three Musketeers of the early Fabian Society, according to George Bernard Shaw, who cast himself as D'Artagnan. Other members such as Hubert Bland were hopelessly outmatched by such talent, Shaw said. It taxed Shaw's diplomacy to the utmost to keep the peace between Bland and the Musketeers, as it did long afterwards between the Webbs and G D H Cole in the latter's very combative phase of Guild Socialism. Beatrice Webb, who was not a member of the Fabian Society in its earliest days, began with an intense contempt for it as a rabble of silly suburban faddists.[34]

Certainly, a group that included Shaw and later H G Wells in its ranks was not short of curious characters. A disaffected Wells was to ascribe Machiavellian traits to the Webbs to explain their position in the Fabians. It did take political skill to maintain a coalition of intellects of the kind that the Fabian

Society became. Sometimes, as with Wells and also with Wallas, the coalition could not be sustained, but more often it was. The Society contrived to be all things to Social Democrats, as the preface to the original *Fabian Essays* termed its contributors. Among the prices paid for a broad political base was un-originality in political and economic theory.

What the original Fabian essayists had in common was a recognition that the nature of capitalism was changing; a realization that the State's economic role had expanded and would continue to expand; and a belief that the State was evolving in the direction of democratic socialism. As for the developments within capitalism, Sidney Webb was able to point to the increased concentration of ownership and the emergence of the business corporation. 'The older economists doubted whether anything but banking and insurance could be carried on by joint stock enterprises: now every conceivable industry, down to banking and milk selling, is successfully managed by the salaried officers of large corporations of idle shareholders. More than one-third of the whole business of England, measured by the capital employed, is now done by joint stock companies.'

As for the role of the State in economic matters, Webb said that the theorists who denounced such activity as repugnant to the sturdy individual independence of Englishmen, and as yet outside the sphere of practical politics, seldom had the least suspicion of the existing extent of such activity. This was because most of it had taken place in the form of municipal socialism, of gas and water socialism. More obviously, the Central Government, in the form of the Post Office, was the largest single employer; and even in the area that private enterprise had left to it, the State subjected it to a wider range of regulation, inspection and control than economic theorists seemed to appreciate. Webb observed that, 'All this has been done by "practical" men, ignorant, that is to say, of any scientific sociology, believing Socialism to be the most foolish of dreams, and absolutely ignoring, as they ought, all grandiloquent claims for social reconstruction. Such is the irresistible sweep of social tendencies, that in their very act they worked to bring about the very Socialism they despised; and to destroy the Individualist faith which they still professed. They builded better than they knew'.

This did not mean that social reorganization could be secured without the conscious efforts of individual reformers; but they did have the advantage of working with the stream rather than against it. Webb then outlined a six point programme for reformers to pursue. Firstly, the complete shifting of the burden of taxation from the workers, of whatsoever grade, to the recipients of rent and interest, with a view to the ultimate and gradual extinction of the latter class. Secondly, the extension of the Factory Acts to raise, universally, the standard of comfort by obtaining the general recognition of a minimum wage and a maximum working day. Thirdly, educational reform to enable all, even the poorest, children to obtain not merely some, but the best education they are capable of. Fourthly, the reorganization of the Poor Law administration to provide generously, and without stigma, for the aged, the sick, and those destitute through temporary want of employment, without relaxing the tests against the endowment of able bodied idleness. Fifthly, the extension of municipal activity to secure the gradual public organization of labour for all public purposes, and the elimination of the private capitalist and middleman. Sixthly, the amendment of the political machinery to obtain the most accurate representation and expression of the desires of the majority of the people at every moment.

This was what Shaw called 'the humdrum programme of the practical Social Democrat today. There is not one new item in it. All are applications of principle already admitted, and extensions of practices already in full activity. All have on them that stamp of the vestry which is so congenial to the British mind. None of them compel the use of the words Socialism or Revolution: at no point do they involve guillotining, declaring the Rights of Man, swearing on the altar of the country, or anything else that is supposed to be essentially un-English. And they are all sure to come – landmarks on our course already visible to far sighted politicians even of the party which dreads them'. A possible collision between an increasingly monopolistic capitalism and democracy as foreseen by another Fabian essayist was not anticipated by either Shaw or Webb. For Webb, socialism was the economic obverse of democracy.[35]

The Fabians' initial strategy was to attempt to permeate the Conservative and Liberal Parties with their ideas. The Liberals seemed the more promising target, and Shaw claimed for himself the credit for committing the Liberal Party to the radical Newcastle Programme in 1891. The Fabians, particularly the Webbs, were by no means always at odds with the Conservatives. At the time of the Boer War, Shaw published a booklet, *Fabianism and the Empire*, which was in favour of 'efficient and sensible' imperialism. The Fabians had some success in helping to shape the Education Act of 1902. There was Fabian support for Joseph Chamberlain's Tariff Reform campaign, while the Labour movement as a whole viewed Protection with some suspicion until the 1930s.

The policy of two way permeation, favoured especially by the Webbs, led to some distrust of the Fabians on the part of Liberal politicians like Asquith, and also within trade union and socialist circles. The Fabian support of Tariff Reform led to Graham Wallas's resignation from the Society. By the mid-1890s, Wallas had been left as the only committed Liberal in the Fabian leadership, and the rejection of Free Trade by the Society was the last of several conflicts of outlook. Even after they had helped to found the Labour Representation Committee in 1900, at least down to the First World War, the Fabians did not limit their energies to its aid. They may have thought with Shaw that the nascent Labour Party was a cork on the Liberal tide in 1906, and that if any 'ism' triumphed then it was Gladstonism not socialism.[36]

In the first decade of the twentieth century, the Webbs came to be the dominant voices among the Fabians. The partnership of Shaw and Sidney Webb gave way to the Partnership of Beatrice and Sidney Webb. The *History of Trade Unionism* published in 1894 was just the first of a massive production line of historical and other political studies that established the Webbs as a formidable intellectual force, whose researches were to impose their findings on secondary authors. Between 1899 and 1929 the Webbs produced ten volumes on the development of English local government, one volume including the Minority Report of the Royal Commission on the Poor Laws of 1905–9, which they had virtually written themselves. According to disciples, that document was a virtual blueprint for the legislation that led to the Welfare State, including the National Health Service Act of 1946.[37] The Webbs' ideas were certainly

influential in the general promotion of administrative rationalization and increased social provision; but theirs was scarcely
the sole influence not least upon the Liberal and Conservative
Governments that passed most of the legislation.

Far from being the authors of the National Health Service,
the Webbs' book *The State and the Doctor* (1910) has been fairly
described as giving aid and comfort to bodies such as the modern
American Medical Association who oppose socialized medicine.
The Fabians viewed the medical profession with distrust as
having a vested interest in the public being ill. Only the Medical
Officer of Health was absolved from this conspiracy because he
was a salaried public official and concerned with what the Fabians
saw as a leading cause of illness, environment.[38] The Webbs
seemed to think that sickness would have no place in their well
ordered Fabian ideal society. In the existing unordered one, the
Webbs opposed the supersession of the Poor Law Medical
Service by 'any system of universal medical insurance'. This
would be 'retrograde in policy, and likely to be fraught with the
greatest dangers to public health and to the moral character of
the poor'. That character was thought to be so weak that the
Webbs could not willingly envisage any system in which poor
persons had any choice of their doctor. To do so would place
the doctor at the mercy of his working class patients who would
demand 'strong medicine' and 'medical extras', and who would
not need to listen to 'the stern advice about habits of life on
which recovery really depends'.[39]

The Webb's commitment to the Labour Party, as opposed to
the promotion of 'national efficiency' through generalized
permeation of all parties, became specific by the end of the
First World War. As Germany was the enemy in the war, one
object of external administrative admiration had to be discarded. The Russian Revolution did not immediately lead to the
rise of a substitute. What the Revolution did seem to be in the
eyes of Arthur Henderson, the leading contemporary figure in
the Labour Party, was the precursor of widespread social
changes even in Britain. Henderson wanted these changes to be
peacefully secured and expecting that the coming extension of
the franchise would be accompanied by an advance in popular
political thought he wanted the Labour Party to provide the
mechanism. The Webbs, in Beatrice's phrase, had come to see

the Labour Party as 'a poor thing, but our own'.[40] By early 1918 Sidney Webb had played a leading part in providing the Party with a constitution and a programme.

Labour and the New Social Order was the programme. It began with the assumption that 'what this war is consuming is not merely the security, the homes, the livelihood and the lives of millions of innocent families and an enormous proportion of all the accumulated wealth of the world, but also the very basis of the peculiar social order in which it has arisen. The individualist system of capitalist production has received a death blow. With it must go the political system and ideas in which it naturally found expression'. The Labour Party had to ensure that what was built in its place was 'a new social order, based not on fighting but on fraternity – not on competitive struggle for the means of bare life, but on a deliberately planned co-operation in production and distribution for the benefit of all who participate by hand or by brain – not on the utmost possible inequality of riches, but on a systematic approach towards a healthy equality of material circumstances for every person born into the world – not on an enforced dominion over subject nations, subject races, subject colonies, subject classes, or a subject sex, but, in industry as well as in government, on that equal freedom, that general consciousness of consent, and the widest possible in power, both economic and political, which is characteristic of true Democracy'.[41]

The Webb drafted document went on to argue that 'the members of the Labour Party themselves actually working by hand or by brain, in close contact with the facts, have perhaps at all times a more accurate appreciation of what is practicable, in industry as in politics, than those in academic instruction or who are biased by great possessions. But today no man dares to say that anything is impracticable . . . What we now promulgate as our policy, whether for opposition or for office, is not merely this or that specific reform, but a deliberately thought out, systematic, and comprehensive plan for that immediate social rebuilding which any Ministry, whether or not it desires to grapple with the problem, will be driven to undertake. The Four Pillars of the House that we propose to erect, resting upon the common foundation of the Democratic control of society in all its activities, may be termed respectively:

(a) The Universal Enforcement of the National Minimum;
(b) The Democratic Control of Industry;
(c) The Revolution in National Finance; and
(d) The Surplus Wealth for the Common Good'.[42]

It was the principle of democratic control of industry that the programme said marked off the Labour Party from the other political parties. 'What the Party looks to is a genuinely scientific reorganization of the nation's industry, no longer deflected by individual profiteering, on the basis of the Common Ownership of the Means of Production; the equitable sharing of the proceeds among all who participate in any capacity and only among these, and the adoption, in particular services and occupations, of those systems and methods of administration and control that may be found, in practice, best to promote, not profiteering, but the public interest'.

Of the Labour Party the programme said, 'it stands not merely for the principle of Common Ownership of the nation's land, to be applied as suitable opportunities occur, but also, specifically, for the immediate Nationalization of Railways, Mines, and the production of Electrical Power ... for the National Ownership and Administration of the Railways and Canals, and their union, along with Harbours and Roads, and the Posts and Telegrams – not to say also the great lines of steamers which could at once be owned, if not immediately directly managed in detail, by the Government – in a unified national service of Communication and Transport ... The Labour Party demands the immediate Nationalization of Mines, the extraction of coal and iron being worked as a public service ... and the whole business of the retail distribution of household coal being undertaken, as a local public service, by the elected Municipal or County Councils. There is no reason why coal should fluctuate in price any more than railway fares, or why the consumer should be made to pay more in winter than in summer, or in one town than another. What the Labour Party would aim at is, for household coal of standard quality, a fixed and uniform price for the whole kingdom, payable by rich and poor alike, as unalterable as the penny postage stamp'. The programme also advocated the elimination of private profit making from industrial assurance, the liquor trade, various services of 'common utility', and the maintenance of the wartime controls of other various commodities and industries.[43]

The financing of these various ventures and also a programme of social reform was not to be borne by its main beneficiaries. 'The Labour Party stands for such a system of taxation as will yield all the necessary revenue to the Government without encroaching on the prescribed National Minimum Standard of Life, of any family whatsoever; without hampering production or discouraging any useful personal effort and with the possible approximation to equality of sacrifice'.

Protection was not to be countenanced, and indirect taxes were not to be imposed on anything but luxuries. For the raising of revenue, the Labour Party was to rely on 'the direct taxation of the incomes above the necessary cost of family maintenance' and of 'private fortunes both during life and at death'. A special Capital Levy was to be raised to pay off the whole or the greater part of the National Debt swollen as it was by the cost of the war. For this, and presumably also its entire programme, for which the individuals concerned would not have to pay, 'the Labour Party claims the support of four-fifths of the whole nation, for the interests of the clerk, the teacher, the doctor, the minister of religion, the average retail shopkeeper and trader, and all the mass of those living on small incomes are identical with those of the artisan'.[44]

The 1918 Constitution of the Labour Party, which was drafted at much the same time as *Labour and the New Social Order*, included as the Party's fourth object the commitment 'to secure for the producers by hand or brain the full fruits of their industry, and the most equitable distribution thereof that may be possible, upon the basis of the Common Ownership of the Means of Production and the best obtainable system of popular administration and control of each industry or service'. It has since been suggested that this socialist objective was successfully urged on an indifferent Henderson by intellectuals such as Sidney Webb and G D H Cole, in the Fabian belief that an important section of the professional and salaried managerial classes were interested in and ripe for socialism.[45] Such an interpretation would need to be substantiated by a fuller study of contemporary trade union attitudes than has yet been undertaken.

The trade union movement as a whole was certainly apathetic about Guild Socialism, a form of 'popular administration and control of each industry and service' which Cole was currently advocating. The Guild Socialists believed that the replacement of the capitalist by the bureaucrat would not essentially change the subordinate role of the working classes. They, therefore, favoured a form of industrial democracy based on producers' control. Essentially, Guild Socialism was a plea for a more active democracy. [46] The trade union leadership, with greater realism, assumed that their rank and file wanted a mainly passive democracy, but one in which their interests were represented. Guild Socialism, a political theory which envisaged a diminished role for the State, withered away. The Webbs, who wanted a more extensive bureaucracy, prevailed.

Fabian Socialism, in the heavily bureaucratic form that the Webbs gave it, became the dominant creed of the Labour Party. Sidney Webb's description in 1923 of 'the inevitable gradualness of our scheme of change'[47] for many came to symbolize the Fabian approach. Given the anticipated 'gradualness' of the demise of capitalism, the Webbs even provided the Labour Party with what purported to be an interim programme to govern in the meantime. [48] The programme was not only scarcely a blueprint for a future mixed economy, but was also not one that proved immediately practicable. The Labour Governments of 1924 and 1929–31 in fact looked to the tenets of Classical Liberalism for guidance, as perhaps the Webbs anticipated in resuscitating Free Trade as an approved principle in *Labour and the New Social Order*.

As for the 'inevitable' side of Webb's formula, this meant much more than a recognition of the slowness of political change in Britain, if indeed in later years the Webbs emotionally accepted even that. 'Inevitable' also meant the overriding of opposition. Politics had no real place in the Webbsian future, as their evidence to the Haldane Committee on the Machinery of Government made clear. When the 1931 political crisis in Britain made it evident that however 'inevitable' socialism in that country was to be in coming, its arrival would be very gradual indeed, the Webbs turned to the Soviet Union. There political democracy was not allowed to interfere with socialism in theory or in practice. [49] The Labour Party recovered from 1931 even if some of its leading intellectuals did not. Such ideas of its own that the Party had in 1945 were essentially those of *Labour and the New Social Order*. The Labour Government elected then, with its nationalization programme and inherited social legislation, made a prominent contribution to the creation of the Managed Economy Welfare State. The crucial contribution of the managing economic theory for the new dispensation, however, was made by a Liberal, Keynes.

Chapter 4

The Keynesian Revolution

'We have to invent new wisdom for a new age', Keynes wrote in 1925, as he surveyed the depressed contemporary condition of British capitalism, scarred by mass unemployment. 'And in the meantime we must, if we are to do any good, appear unorthodox, troublesome, dangerous, disobedient to them that begat us. In the economic field this means, first of all, that we must find new policies and new instruments to adapt and control the working of economic forces, so that they do not intolerably interfere with contemporary ideas as to what is fit and proper in the interests of social stability and social justice.' In terms of economic theory, what Keynes had to bring himself to do was to destroy the grip on it of the Marshallian School. What W S Jevons had called 'the noxious influence of Authority' in economics had passed from J S Mill on to Alfred Marshall. The period from the mid-1880s down to 1914 was emphatically the Marshallian Age in British economics.

Marshall created a genuine School which included in its ranks A G Pigou and D H Robertson, his successors in the Chair of Political Economy at Cambridge, and, until 1930, Keynes. When Jevons had led 'the marginal revolution' in economic theory with his *Theory of Political Economy* in 1871, he had aimed at nothing less than 'the overthrow of the Ricardo-Mill Economics'. His early death, among other factors, left the way clear for a sort of pious counter-revolutionary restoration or retention of some of the Classical terminology and concepts, in which, for example, Say's Law was retained, and even Malthusian population theory was not entirely discarded.[1] The architect of the restoration was Marshall, whose *Principles of Economics*, first published in 1890, became what J S Mill's *Principles of Political Economy* had been before, *the* book on economics.

Other magisterial volumes followed. The internal free market, external Free Trade, and the Gold Standard were all treated with sophisticated approval. The Ricardian assumption of economies tending towards full employment was retained. As the first conventional liberal economist to recognize that the facts of the post-1918 world no longer fitted the economic theory, it fell to Keynes to overthrow the Marshallian School in which he had been trained himself. The sound and the fury of the attack, and the change that it swiftly wrought in British economic practice, tended to obscure the fact that in the sphere of economic theory the Keynesian Revolution was importantly incomplete. Keynes had not been able to fully break the grip of his Marshallian intellectual inheritance, an examination of which is crucial to the understanding of what Keynes was fighting for, and against.

I. THE MARSHALLIAN SCHOOL

Alfred Marshall was the dominant figure of Neo-Classical Economics.[2] He was the most prominent architect of the Great Theory of Economics that so well suited the decades immediately before 1914 in which the free market was dominant and legally entrenched, perfect competition if not a fact was not yet a gross and obvious absurdity, resources were allocated by a market where the value of the currency was stable, and one could seriously think in terms of a 'long run' including further decades of family and business prosperity where the harvest sown with labour and thrift would be gathered in due course. For such a world, 'general equilibrium' was an image miraculously successful in combining simplicity with an all inclusive explanatory power and a recognizable resemblance to the facts.

Marshall was well aware that in practice imperfections of the market existed, devoting a part of the *Principles* to what he described as the theory of monopoly. Moreover, Book III of his classic *Industry and Trade* was about 'Monopolistic Tendencies', and included chapters on American and German trusts and cartels as well as British developments in this direction. Nevertheless, to the end of his career, he wrote in terms of a constant increase in the forces that tended to break up monopolies, and 'to offer to men, who have but little capital of their own, openings both for starting new businesses and for rising into posts of command in large public and private concerns'. His basic theoretical model remained that of perfect competition in which 'the forces of supply and demand have free play' and in which there was perfect knowledge and foresight. [4]

Although his major contribution to economics was theoretical, Marshall did not assign himself the role of disinterested but yet exclusively informed spectator, which, as late as the first part of the 1930s, Lionel Robbins was ascribing to economists. Economics is neutral between ends, Robbins proclaimed, but Marshall was very clear about the ends that the study of economics should be pursuing. Even in the *Principles*, he felt the need to emphasize that 'the dominant aim of economics in the present generation is to contribute to a solution of social problems'. In Keynes's opinion, 'Marshall was too anxious to do good. He had an inclination to undervalue those intellectual parts of the subject which were not directly connected with human well-being or the condition of the working classes or the like, although indirectly they might be of the utmost importance, and to feel that when he was pursuing them he was not occupying himself with the highest'. Indeed, prominently displayed in his college rooms, Marshall kept a portrait of a 'down and out' whom he called 'my patron saint' as a constant reminder of the need not to become 'a mere thinker'. [5]

The main problem facing the economic and social system of his time, Marshall felt, was 'how to get rid of the evils of competition while retaining its advantages'. As things stood, the really poor were 'used up in a hand to mouth struggle for existence' which meant that they did not develop as they should. Marshall's interest in increased State educational provision was mainly directed towards the minimization of the loss of talent in the working classes. He was also concerned about the poor quality of working class housing, and he was an advocate of town planning. He wrote with approval in 1909 of copying German methods of helping what he called 'our Residuum', or the lower part of the working classes, and he came to see old age pensions and social insurance provision as valuable palliatives for extreme inequality of wealth.

Marshall favoured redistributive taxation measures, including a large use of steeply graduated taxes on incomes and property, and a moderate increase in death duties. He struck a familiar nineteenth century note in emphasizing that he wanted 'even the poorest class of genuine workers' to pay some taxes so that they would remain 'full, free citizens, with a direct interest in public finance', with the promise that 'the greater part of what they contribute directly to the Exchequer should be returned to them indirectly by generous expenditure from public funds, imperial and local, for their benefit'.[6]

The duties that Marshall accorded to the State in the economic sphere, however, were fairly restricted. He wrote in 1907, 'If government control had supplanted that of private enterprise a hundred years ago, there is good reason to suppose that our methods of manufacture now would be about as effective as they were fifty years ago, instead of being perhaps four or even six times as efficient as they were then' and that 'the total real income of the country would be about half of what it is now'. Although at one time attracted by socialist ideas, he had eventually come to consider that 'no socialistic scheme, yet advanced, seems to make adequate provision for the maintenance of high enterprise and individual strength of character; nor to promise a sufficiently rapid increase in the business plant and other material implements of production, to enable the real incomes of the manual labour classes to continue to increase as fast as they have done in the recent past, even if the total income of the country be shared equally by all'. He believed that the problem of poverty was 'a mere passing evil in the progress of man upwards'. In fact, he thought that through greater mechanization the condition of even 'the humbler classes of mankind' could be raised because they would have mechanical slaves to do the routine things that at present dominated their lives, thus making possible greater leisure for them and, aided by improved educational provision, higher quality work too. Indeed, assuming that human and material resources were better utilized, Marshall had 'large hopes' about the future provided that it was entrusted to a basically private enterprise economy.[7]

It was primarily through Pigou that the Marshallian tradition was handed down and became the Cambridge school of economics. He brought up a generation of Cambridge economists in the conviction that 'it's all in Marshall'. Pigou once wrote that many times he had imagined that he had made an original contribution to economic thought only to turn to Marshall's *Principles* and 'almost inevitably in some obscure footnote there was half a clause, inside a parenthesis perhaps, which made it obvious that Marshall had solved this problem long before but had not thought it worthwhile to write the answer down'. Pigou in fact substantially developed what he interpreted as Marshallian thinking, perhaps beyond the point which Marshall wished it to be taken, to judge from the latter's private comments on Pigou's *Wealth and Welfare*.[8]

The tone of Pigou's work was set in this book, first published in 1912, in which he emphasized that 'the complicated analyses' made by students of economic science were 'instruments for the bettering of human life. The misery and squalor that surround us, the injurious luxury of some wealthy families, the terrible uncertainty overshadowing many families of the poor – these are evils too plain to be ignored'. Pigou in fact promoted the study of welfare economics which he took to be concerned 'to investigate the dominant influences through which the economic welfare of the world, or of a particular country, is likely to be increased. The hope of those who pursue it is to suggest lines of action – or non action – on the part of the State or of private persons that might foster such influences. Nobody supposes that economic welfare is coincident with the whole of welfare or that the State ought to pursue it relentlessly without regard for other goods – liberty, for instance, the amenities of the family, spiritual needs and so on'.[9]

Pigou's *Wealth and Welfare* (and the subsequent versions of it that appeared as *The Economics of Welfare*) were based on the pragmatic utilitarianism that Pigou, like Marshall before him, had imbibed from Cambridge's Henry Sidgwick in preference to the more fashionable Oxford Idealism of Green.[10] Unlike his successors in welfare economics, Pigou was primarily concerned with practical applications of theory. In other words, where there was a divergence between private and social product what measures might be taken to bring the two into equality. Pigou came to believe that under an unregulated private enterprise system, disharmonies occurred in production, in distribution and in the occurrence of industrial fluctuations. In the sphere of production, for instance, he thought that the State should intervene to ensure the 'husbanding of natural resources, the need for which was not always comprehended by the current generation', to regulate the social costs of production, such as pollution, and to either control or manage monopolies. [11]

As for the disharmonies associated with industrial fluctuations, Pigou said in 1935 that economists had for some time recognized the need for State intervention through the banking system to moderate the effects of the trade cycle provided that it could be done successfully, a matter on which he did not commit himself. Regarding the unemployment that could result from industrial fluctuations and from other changes in the economy, he specifically rejected the Ricardian view, or, as it had come to be in his time, the 'Treasury view' that public works did not increase aggregate employment but simply diverted it from the private to the public sectors. Indeed, in his Inaugural Lecture in 1908, Pigou dealt with the issue of levying rates and taxes for the purpose of setting unemployed men to work, recording that it had been recently said in Parliament that 'if you employ public moneys in this way, you take funds, which would have been used by private persons in the employment of better workmen on tasks that are wanted, to use them in employing worse workmen on tasks that are not wanted. You therefore, tend to impoverish the community without really lessening the aggregate mass of unemployment. This view is attractively simple; but economic analysis shows that it ignores two important considerations.

'First and most evidently, it ignores the fact that in the twentieth century the unemployed cannot be allowed to starve; that, therefore if they are not given work, they will certainly be given maintenance either by private charity or by the Poor Law, that, therefore, the money spent in setting up relief works and so on is, in great measure, money that would otherwise have been spent in charitable and Poor Law grants, and not money that would have been used in employing labour in private industry.

Nor is this all. Even apart from that consideration, it would not be true that the levying of rates and taxes for relief works would contract private industry by an amount *equal* to the expansion of public industry. It would, no doubt, contract it to some extent. But it is probable that only a part of the extra taxes people had to pay would be taken from funds they would otherwise have devoted at that time directly or indirectly to wage payment. Hence, the true result of relief works and so on is not to leave the aggregate amount of unemployment in the country unaltered, but to diminish that amount. There are more people at work than there would otherwise have been'.

On the other hand, Pigou was subsequently critical of the manner in which the Minority Report of the Royal Commission on the Poor Law handled the subject, arguing that they had seriously underestimated the cost, and emphasizing that the efficacy of a public works policy depended upon mobility in the labour market.[12]

In his Inaugural Lecture, Pigou had used the problem of unemployment to illustrate the practical uses of economic analysis, and his classic work *Wealth and Welfare* had originally developed from a study of the causes of unemployment. He should, therefore, have been well placed to make the theoretical breakthroughs that could have led to more effective measures to combat the mass unemployment problem of the inter-war years, especially as for some time in the 1920s economists generally treated the problem as simply a particularly severe example of the downward phase of the trade cycle which would shortly correct itself.

Pigou, as we have seen, an advocate of counter-cyclical public works, did publish in 1929 something approaching a modern multiplier theory. However, he was generally not able to break out of the current discussion in terms of wage cuts as a means of encouraging employment, an approach which he was not confident would work, and about the mobility of labour. In the sphere of practical policy, he was associated as a member of the Cunliffe and Bradbury Committees with the return of the Gold Standard in the 1920s, which scarcely made for a solution of the unemployment problem. In his published work about unemployment, Pigou became much more theoretical in outlook.

At the beginning of his book, *The Theory of Unemployment,* published in 1933 at a time when he himself said that 'the tragedy of unemployment is of unexampled magnitude', Pigou declared the aim of his study to be 'to clarify, not to advocate a policy. While it is natural and right in the present deplorable state of the world's affairs that many should seek to play a part in guiding conduct, that is not their primary business. They are psychologists, not clinical practitioners; engineers, not engine drivers. The main part of such contribution as they may hope to make must be indirect; in the study, not in the pages of newspapers and even in the council chamber'.[13] Keynes, given to publicity and committed to finding a practical solution to the problem of mass unemployment, made Pigou's work a prime target of his assault on the prevailing economic orthodoxies.

The Marshallian School, indeed, was in retreat by the time that Pigou has been succeeded in Marshall's old Chair by D H Robertson, who was to hold the Professorship between 1944 and 1957. Robertson was even more of a Marshallian than his seniors and he was certainly an adherent of Pigou's belief that 'it's all in Marshall'.[14] Robertson had been tutored by Keynes in his Cambridge undergraduate days, and he closely collaborated with him in the 1920s. In very early career, Robertson had dismissed the 'Treasury view' on public works as expounded by R G Hawtrey, and he had given 'cordial support' to the Minority Report proposals that Pigou had shown reservations about.[15] Robertson was associated with Keynes in the publication of the Liberal Party's Yellow Book, *Britain's Industrial Future* (1928), which advocated a large scale public investment programme to try to lift the depressed British economy in the direction of fuller employment. Robertson, however, vehemently dissented from Keynes's later ventures, arguing, among other things, and not without point, that the commitment that Keynes wanted to see made to the maintenance of full employment was bound to be inflationary. The Marshallian School finally died with Robertson in 1963. Insofar as its demise was caused by other intellectual influences, those provided by Keynes, a former subscriber to the faith, were the most decisive.

The attitudes of the Marshallian School to the role of government differed in emphasis between its members, but they were

generally more favourable to State activity in the social policy
sphere rather than in economic matters. Pigou must certainly
be exempted from association of welfare economics with the
general advocacy of *laissez-faire*.[16] As for Marshall himself, he
made it clear that 'there is no general economic principle which
supports the notion that industry will necessarily flourish best,
or that life will be happiest and healthiest, when each man is
allowed to manage his own concerns as he thinks best'.

As we have seen, Marshall envisaged the State taking on a
variety of social functions, but in economic affairs he thought
that 'the heavy hand of government tends to slacken progress
on whatever matter it touches'. He seemed to fear that business
and politics could be mutually corrupted by more contact.
Marshall thought that Pigou had gone too far in *Wealth and
Welfare* in writing down the value of the competitive system.
Moreover, he was less convinced than Pigou about the remedial
effects on unemployment of public works. If the State had to
act, Marshall generally preferred 'an extension of local responsibilities whenever possible'. Pigou thought that if Marshall had
lived into the 1930s his distrust of central government economic
activity would have been diminished, because the invention of
public corporations 'not directly subject to political control' had
'greatly widened the range of what is practicable'. Pigou considered, however, that Marshall would have 'put the burden of
proof squarely on those who wished to supersede private enterprise by such devices', and that even in monopolistic situations
he would have preferred government control to government
operation.

Writing in 1937, Pigou himself envisaged the nationalization
of the Bank of England (with instructions being given to it to
use its powers to mitigate, as far as possible, violent fluctuations
in industry and employment) and certainly also the manufacture
of armaments, probably the coal industry and possibly the
railways. If all went well, Pigou said, one could go farther in
gradually modifying the general structure of capitalism not only
by more acts of nationalization but also by exercises in redistributive taxation with 'the deliberate purpose of diminishing
the glaring inequalities of fortune and opportunity which deface
our present civilization'.[17]

The Marshallian School has been associated with the intellectual authorship of the Welfare State.[18] Certainly, it helped to turn liberal economic theory in that direction, in much the same way as Green turned liberal political theory. Nevertheless, for all the social concern which brought Marshall and Pigou to the study of economics, and Robertson too, theirs was not the crucial contribution made by economists to the development of the Welfare State. The ending of Free Trade in the 1930s and not the failure to find a solution to mass unemployment was what led Pigou to fear in 1939 that the study of economics was redundant in practical terms for the present. Pigou was closely involved in the policy of returning to the Gold Standard, which had the effect of making industrial recovery more difficult, and with it the amelioration of unemployment. When Robertson received an honorary degree at Harvard in 1936, he warned his audience against doing too little about the persisting high level of unemployment, but he warned even more against doing too much.[19] The situation demanded an urgency that Marshall's faithful disciples did not display, leaving an unfaithful one, Keynes, to construct the essential apparatus of economic management for the Welfare State.

II. J M KEYNES

However inhibiting 'the Marshallian dictatorship'[20] was on the development of British economics, events were pressing for change, and so were economists undeterred by the dominant tradition. Keynes and those who allied themselves with him such as R F Kahn, Joan Robinson, and R F Harrod, were to play a major part in an immense creative spasm in economics, which began in the mid-1920s and which lasted until the Second World War. This yielded six or seven major innovations of theory, which together completely altered the orientation and character of economics. Until the 1930s, economics was the science of coping with basic scarcity. After the 1930s, it was an account of how men coped with scarcity and uncertainty. One thing above all divided the new theory from the old: the discarding of the assumption (which has often been quite tacit) of universal perfect knowledge. At the opening of the 1930s, economic theory still rested on the assumption of a basically orderly and tranquil world. At their end, it had come to terms with the restless anarchy and disorder of the world of fact.[21]

A leading casualty of bringing economics more in line with the world of fact as it seemed in the inter-war period had to be the Marshallian School, and its overthrow was all the less peaceful for being largely accomplished by economists from Marshall's native Cambridge. Joan Robinson's work on imperfect competition is illustrative of the changes that took place in economic theory. Mrs Robinson saw herself as building on the foundations laid by Marshall and Pigou; but as mainly following the suggestion of another Cambridge innovator, Piero Sraffa, about the need to develop monopoly analysis. Writing in 1933, she said that 'we see on every side a drift towards monopolization under the names of restriction schemes, quota systems, rationalization, and the growth of giant companies'. There was what she called 'a world of monopolies'. Yet, she said, it was still customary in setting out the principles of economic theory, to open with an analysis of a perfectly competitive world, and to treat monopoly as a special case. Mrs Robinson argued that this procedure could with advantage be reversed.[22]

The task of a more general attack on the prevailing orthodoxy fell to Keynes. Trained in economic theory under the auspices of Authority at Cambridge, Keynes had by the mid-1930s a long record of conflict with authority in economic policy in the shape of the Treasury and the Bank of England. Indeed, Keynes's public reputation had been made when he had resigned from the Treasury in protest against what he saw as the severity and economic nonsense of the Versailles Settlement, and had made his views known to the world in his polemic, *The Economic Consequences of the Peace*.

Conflict with the Bank of England and the Treasury followed over the return to the Gold Standard in 1925, which Keynes opposed. Conflict with the Treasury occurred again over the Liberal Yellow Book proposals, which aimed to ameliorate mass unemployment mainly by means of a public works programme. The Macmillan Committee on Finance and Industry of 1929–31 provided the arena for yet more combat between Keynes and the 'Treasury view'. As he saw things, the problem of mass unemployment needed a swift solution. 'It is certain that the world will not much longer tolerate the unemployment which, apart from brief intervals of excitement, is associated – and, in my opinion, inevitably associated – with present day capitalist individualism'. All that current economic theory and policy offered was the long run resolution of the unemployment problem. This was not good enough. In Keynes's opinion, 'this long run is a misleading guide to current affairs. In the long run we are all dead. Economists set themselves too easy, too useless a task if in tempestuous seasons they can only tell us the storm is long past and the ocean is flat again'. He believed that, more immediately, it was possible 'by a right analysis of the problem to cure the disease' of unemployment, 'whilst preserving efficiency and freedom'.[23]

The propagation of his 'new wisdom for a new age' meant for Keynes that this time he had not merely to quarrel with the Treasury and the Bank of England. He had now to make war on many of his fellow economists, including his own Professor, Pigou; and, as difficult, he had to combat the memory of Marshall. Keynes had written a superb biographical study of Marshall, but his deference had always known limits.[24] Nevertheless, although Keynes was not as restricted as Pigou had been by the need to follow in Marshall's intellectual footprints, on the journey towards and even beyond the *General Theory*, he 'carried a good deal of Marshallian luggage with him and never thoroughly unpacked it to throw out the clothes he could not wear'. His 'long struggle of escape' from 'habitual modes of thought and expression' was an incomplete one.

This failure to entirely discard Marshallian intellectual impedimenta was hidden from many friends and foes by the controversial manner in which he signalled his departure from what he portrayed in the *General Theory* as the prevailing orthodoxy. Pigou said in his review of that book that Keynes had learnt in writing *The Economic Consequences of the Peace* that 'the best way to win attention for one's own ideas is to present them in a matrix of sarcastic comment upon other people'. Whether this was true or not, Keynes's scholarly two volumes *Treatise on Money* had failed to attract the favourable critical reception he had hoped for when it had been published in 1930. This had been particularly disappointing as it had indicated possible ways out of the unemployment situation. He seemed to resolve to write another book that could not be pushed to one side. So that, while Keynes said at the outset of the *General Theory* that he wished it could have been written with less controversy, he seemed to set out to make the book as provocative as possible.

In the opinion of one disciple, he went out of his way to pick out 'the interpretation of Marshall most adverse to his own views, to pulverize it, mock it and dance upon the mangled remains, just because he thought it a matter of great importance – of real, urgent, political importance – that people should know that he was saying something fresh. If he had been polite and smooth, if he had used properly scholarly caution and academic reserve, his book would have slipped down unnoticed and millions of families rotting in unemployment would be so much the further from relief. He wanted the book to stick in the gizzards of the orthodox, so that they would be forced either to spew it out or chew it properly'. His loyalty to Marshall made Pigou spew it out.[25] In the meantime Keynes had secured the attention for his ideas that he wanted.

The debating tone of the *General Theory* was set from its very beginning, when Keynes anticipated the response of his potential antagonists by suggesting that they would 'fluctuate between a belief that I am quite wrong and a belief that I am saying nothing new'. The only sensible course, seemingly, was to concur with his view. He did not handicap himself either with suggestions that the contribution to economics represented by the *General Theory* was an unimportant one. The general applicability of his theory was emphasized, while that of his predecessors was said only to apply to a special case. Although Keynes was well aware of a more conventional use of the term, he chose to call his predecessors since Ricardo 'Classical Economists'. Moreover, he portrayed their views in such a manner that those still available for comment found it difficult to recognize themselves.

Indeed, he had some trouble in finding published works that fitted the picture that he drew of his adversaries. He relied largely on Pigou's *Theory of Unemployment*, published only three years before, and fairly described by one reviewer as containing doctrines 'quite as strange and quite as novel as the doctrines of Mr Keynes himself'. As the *General Theory* itself was not easy to read and master, this led to a succession of interpretative texts that may have helped to keep the Keynesian momentum going for some time afterwards. In addition, it could be suggested that by inventing his own terms (such as the propensity to consume, liquidity preference, and the marginal efficiency of capital), and seeming to introduce a new language of economics, he made his theory attractive to the younger generation of economists. He seemed to be declaring redundant not only the learning of the older economists but also those economists themselves, thus opening the way for the adherents of the 'new economics'.

Neither Keynes nor his disciples were probably as calculating as a collection of unfavourable interpretations of their behaviour suggest; but it does seem reasonable to agree with one disciple that Keynes 'lacked the scruple of a scholar'. This was hard to bear for those criticized. Yet, as Keynes himself said, 'the matters at issue are of an importance which cannot be exaggerated'.[26] For his overriding concern was with finding a means of curing mass unemployment, not in respecting academic niceties. Like Smith's *Wealth of Nations,* Keynes's *General Theory* was both a major contribution to the development of economics and a tract for the time.

The *General Theory* was bang on the central economic problem in British capitalism in the 1930s. While on the way disposing of such concepts as the quantity theory of money, until then everybody's theory of money, Keynes made straight for the crucial flaw in contemporary economic theory. As one modern monetarist theorist has put it, 'in directing his attack at the Neo-Classical concept of an economic system equilibriating at full employment, and presenting a general theory of underemployment equilibrium of which Neo-Classical Theory was a special case, Keynes's polemical instinct was surely right, both because Neo-Classical ways of thinking were then a major obstacle to sensible anti-depression policy and because, for professional economists, the concept of equilibrium has always had far more intellectual sex appeal as an analytical companion than its opposite, disequilibrium'.[27]

When Keynes said that the Neo-Classical Economists had not revised their 'fundamental theory' to exclude 'the notion that if people do not spend their money in one way they will spend it in another', he was more accurate than when he made Say's Law the central tenet of that School's theoretical position. Say's Law may have been a straw man in Keynes's attack on the Neo-Classical School but one body that still seemed to take its attitude to public works expenditure from the teachings of Say and Ricardo was the Treasury. That Keynes for his purposes treated Treasury and Neo-Classical attitudes towards public works programmes as similar was unfair to the latter, because, as we have seen, Pigou and Robertson favoured such measures.

Keynes was less unfair to the Neo-Classical Economists as a group when he associated them with the advocacy of wage cuts to promote employment. This was probably true of a majority of them, although Pigou's position was heavily qualified, and Robertson was opposed to such policies. Nevertheless, it remains the case that before Kahn and Keynes there was no employment theory in economics, only trade cycle theory where general unemployment was a transient phase and not a state of repose.[28] The importance of Kahn's multiplier as a theoretical innovation may have been exaggerated,[29] but the concept was an invaluable one in demonstrating the employment benefits that would follow from increased investment. One result of the Keynesian assault on what he defined as the prevailing orthodoxy was to strengthen the case for public works and to place the burden of proof on anyone who would seek to remedy unemployment by depressing the wage rate.[30]

Before turning to Keynes's views on the role of the State in the economy, one thing needs to be emphasized. Although he had put right Ricardo's regretted victory over Malthus on effective demand, and then supplanted Marshall as the Authority in economics, Keynes's 'struggle' to shed former influences upon him was not entirely successful and this made his work less complete than it would otherwise have been. Although Keynes's macroeconomic theory provided the necessary tools for the subsequent development of dynamic economics, his own system (as Harrod said at the time) was essentially a static one. Harrod could have added that the system was made to sustain more than it could. Keynes's *General Theory* was an example of the Ricardian Vice of piling a heavy load of practical conclusions upon a tenuous groundwork, which was unequal to it, yet seemed in its simplicity not only attractive but also convincing.

The model that Keynes used was a closed economy. Taken as given were 'the existing skill and quantity and quality of available equipment, the existing technique, the degree of competition, the tastes and habits of the consumer, the disutility of different intensities of labour and of the activities of supervision and organization, as well as social structure'. Indeed, Keynes's macroeconomic theory rested on a Marshallian microeconomic base. He said himself that at full employment Neo-Classical Economics came into its own again.[31] However, this view, like his model, rested on an assumption of an underlying competitive market system that, as he elsewhere recognized, was increasingly less likely to exist, a tendency which had implications for the applicability of his favoured policies.

Those policies entailed an extended economic role for the State compared with that envisaged by Marshall, and a more general one in terms of broad management of the economy than Pigou had proposed. Keynes believed that 'the outstanding faults of the economic society' of the inter-war years were 'its failure to provide for full employment and its arbitrary and inequitable distribution of wealth and incomes'. The latter remark struck a radical note often to be found in his work, such as when he cast doubt on the social virtue of saving and anticipated 'the euthanasia of the rentier'. On further examination, his radicalism was often milder than it first seemed. For example, he thought that current disparities in wealth and incomes were too great, and that higher death duties were needed to reduce inherited advantage. However, he also believed in the desirability of 'significant inequalities' in rewards, because 'there are valuable human activities which require mature ownership for their fruition'.

He was no socialist. He found Marx's writings an irrelevance. He said of the Labour Party, 'it is a class party, and the class is not my class. If I am going to pursue sectional interests at all, I shall pursue my own. When it comes to the class struggle as such, my local and personal patriotisms, like those of every one else's, except certain unpleasant zealous ones, are attached to my own surroundings. I can be influenced by what seems to me to be justice and good sense; but the class war will find me on the side of the educated bourgeoisie'. There is something in the view that Keynes's personal history, and the affiliation of liberals and radicals with Keynesian doctrine, obscured the vital point that the techniques of Keynesian economics were simply neutral administrative tools. Keynes, however, was by no means neutral. He himself described his *General Theory* as being in some respects 'moderately conservative in its implications'.[32] What was to be moderately conserved was the private enterprise system.

Although 'in many ways' he found it 'extremely objectionable', Keynes believed that 'capitalism, wisely managed, can probably be made more efficient for attaining economic ends than any alternative system yet in sight'. This did not mean, however, the continuance of *laissez-faire*. Keynes wrote, 'Let us clear from the ground the metaphysical or general principles upon which, from time to time, *laissez-faire* has been founded. It is *not* true that individuals possess a prescriptive "natural ability" in their economic activities. There is *no* "compact" conferring perpetual rights on those who Have or on those who Acquire. The world is *not* so governed from above that private and social interest always coincide. It is *not* so managed here below that in practice they coincide. It is *not* a correct deduction from the Principles of Economics that enlightened self interest always operates in the public interest. Nor is it true that self interest generally *is* enlightened; more often individuals acting separately to promote their own ends are too ignorant or too weak to attain even these. Experience does not show that individuals, when they make up a social unit, are always less clear sighted than when they act separately'.

Nonetheless, he said, the Treasury and the Bank of England continued to pursue policies based on the premisses of *laissez-faire*, despite the fact that, for instance, the trade unions were 'strong enough to interfere with the free play of the forces of supply and demand', and the divorce between ownership and control in private companies made them more like the growing number of public corporations and more concerned with their general stability and reputation than with profit maximization. He said that 'our philosophy of economic life' had changed, but that this had taken place 'without changing our techniques or our copybook maxims'. As Keynes saw things, the current orthodoxy might represent the way in which we should like our economy to behave, but as it did not, corrective measures were needed which would ensure the sufficiency of demand that would secure the full employment of resources.[33]

The central controls necessary to ensure full employment, Keynes recognized, would involve 'a large extension of traditional functions of government'. He believed that 'the State will have to exercise a guiding influence on the propensity to consume partly through its scheme of taxation, partly by fixing the rate of interest, and partly, perhaps, in other ways. Furthermore, it seems unlikely that the influence of banking policy on the rate of interest will be sufficient by itself to determine an optimum rate of investment'. However, 'apart from the necessity of central controls to bring about an adjustment between the propensity to consume and the inducement to invest', he thought that 'there is no more reason to socialize economic life than there was before'. He wanted to see 'a wide field' retained 'for the exercise of private initiative and responsibility' within which 'the traditional advantages of individualism will still hold good'. As he saw them, they were 'partly advantages of efficiency – the advantages of decentralization and of the play of self interest', but, above all, be believed, 'individualism, if it can be purged of its defects and its abuses, is the best safeguard of personal liberty in the sense that, compared with any other system, it greatly widens the field for the exercise of personal choice, the loss of which is the greatest of all losses of the homogeneous or totalitarian State. For this variety preserves the traditions which embody the most secure and successful choices of former generations; it colours the present with the diversification of its fancy; and, being the handmaid of experiment as well as of tradition and of fancy, it is the most powerful instrument to better the future'.

Although the attainment of full employment required government intervention, particularly in the field of investment, Keynes considered that 'beyond this no obvious case is made out for a system of State Socialism which would embrace most of the economic life of the community. It is not the ownership of the instruments of production which it is important for the State to assume. If the State is able to determine the aggregate amount of resources devoted to augmenting the instruments and the basic rate of reward to those who own them, it will have accomplished all that is necessary'.[34]

Provided that the economic system remained essentially capitalist, there were few economic shibboleths that Keynes was not prepared to sacrifice to remedy the mass unemployment problem of the inter-war years, even temporarily, Free Trade. He did not spare those of his fellow economists who had either trained him or worked with him. Pigou was later to concede that the 'dogmatic slumber' into which British economics had fallen after Marshall had needed to be ended. Yet, for all the sound and the fury of Keynes's assault upon almost all other British economists since Ricardo, his departure from accepted theory was less fundamental than it seemed. To say this is not necessarily the same as concurring with the currently fashionable trait of writing Keynes down. Not only did Keynes's theoretical work point the way out of the Depression, but also, as Harrod has said, he was 'the father of dynamic economics' – providing the macroeconomic theory of statistics that was an indispensable foundation – and he gave a great stimulus to subsequent work in economic statistics. Moreover, although the *General Theory* was 'the Economics of Depression', Keynes did himself use his analytical tools in *How to Pay for the War* (1940) to show how they could be applied to an entirely different situation.

The obvious weakness in Keynesian macroeconomics was that it was constructed on an assumption of a competitive market below it that was increasingly less likely to be there. That Keynes should make such an assumption was doubly curious. Firstly, because he was well aware of the study of imperfect competition made by his disciple, Joan Robinson. Secondly, because, as we have seen, he had elsewhere recognized that the market situation was being changed partly by the emergence of a public sector, partly by the changing nature of private enterprise organization, and partly by the advent of powerful trade unions. There had come into being, as Abba Lerner later put it, individuals or committees who had the power to countermand the automatic market forces.[35] What Keynes failed to do was to incorporate these tendencies into his theory for the economic management of domestic capitalism. Another flaw in the *General Theory* was that – in contrast with

G

his other work – Keynes treated the role of money in a cavalier manner.[36]

It was a flaw, too, that, in a book self consciously designed as the bible of a new creed, international economic arrangements found little place in the *General Theory*. The *Treatise*, which did contain such arrangements, was bound to become relatively disregarded. Keynes's later efforts to promote a new international economic order never met with the success he hoped for and the West needed. Nevertheless, however imperfect their workings might well have seemed to him, Keynes was one of the architects of the Bretton Woods institutions – the International Monetary Fund and the World Bank.[37]

Keynes has been well described as a defender of capitalism.[38] His aim was to make the capitalist system function more smoothly and fairly. In his opinion, 'the important thing for government is not to do things which individuals are doing already, and to do them a little better or a little worse, but to do those things which at present are not done at all'. He did not exclude 'all manner of compromises and of devices by which public authority will co-operate with private initiative'.[39] Yet he was more wedded to private enterprise than, for instance, Pigou had been, and shortly before his death in 1946, he expressed his antipathy towards large scale nationalization.[40]

This distaste for widespread socialization in the economic sphere, however, accompanied an approval of the development of the social services that was very much in the Marshallian tradition. Keynes was an advocate of family allowances. The general philosophy of the Beveridge Report accorded with his views.[41] Keynes had made an essential contribution to the working of the modern British Welfare State by providing it with its operating economic theory. Compared with the attitudes that had been dominant since the demise of Mercantilist notions, Keynes's ideas had promoted a radical change in the responsibilities of the State in a capitalist economy.

Experience slowly, if unsurely, has shown up the flaws in the Keynesian model, certainly as practised in his native Britain. Keynes has been deposed as Authority. Ironically, the earliest contenders for his intellectual throne were those who looked back beyond Keynes to the ideas that he had spurned, and took inspiration from them.

PART TWO

THE DEVELOPMENT OF THE MACHINERY AND FUNCTIONS OF GOVERNMENT SINCE 1780

Chapter 5

The Eighteenth Century Inheritance

The intellectual beauty of the mercantilist model that Adam Smith constructed in order to demonstrate its flaws seems to have encouraged others since, including Keynes, to believe that the system which Smith described accorded with the reality of his time.[1] Prevailing ideas before Smith wrote often did favour a purposive role for government in the economy and in social provision. This does not mean, however, that effective practice followed suit, and this was also the case with Acts of Parliament. What rendered the pervasive Mercantilist State an illusion was the absence of the necessary governmental framework to render it fact. This is not to say that important changes in the machinery of government did not take place, for example, in the 1530s,[2] or, again, at and after the Restoration of 1660. Nevertheless, in the mercantilist period as a whole, the continuities in administration were as remarkable as the changes. At the centre, the old administrative system generally seems to have survived down to the age of Economical Reform.[3]

Even more important, not least given the problems then posed by distance, was the continuing undeveloped condition of local administration, which placed severe limits on the effectiveness of government. It may be that, on paper, compared with her European neighbours, England had the only really effective national system of poor relief in the form of the Elizabethan code of 1601.[4] In practice, however, when social problems were not able to be met by the individuals and families most closely concerned, private philanthropy was the most likely source of aid.[5] In the economic sphere, even if a form of Colbertism was desired, the machinery did not exist to implement it.[6] Private initiative in practice dominated the economy. What was the world's first Industrial Revolution was mainly the work of private enterprise.

The role of the State in eighteenth century Britain was largely confined to law and order, national defence, the conduct of foreign policy, the promotion of trade and some attempt at imperial management, various local functions (chiefly, poor relief), and the collection of the revenue to sustain these activities. This role was fairly simple. The central administrative structure was complex but small, and only slowly and imperfectly rationalized after 1780. The central government still lacked a means of controlling what passed for the local government system. The international pre-eminence that Britain enjoyed by 1815 followed a century and more in which the domestic practice of government, if not the prevailing philosophy of the time, was that governments which governed least governed best.

I. CROWN, PARLIAMENT AND ADMINISTRATION

In the years after 1688, the way was pointed in the direction of constitutional monarchy, cabinet government, and parliamentary democracy; but this is only evident in retrospect, and it was not a conscious part of the Revolution Settlement. What that Settlement did achieve at the very outset was to make it clear that the King had to rule through Parliament, while leaving him the means of doing so. However, what the precise relationships of King, Lords and Commons were supposed to be in the eighteenth century mixed form of government were as unclear in constitutional practice as the misty prose of Sir William Blackstone was in constitutional theory. The confusions followed from an executive monarchy being combined with what can now be seen as the beginnings of parliamentary government. Thus, when George III came to the throne in 1760 determined to change the Ministers and the policies that he had inherited, he was more ignorant of contemporary political realities than of his constitutional rights, literally interpreted.

With the arrival of Parliament as an essential part of the governmental system, the monarch needed a Minister or Ministers to run the institution. In the relationship between the King and Minister or Ministers, who was who's creature partly depended on the individuals concerned. The eighteenth century witnessed changes in the relationship between the Crown, the Cabinet Council and Parliament, but the Crown was by no means pushed to one side.[7]

For much of that century, it remained the case, as David Hume said in 1741, that 'the Crown has so many offices at its disposal, that, when assisted by the honest and disinterested part of the House, it will always command the resolutions of the whole so far, at least, as to preserve the ancient constitution from danger'. The Government normally consisted of an alliance between a group of politicians, and a Court and Administration group (placemen). To Crown patronage was added the political ability of parliamentary leaders. The Court could supply numbers, but not political leaders and a parliamentary facade. The Opposition consisted of politicians currently out of favour, and independent country gentlemen uninterested in office and suspicious of those who felt differently. Divisions between Tory and Whig seem to have meant a good deal at local level particularly on a religious basis: High Church versus Low Church and Dissent. They do not seem to have mattered much in mid-eighteenth century Westminster politics, although this was perhaps not so at other times. The controversies over George III's initial political behaviour stirred the political pot a little. The American and French Revolutions stirred it a lot. The origins of the Liberal and Conservative parties that governed Britain in the nineteenth century have been traced by some to the political debates of the period of the French Revolution. Nevertheless, modern political parties did not characterize British politics until the extension of the franchise made the electorate the decisive force in the choice of the government.[8]

The ability of Ministers of the Crown to use patronage to ensure a governmental majority in the Commons was a continuing source of controversy, and of resentment among politicians excluded from favour. At the time of the Revolution Settlement the number of placemen in the House had been objected to. It was also one of the discontents indicated in Edmund Burke's *Thoughts on the Present Discontents,* published in 1770. In fact, Burke, initially, was one of the leaders of the Economical Reform movement of the 1780s, which had some small success in reducing the 'influence of the Crown' in Parliament. A Commission on Public Accounts set up in 1780 marked the beginning of a process in which, as the result of legislation and administrative reform, by 1832 the Crown was left without the means of ensuring a governmental majority in the Commons.[9]

The Educational Reform movement had less immediate political impact than its leaders had hoped for, but it certainly had an immediate administrative impact. As early as 1787 it had yielded important administrative results. A rough separation had been effected between the expenses of the Household and those of civil government in general. The great spending departments of the Navy, Army and Ordnance had been regulated. The revenue had been consolidated into a single fund, the offices of receipt had been partly amalgamated, a new system of audit had been devised, and the old Exchequer had been twice reformed. A beginning had been made in the substitution of salaries for fees and perquisites in public offices. The Revolutionary and Napoleonic Wars with France may have distracted the Younger Pitt from further essays in Economical Reform; but the financial pressures of the war and immediate post-war period kept attention on ways of reducing and regularizing public expenditure. A succession of commissions and committees looked at the matter and slow change followed. Some pattern to it was given by the fact that many of the reforms advocated by the Commissioners on Public Accounts of 1780–85 were gradually introduced between 1782 and 1830. However, the pattern was sometimes confused. An Act of 1810 established a general and comprehensive superannuation scheme for all public officers well before the establishment of any unified regulations for salaries of public officers.[10] A rationalization of the central administrative structure took place in the half century after 1780, which brought it under closer parliamentary control, notably for finance. Nevertheless, the structure largely remained otherwise uncoordinated and a collection of public offices still recruited by patronage.

II. THE MACHINERY OF GOVERNMENT AND ITS 'TRADITIONAL' FUNCTIONS

The 'traditional' functions of the State accounted for most of the changes that took place in the machinery of government in eighteenth century Britain. However, the general scale of change was modest even in the spheres of law and order, colonial management, defence, the conduct of foreign policy, and the raising of revenue.

(i) Law and Order

An independent judiciary and the establishment of the Home Office can both be traced to the eighteenth century. Nevertheless, that century does seem to have been a static age in legal development. The system of English judicial administration remained essentially that of the Tudors who themselves had inherited a fairly comprehensive, if complex, system which, to some extent, they had elaborated. Provision for police remained minimal. The militia were a potential instrument for sustaining internal law and order, even if those expected to keep order were sometimes little different from those who either did, or were expected to, break the law. Even after the Act of Union of 1707, the Scots retained their separate legal system and their own local government arrangements.[11]

The Justices of the Peace represented the lowest rung of the English judicial system. They were also at the heart of the major arrangements for English local administration, sharing with, or being the same people as, the Corporations in incorporated urban areas. The institution dated from the middle of the fourteenth century. The appointments were made by the Crown, and made from among the gentry and nobility. The involvement of the nobility, unique to England, was thought by Francis Bacon to make for social stability.

Besides their legal tasks, for which some were formally qualified, the Justices were expected to implement economic and social legislation. They also came to assume greater responsibilities in relation to the Constable, the leading figure of the four principal annually elected officers of the parish (the others being the Churchwarden, the Surveyor of Highways, and the Overseer of the Poor). The Constable's position was gradually diminished, although the process was by no means a uniform one; and a tradition of independence was handed on to the later professional police. Prisons were also locally administered, even if the Justice's responsibilities for them, aside from raising the necessary finance, were vague.[12]

(ii) Defence Organization

With military costs a major source of expenditure, the organization for war was one of the chief concerns of eighteenth century government. The Admiralty in general – and the Navy Board in particular – largely kept to the practices inherited from the era of Pepys, at least down to the 1780s, when administrative reform struck. The organization was haphazard at times, but sufficiently effective. For instance, two-thirds of the fleet on the eve of the American Revolution was built in the navy's own dockyards.[13] Moreover, except in that particular conflict, the Royal Navy was on the winning side.

The remainder of the organization for war mainly involved the Ordnance Office and the Secretary at War. In peacetime, there was little central administration to be done since the army was little more than a collection of regiments, and each regiment's agent dealt with most of the business. The gentlemen of the War Department (or, more accurately, war departments) have been described as leading an administrative life of exquisite confusion. This was a confusion that Economical Reform only temporarily modified. In the early 1780s, the payment of troops and expenditure on recruiting, which had been in the hands of the regiments, was made the responsibility of the Secretary at War; and he was made more obviously accountable to Parliament.

However, this rationalization was followed by further confusion in 1793. Then, the Crown not only appointed a Commander in Chief (previously the monarch himself), but also a Secretary of State for War. The Commander in Chief quickly claimed the entire control of military administration as the monarch's representative. This claim was disputed by the Secretary at War. The administrative battle rumbled on until 1812. Then, the Secretary at War's financial control was conceded. It was, however, made subject to agreement with the Commander in Chief and, in the absence of such agreement, resolution by three Ministers. One of these was the Secretary of State for War who, since 1801, had also assumed responsibility for the colonies. Meanwhile, the wars with France continued. At the end of them, there were no less than fifteen government offices concerned with army affairs.[14]

(iii) *Imperial Management*

Trade and colonies were among the prizes of the many wars of the eighteenth century, but they were initially costly prizes. The financial situation left by the Seven Years War was sufficiently serious for the British Government to try to rationalize its relationship with its colonies. Down to the Treaty of Paris of 1763 – when Quebec was added – the First British Empire had been an empire of outposts – consisting of islands, trading stations in India and West Africa and a stretch of inhabited coastline in North America. Britain was now in a dominant position in Canada and India. How was the new, larger empire to be run? The East India Company had to formally acquiesce in the arrangements indicated by North's Regulating Act of 1773. The Quebec Act of 1774 was acceptable to the French inhabitants there as it respected their legal and political traditions.

However, the inhabitants of the thirteen American colonies did not feel the need to be run at all, even on the loosest rein. The eventual result was the American Revolution, and the loss of the Thirteen Colonies which is traditionally taken to mark the end of the First British Empire. The Second British Empire was a development, not a departure from, the First. The commercial attractions of the lands in and around the Indian and Pacific Oceans were such that the swing to the East had begun before the losses in the West Indies had taken place. As it had taken shape by 1815, the Second British Empire was made up of many different communities: real English colonies in Canada and the West Indies; penal settlements, growing into colonies, in the Southern Pacific; conquered European colonies in Canada, South Africa and the West Indies; kingdoms annexed in India, Ceylon and the Malay Archipelago; some footholds in tropical Africa, and strategic posts guarding the trade routes in the Mediterranean, the Caribbean Sea, the

South Atlantic and the Indian Ocean. There was a vast diversity of race and religion.[15]

The most spectacular developments had taken place in India. There, in 1785 – at the time of the departure of Warren Hastings – British possessions had been confined to the province of Bengal, and a handful of trading posts like Bombay and Madras. In the seven years up to 1805, one of Hastings's successors as Governor General, Sir Arthur Wellesley – the future Duke of Wellington – had added an area to the Empire which in terms of size could be compared with the conquests of Napoleon, and lasted much longer.[16] The pace of annexation was not matched later, even during the era of the dynamic Lord Dalhousie. Nevertheless, by the mid-1850s, the area within the natural geographical boundaries of India had all been brought under some sort of British rule, including much of Burma. With the loss of the Thirteen Colonies, India became the centrepiece of the overseas Empire, and thereafter it was always placed in a special category.

Responsibility for the colonies was often shared between several departments although, from 1696, an agency with some element of permanence for advising on colonial matters was created in the Board of Trade and Plantations. This Board of eight men (who included such worthies as the Bishop of London) became the most important advisory body to the Privy Council on colonial matters for most of the eighteenth century, operating with widely varying degrees of efficiency. The Board of Trade was also a centre for the promotion of overseas trade, and for the intermittent collection of trade information from consuls abroad. The Board of Trade was a temporary casualty of the Economical Reform movement. It was abolished in 1782, but reconstituted in 1786 as the Committee of the Privy Council for Trade and Foreign Plantations.

The new Board of Trade included, among others, the First Lord of the Treasury, the Chancellor of the Exchequer and the Secretaries of State, together with the Board's President and an enlarged clerical staff. In 1784, the Board of Control was created by the Younger Pitt. It consisted of six unpaid Privy Councillors, and it had responsibility for the political and revenue administration of India. Pitt left the Court of Directors of the East India Company with its original authority in commerce. This proved to be a formula for administrative conflict that was only partly modified by the appointment of a regular President of the Board in 1793 – the precursor of the Secretary of State for India. As for the central control of the other colonial arrangements, the volume of business was deemed to be such that in 1768 a Secretary of State for the Colonies was appointed. The post was a victim of Economical Reform. The responsibilities were transferred to the Home Office in 1782. There they stayed until 1801. Then the Secretary of State for War had Colonies added to his title, and there then began half a century in which colonial affairs were the responsibility of the War Department.[17]

(iv) *The Conduct of Foreign Policy*

The abolition of the Colonial Secretaryship in 1782 was accompanied by a rationalization of the roles of the remaining Secretaries of State. That these roles had stayed undefined for so long was testimony to the indifference to administrative arrangements which seemed to characterize British government for most of the eighteenth century. The Secretaries of State tended to divide all domestic business between them, apparently on the basis of competition for fees and perquisites. The division of responsibility for foreign affairs was based on the Southern Secretary taking all the business connected with Roman Catholic countries; the Northern Secretary dealing with the Protestant countries, and also Poland and Russia. While the monarch continued to play an active part in foreign policy, the division of responsibility was sometimes blurred. The duties of the Secretaries of State in domestic affairs were neither very numerous nor, apart from criminal business, very important. The Secretaries had an often confused collection of responsibilities for Scotland, Ireland, the colonies, and for military matters. Some of these responsibilities came to be governed by erratically observed conventions. The Southern Secretary usually took responsibility for Irish and colonial affairs. At certain times in the eighteenth century, there were three Secretaries instead of two, as we have noted regarding the colonies. Another example was that between 1709 and 1746 there was intermittently a third Secretary, whose province was Scotland, and who was always a Scot.[18]

The original initiative for rationalizing the responsibilities of the Secretaries of State seems to have come from George III in 1771. He was under the erroneous impression that in all the other leading European countries there was a division between home and foreign policy making arrangements. The monarch's desire for a sensible division of administrative labour was added in 1782 to the parliamentary desire to save money: hence the creation then of the Home Office and Foreign Office.[19]

(v) The Treasury and Finance

The eighteenth century Treasury was the main source both of political patronage and of internal financial control of the public offices. This can now be seen to have been a conflictual role, but it was one that for a long period after 1714 was generally deemed to be both practicable and desirable. The years immediately before 1714 had seen what seemed to be the beginnings of a tradition of professionalism in the Treasury, but this did not survive the political demise of the main Minister concerned, Sidney Godolphin. Thereafter, the Treasury's management of its own group of subordinate departments fell away into an amiable compromise between fiscal responsibility and political responsibility. The Revolution Settlement had left the House of Commons with substantial formal control over Crown revenue and expenditure, and something akin to a Budget Statement emerged. The Commons did occasionally object effectively to levels of taxation and to particular expenditure, but the Budget itself had an easy passage. There was in practice, little effective control over excessive expenditure.

For most of the century there seems to have been little knowledge, understanding or interest in financial matters in the Commons. Such knowledge was disparaged as 'clerk-like', The reverses of the American War of Independence undermined this apathy. With the Commission on Public Accounts insisting that 'every office should have a useful duty annexed to it', the reform of the Treasury was bound to occur. Burke envisaged a partnership in government between a sovereign legislature and an omnipotent Treasury. He wanted an effective Treasury control as a condition of effective parliamentary control. In 1782, the Treasury was recast on a divisional basis with each division having some solid core of responsibility. Some able clerks were sent out to colonize subordinate departments, and an attempt was made to regularize the conditions of service of the staff who remained, some of whom were inept. An investigation in 1784 found the new arrangements not far short of perfection.

Nevertheless, others were less complacent. In 1804, the Treasury Board formally divided business between the two Secretaries to the Treasury by assigning the financial duties to one, and the non-financial (including the distribution of patronage) to the other. The following year saw a further important change when the Board appointed a Permanent Assistant Secretary, who was ineligible for Parliament. The arrangements arrived at by 1805 were to prove durable: a Permanent Secretary – chief of the permanent staff – in charge of the office; a Financial Secretary assisting the Chancellor of the Exchequer, both politicians; and a Parliamentary Secretary (or patronage secretary) assisting another politician, the First Lord of the Treasury, in the management of the House of Commons.[20]

The revenue departments similarly attracted the attention of reformers from the 1780s onwards. The major departments – the Commissioners of Customs, of Excise and the Office for Taxes – survived the period, but not unchanged. For most of the period, the departments, recruited by patronage, and – in the case of Customs and of Excise – paid directly in terms of a share of the revenue raised, were able to shuffle along in a general atmosphere of administrative somnolence. Even the politically masterful Walpole failed to secure his Excise Bill of 1733. This, ideally at least, would have shifted the emphasis of taxation from land and commerce to consumption. The Excise Office did not eventually escape the reformers, although as late as 1797 expensive abuses were still being discovered there. The reform of customs administration was first effectively under-taken by the Younger Pitt. Customs administration, on the face of it, was both inefficient and corrupt. It was challenged by perennial smuggling. It was staffed both centrally and locally by the products of patronage.

Nevertheless, customs duties, where effective, did serve a

function of protecting domestic industry at a crucial period of economic development. Presumably they also provided a net gain to the Exchequer, if one secured at a high administrative cost. The main business of the Office of Taxes – at least from 1693 – was concerned with the controversial land tax. Some of the political pressure of the tax was eased by the fact that its local administration was in the hands of the very landowners on whom it was levied. This probably led to deficiencies in assessment and collection. The appointments of paid officials in the Office of Taxes were closely supervised by the Treasury in the interests of patronage. Otherwise, the Office was left for decades to its own devices. It even survived the immediate impact of Economical Reform; but not without having major duties transferred to it by Pitt in 1795 that increased the scope and pace of work. A rationalization of staff preceded Pitt's decision in 1798 to use the Office as the best instrument to run his income tax. Another rationalization followed Addington's use of the Office as a source of assessments to make the income tax more effective.[21]

III. THE MACHINERY OF GOVERNMENT AND ITS ECONOMIC AND SOCIAL POLICY FUNCTIONS

Whatever its formal powers and ambitions, the eighteenth century State was without the machinery of government to effectively and consistently intervene in the domestic economy. Its role in social provision was restricted too.

The eighteenth century British economy was dominated by private enterprise. Indeed, the part played by the State in the economy during the British Industrial Revolution was as small a role, if not smaller, than any government was later to play in promoting that level of economic development. The State ran the Post Office. It ran some military and naval establishments. These may have been examples of large scale enterprise which private entrepreneurs later copied; but they were not intended as such. The system of public finance – which by the time of the Younger Pitt already had 'Gladstonian' overtones of economy and debt redemption – was one that at the time commanded confidence. It was a system which did not bear heavily on the investing classes. Their sense of financial security compared with, for example, their French counterparts may well have been an important factor in the greater economic development that took place in Britain.

Again, the State's role was indirect. It may be that the liberal and also secure atmosphere which government helped to create was the right context for the crucial technical innovations to occur which led to the Industrial Revolution. Whether this was so or not, Britain was the place where all the basic inventions which created modern industry were made, perfected and introduced into industry, including, most revolutionary of all, the steam engine. These crucial innovations were the work of individuals. The State did try to promote the commercial health of the country. Its Consuls abroad had instructions to further British trading interests, which some of them may have done. The practice of establishing State favoured overseas trading companies did not survive the South Sea Bubble of 1720; although the East India Company, for instance, was able to retain some of its trading privileges until as late as 1833. The Navigation legislation survived beyond that in a modified form. The system of protective duties and associated arrangements developed from 1690 continued to be elaborated down to the time of Adam Smith.

His ideas were then one influence which led William Pitt's Government to conclude the Anglo-French Commercial Treaty of 1786. Whatever its importance as an example later, at the time the Eden-Reyneval Treaty was a short lived exception to a situation in which government intervention was a common feature of external trade. Eighteenth century governments extended Protection to industry and commerce, while leaving private enterprise to dominate the actual activities. Similarly, in relation to agriculture, the State confined itself to presiding over the continuing process of change, providing Protection through the Corn Laws and a legal means through which enclosures could proceed.[22]

The role that government played in social provision in eighteenth century Britain was also overshadowed by private activity. Arrangements differed too between England and Scotland. The Church played a prominent part in poor relief administration in Scotland, where local government involvement in education was also important. In England, the 'volun-

tary principle' was dominant in education; but the State did
play a larger part in administering poor relief. There was some
extension of local authority functions, mainly in the form of
rudimentary arrangements for safeguarding public health. The
social structure continued to rest on the family, on which, from
the middle of the eighteenth century onwards, industrialization
and urbanization placed massive strains.

Where the family and friends were not able to cope, the main
burden of social welfare was met by private philanthropy and
voluntary action rather than by the State, or not at all. The
main framework for governmental social provision in eighteenth
century England continued to be the Elizabethan Poor Law,
modified as the century progressed. In its general operation,
the Old Poor Law was not the same as a minimum wage allied
to child allowances as it was later portrayed, even if it may have
been in some areas. The overall position in social provision was
well summarized by a contemporary, Sir Frederick Eden, when
he said that the nation in its collective capacity was committed
only to 'the removal of extreme wants in cases of extreme
necessity', and not 'to educate the orphan, feed the ancient and
impotent, and provide employment for the industrious'. The
State thus acted only within narrowly prescribed limits, 'leaving
the rest to the faithful trusts of the sentiments of our minds, the
feelings of our hearts, the compunctions of our consciences' as
friends of the poor.[23]

The machinery of central government reflected the limited
economic and social role played by the State. Arsenals, dockyards, and the Post Office accounted for what the State did as a
direct producer. The Post Office, founded in 1662, proved to be
a durable institution. It was much more than a means of
delivering mail, a source of revenue, or even a centre for
imperial communications. It was an important source of
patronage. Such were the pickings that Sir Francis Freeling, the
Office's Secretary between 1797 and 1822, had built up his
income to £4200 a year by the end of his career. Before 1815, the
Post Office was notably successful in avoiding the administrative
reformers. The Board of Agriculture and Internal Development
was a more short lived but also curious part of central government. It was established in 1793 with a grant from Pitt's
Government, mainly as a reward for political services rendered

by an independent parliamentarian, Sir George Sinclair, who subsequently ran the Board as if it was his private property.

The formal relationship of the Board with the rest of central government was obscure. The Board had no executive authority. It reflected the character of the Royal Agricultural Society, which permeated it until the Board's demise in 1882. Of the other parts of central government, the Treasury, the revenue offices, and the Board of Trade were economic departments. There was no department which was responsible for social policy, beyond the Privy Council or the Home Office preparing social legislation for local implementation. [24]

The basic arrangements for local administration in eighteenth century England remained essentially what they had been in Tudor times. As the Webbs said, if any of the Dutch gentlemen who landed at Torbay with William III had asked a Lord Lieutenant or a Justice of the Peace to describe the local government of England, he would have been met with a blank ignorance of any such order of things. The rulers of a county would have thought of themselves not as local authorities at all; but as deputies of the King, with an obligation to provide what was requisite for the King's soldiers, to hold the King's Courts, and to maintain the King's peace. They saw themselves as having a general commission to govern their own county as they thought right and especially to supervise all other citizens in fulfilling their respective obligations.

They would probably have been aware that there were exceptions to such government by the landed gentry in areas like the City of London and the many and various boroughs, although these were run by their urban social equivalents. There existed something which the Webbs called the anarchy of local autonomy. As in Tudor times, what sustained the local bodies was the continuing obligation to serve unpaid as Constable, Surveyor of Highways, Churchwarden, or Overseer of the Poor. The sheer persistence of these arrangements was remarkable. However, as the eighteenth century progressed, it became increasingly clear that they could not perform adequately even some of their traditional functions, let alone deal with the problems that industrialization either created or emphasized. So, by the side of the conventional local authorities, and in some cases directly connected with them there developed statutory authorities for special purposes. These were local governing bodies established by special Acts of Parliaments or Royal Commissions. To the Commissioners for Sewers – who dated from Tudor times – were added Guardians of the Poor (administering poor relief for groups of parishes), Turnpike Trusts (responsible for road building and maintenance), and, perhaps most important of all, Improvement Commissioners. The latter made most impact on the ordinary local inhabitant. For him, the routine of administration of the sluices and embankments excited little attention. While he might grumble at the state of the roads or the turnpike tolls, in only a minority of places was he occasionally called upon to pay either a sewers rate or a highway rate.

To the average householder, a change in the method of governing the poor only mattered if it affected the poor rate. On the other hand, the bodies of Police, Paving, Street, Lamp or Improvement Trustees or Commissioners, dealt with matters of daily life which were important for every household. They set going public services of an altogether novel kind. They introduced a new regulation of individual enterprise and personal behaviour. They levied on every householder new and extra taxation constantly increasing in amount. The establishment between 1748 and 1835 in nearly every urban centre, under one designation or other, of Improvement Commissioners, the Webbs thought pointed towards the modern development of town government.[25] Nevertheless, for most of England, it was still local government mainly by the Justices of the Peace.

The administration of the Old Poor Law involved about 15,000 parishes in England and Wales. It seems likely that there was no uniformity and that the attitude and practice, not only of neighbouring counties, but even of neighbouring parishes, were diametrically opposed. The English Poor Law seems as often as not to have followed local practice as initiated it. This was the case with relief given outside institutions. Individual parishes had given allowances in aid of wages for many years, particularly to labourers overburdened with children. The Webbs noted the existence of this practice at Colchester even from the time of the 1601 Act itself. There is other evidence of the practice in Cambridgeshire soon afterwards. The early and middle years of the eighteenth century probably witnessed an extension of such outdoor relief. In the last quarter of that century – perhaps as a result of the example of Gilbert's Act of 1782 – these allowances may have been further extended and regularized.

The development of outdoor relief has been commonly associated in books with Speenhamland, a place near Newbury in Berkshire. There, in 1795, in the midst of economic distress and some fear of possible Jacobin risings, the local Justices laid down a scale of allowances in aid of wages that was related to bread prices. The Speenhamland system is sometimes said to have become the law of the land over most of the country-side, and even, in a much diluted form, in a number of factory towns. In fact, the Speenhamland programme seems to have been merely a sophisticated elaboration of earlier Berkshire models. It was anticipated in other counties. It was probably not even widely applied as such in Berkshire itself.[26] Allowances were associated with the Old Poor Law which were paid to, among others, the able bodied outside institutions. The basis, availability, and even existence of such relief depended on local decision.

IV. THE EIGHTEENTH CENTURY INHERITANCE

The eighteenth century tends to be seen in terms of administrative quiescence. Whole areas of State responsibility such as the legal system were left largely unchanged. Even when administrative changes did take place – such as when the Church of England's relationship with the State was changed in 1704 with the establishment of Queen Anne's Bounty – they seem dwarfed by later developments. Eighteenth century governmental machinery was a modest affair. The central administration employed perhaps 17,000 people (about 14,000 in the revenue departments), although about 10,000 more worked in naval dockyards. The armed forces employed on average a further 70,000. Hence, an estimate that government employment accounted for between 4 and 5 per cent of the adult male population. This meant that Britain probably had more public servants than the contemporary United States Federal Government, but probably fewer than France at least under the monarchy. There was nothing that as yet could be called a Civil

Service (although there was a Diplomatic Service of sorts).[27] Local authorities had few effective links with the centre or, for that matter, with each other. Some developments pointed to a more extensive future role, but, generally, local government was unambitious in its aims. The conventional view of the eighteenth century machinery of the State as a whole seems to be that it was ineffectual, certainly before the 1780s when the Economical Reform movement began the rationalization of the old administrative system.

Yet, the century witnessed domestic expansion in the form of formal unions with Scotland and Ireland. Externally, the First British Empire grew and grew until the loss of the American Colonies. Even then a Second British Empire developed. In the many wars of the century, Britain was only on the losing side once. So, eighteenth century government had its successes in its 'traditional' activities. Whether the machinery of the State was effective in the economic and social spheres in relation to chosen goals is difficult to establish. For some, the mounting cost of poor relief meant that the State was only too effective. The devotees of Free Trade certainly felt that the State regulation of external trade was sufficiently effective to need campaigning against. Nevertheless, economic and social legislation probably did not often – and certainly did not always – mean that practice followed suit.

In practice, eighteenth century governments left the main responsibilities for economic advance and social provision to private initiative. A fully fledged Mercantilist State existed in Adam Smith's imagination and then on the pages of the *Wealth of Nations*. The conditions for the British Industrial Revolution were laid down, and the Revolution itself took place, in a country in which the touch of government on the fabric of society was still a light one.

Chapter 6

The Machinery and Functions of Nineteenth Century Government 1815 - 1914

What made the nineteenth century unique was that for most of it the dominant ideology was that of the Classical Economists, who favoured *laissez-faire* in principle or on utilitarian grounds. The middle quarters of the nineteenth century in particular represented the Golden Age of Classical Liberalism. The chopping away of the mercantilist framework did not fundamentally alter the role of the State in the economy and in social provision in actual practice. Private initiative remained paramount in both the economic and social policy spheres. Where the State did act it normally did so at local rather than central government level. What made the major part of the nineteenth century different was that this role for the State was ideologically preferred.

Moreover, this preference was sustained even in the context of the economic and social problems either created or illuminated by industrialization and urbanization. The teachings of T H Green and the Marshallian School eventually shifted the burden of proof away from the advocates of State activity, especially in relation to social legislation. This occurred too late in the century to change the general picture, which was that the nineteenth century was characterized by the growth of government, but not by its growth in relation to the Gross National Product.[1]

The first industrialized society was characterized for most of the nineteenth century by a limited role for the State in the economy, and a restricted but slowly growing one in social provision. The Poor Law remained the main mechanism through which the State met its responsibilities for social welfare, although it also came to acknowledge them in education and public health too. The social reforms of the latter years of the nineteenth century and the first decade or so of the twentieth century can now be seen to point to a more expansive role. The chief emphasis of the central government's economic role, however, remained regulative right down to 1914, although 'gas and water socialism' was one characteristic of the supposed golden era of local government. That it took over sixty years to recast the structure of local government was one indication of the slowness of administrative change. That the reforms of the Civil Service were incomplete at the end of the nineteenth century was another. Yet, with reforming activity extending to such resistant areas as the judicial system, it could not be said to be minimal in its range, even if such rationalization of government that took place fell well short of Benthamite ideals. The modesty of expectations in relation to State activity compared with the mercantilist era proved no guarantee of the realization of ambitions. The nineteenth century certainly witnessed important changes in the machinery of government and in what the State did. Nevertheless, "traditional" functions continued to dominate the role of the State. The general scale of change was substantial but not revolutionary.

I. CROWN, CABINET, PARLIAMENT AND ADMINISTRATION

The nineteenth century was when British government took on a form easily recognizable to the twentieth century eye, with marked developments in the direction of constitutional monarchy, a non-political Civil Service, Cabinet government, and parliamentary democracy. However, the pace of change was normally a slow one.

The cumulative effect of the three Representation of the People Acts passed in the nineteenth century was a dramatic extension of the electorate, to whom the choice of government passed. The immediate effect of these Reform Acts on political practice was often less dramatic. The proportion of the adult male population in England and Wales who could vote after

1832 was 1 in 5 (1 in 8 in Scotland), 1 in 3 after 1867 (1 in 3 in Scotland also), and perhaps 2 in 3 after 1884 (3 in 5 in Scotland). The Irish figures were much lower. Whereas the British electorate had numbered only about 450,000 in 1831, by the 1886 Election it had grown to about five millions. Nevertheless, this did mean that before the 1918 Reform Act, at the most only 60 per cent of the adult male population was enfranchised, and that 70 per cent of the adult population did not have a vote.

Groups such as the Chartists, who pressed for universal male suffrage in the 1840s, made little immediate impact. Indeed, in 1848, when the Chartist agitation reached its climax, many of Britain's major European neighbours faced political revolutions, some successful. What the 1832 legislation had done was to attach the middle classes to the aristocratic constitution. The framers of the legislation had accepted that with the Industrial Revolution a new type of property owner had arisen by the side of the traditional landed interests and that this class was powerful enough to demand and to deserve recognition. If there was to be a clash between the opposed interests of agriculture and industry, it was thought better that such a collision should take place within the parliamentary field. There, its worst effects would be subdued by the responsibilities of office and the ties of party. It would not take the form of a landowning Parliament opposed to an unenfranchised industrial population of employers and employed.

The implicit strategy behind the 1832 legislation proved correct. When the big clash between the landed interest and the holders of other forms of wealth came over the Corn Laws in 1846, it was settled within the parliamentary framework. There was no necessary next step in extending the franchise, and the legislation of 1867 was passed in a confused political situation. It was not until the legislation of the 1880s that a radical redistribution of seats took place. The advance towards political democracy was slow and haphazard. [2]

The balance of constitutional power between King, Lords and Commons was changed by the extension of the franchise, but not precipitously and sometimes uncertainly. It was not until after the resolution of the constitutional crisis of 1909–11 that the hereditary House of Lords was firmly relegated to a lesser position than that of the Commons. Moreover, that crisis showed that, in particular circumstances, the hereditary monarch was still politically important. Generally, though, that importance was much diminished compared with before 1832, even in the case of Queen Victoria. Her influence normally seems to have been determined by the extent to which her views were acceptable to the Prime Minister and Cabinet of the day.

The 1837 Election was the last in which royal disapproval cost a party victory. Such disapproval did not prevent Sir Robert Peel's success in 1841. Peel became Prime Minister as the leader of the Conservative Party. Yet, his fundamental outlook, conditioned by his first twenty years in politics, was executive and governmental. He failed to see that his attachment of overriding importance to his responsibilities as a servant to the Crown could conflict with his role at the head of the Conservative Party, which he split over the Corn Laws in 1846, the repeal of which he deemed in the national interest.[3]

The party system was still in its infancy in Peel's day, as his own attitudes testified, and when the creature was more fully developed, it took the form of two major parties, not just two parties. Peel had seen that the landowning interest was too small a base for the Conservatives. His attempt through the Tamworth Manifesto to broaden their appeal to embrace the urban and industrial classes was more forward looking at the time than was Disraeli's opposition to the removal of the Corn Laws. Disraeli later recognized that for the foreseeable future Protection was politically dead; but it was not until the later extensions of the franchise that the Conservatives established themselves as a governing party. Disraeli came to adorn Peelism with imperialism and social reform. He thus drove a wedge into the potential Liberal vote, and ensured a working class following for his Party. Some socialists found working class Conservative voters a curiosity, but as many manufacturers were Liberals such allegiance was unsurprising.

Nevertheless, although the Conservatives successfully laid claim to English nationalism, the Liberals were dominant intellectually. The pages of the leading Liberal ideologue, J S Mill, extolled the virtues of Free Trade, the Gold Standard, the domestic free market, economy in public expenditure, representative government, local initiative and personal liberty. Whatever its consistencies on paper, Liberalism in practice was confused on several counts. Social reform was looked on favourably (particularly after Green and Marshall had given Liberalism a positive twist); but the public expenditure needed to make it work was less easily countenanced. There was an inclination to give a leg up to the working classes which ensured links with the trade unions; but the tolerant virtues of Liberalism were difficult to transplant below. There was an ambivalence in Liberalism about imperialism; but, in practice, Gladstone and other Liberals acquired colonies as did Conservative Governments.

Moreover, the Irish Question provided a perennial problem that defied a Liberal solution. When Gladstone embraced Home Rule for Ireland, he split his party. The disruptive appearance of the Irish Nationalists on the parliamentary scene was mainly at the expense of the Liberals. Similarly, with the formation of the Labour Representation Committee in 1900, it was the Liberals who felt the need for an alliance. The Conservatives, short of ideas, if not usually of votes (at least after 1874), were in no position to challenge the Liberal intellectual dominance, until Joseph Chamberlain joined their ranks. Even his allegiance eventually proved to be a mixed blessing, because his advocacy of Tariff Reform was electorally unpopular. The Liberals and Conservatives were agreed about the continued dominance of the means of production, distribution and exchange by private ownership; but such agreement still left room for debate and sometimes bitter controversy.

The split in the Conservative Party over the Corn Laws ushered in the supposed Golden Age of Parliament, that lasted until 1867, in which the House of Commons made and unmade governments. That minority governments and coalitions came and went during a twenty-one year period within the nineteenth century, did not mean that over the century as a whole Ministerial control of the Commons was being continually undermined. Even before the commonly recognized changes in parliamentary procedure of 1902, which worked in their favour, governments usually had plenty of room for manoeuvre. Bodies such as the Select Committee on Public Accounts – founded in 1861 – made governments run the gauntlet of parliamentary financial criticism. The Commons, however, was only expressing the prevailing attitude to public expenditure in the political nation, and in governments of all colours. The developing constitutional conventions of Cabinet collective responsibility and individual ministerial responsibility could not only be used by, but also against, Parliament. Groups of politicians or individual politicians survived if they had sufficient support, and they normally did have. Governments had inherited the Crown's prerogatives of executive initiative, and usually took effective advantage of them in relation to Parliament.[1]

With the Crown gradually eased to the side of the political arena, the Civil Service similarly followed, some think necessarily. The arrangements for staffing central government were certainly one area which showed substantial change over the period between, say, 1780 and 1914; but it was usually slow, often very slow, change. Before the period 1780–1830, there was definitely no body that could be seriously called a Permanent Civil Service. Even after that, the development of such a Service was a gradual and often uncertain one. The reason why this is not always thought to be so is the reputation of the Trevelyan-Northcote Report of 1853. Sir Charles Trevelyan had been a civil servant in India. He was a relative and admirer of Lord Macaulay. What Macaulay aspired to do for the Indian Civil Service, Trevelyan – by 1853 at the head of the Treasury – aspired to do for the Civil Service at home. After reviewing the organization of various government departments, he was appointed – together with Sir Stafford Northcote – to review the organization of the Civil Service as a whole.

The main recommendations of the Trevelyan-Northcote Report are well known. They advocated a more unified Service; with its work subjected to a satisfactory division between intellectual and mechanical duties; with its direct entrants recruited by open competitive examinations, instead of by patronage; and with promotion within the Service being based on merit and not seniority. The Report was brief and trenchantly written. It was too forcefully written for the tastes of the more conservatively minded leading Civil Servants, some of whom protested that its portrayal of the existing arrangements as grossly inefficient was wrong. Some of them also pointed out that the existing tasks of even the leading Civil Servants scarcely merited the talents that the reformers wished to see recruited from the universities to do the supposedly 'intellectual' duties.

The opportunities for middle class youth that were opened up seem to have been an important factor in some of the initial support that the Report secured. Among the leading supporters was the ubiquitous J S Mill, at the time a Civil Servant in the India Office. He described 'the proposal to select candidates for the Civil Service . . . by competitive examination' as 'one of those great public improvements the adoption of which would form an era in history. The effects which it is calculated to produce in raising the character both of public administration and of the people can scarcely be overestimated'.[5]

Even with this sort of influential support, however, the implementation of the Trevelyan-Northcote Report was a slow business. Admittedly, the Civil Service Commission was established as early as 1855 to supervise recruitment, and the important superannuation legislation of 1859 soon extended its powers. Nevertheless, the Commission spent its first decade and a half administering what was really a system of limited and permissive competition. It was not until 1870 that open competition was introduced into most of the major departments. The Home Office held out until 1873. The Education Office did not comply and neither did its successor until 1914. At that date, the second Board of Agriculture – formed as late as 1889 – appointed to its leading posts by patronage. The Foreign Office kept to separate arrangements until 1905. Sir George Murray was an example of a patronage appointee whose career as a leading Civil Servant lasted nearly until the First World War. He was a Permanent Secretary to the Treasury between 1903 and 1911. Murray told a Royal Commission in 1912 that the examination entrants were less capable than his own generation.

Whether this was so or not, after 1870 what came to be called the First Division of the Civil Service was mainly recruited by open competitive examinations from among middle and sometimes upper class Oxford and Cambridge university graduates who had normally read subjects unrelated to their future work. They were assigned what were defined as the 'intellectual' duties of the Service, facing a career in which promotion was formally based on merit. The common mode of entry may have eventually made for a collective sense of identity in the First Division. Generally, though, the Service is best described as fragmented until the National Insurance episode of 1911–12 led to some breaking down of departmental barriers. Then, the First World War broke down some more. Those who dispute this interpretation can turn to Sir Warren Fisher's evidence to a Royal Commission in 1930. 'Until relatively recent years', said the then Head of the Service, 'the expression "Civil Service" did not correspond either to the spirit or to the facts of the organization so described'.[6]

The development of a means of staffing government departments independently of Ministers was promotive of the convention of ministerial responsibility. The convention was promoted also by the advent of a career service which the administrator came into young with little opportunity to make a public mark in his field of work. Only the anonymous Civil Servant could be granted anonymity. Sir James Stephen's pleas for it when he was widely – but wrongly – thought to be running colonial policy in the 1830s were understandably resisted. Of course, some later Civil Servants did run their Ministers, but the formal position had changed and, importantly, was seen to have done so. That was a difference between the constitutional situation which developed after 1870 compared with that which prevailed, for example, in 1830. It was not until the second half of the nineteenth century that the political and constitutional climate even ensured that administration by a ministerial department was orthodox and that by a board, suspect. Even this disapproval of central boards was relaxed after 1906.[7] The halcyon era of ministerial responsibility was a short one. Even during it there were the exploits of Civil Servants such as Sir Robert Morant.

By the time of the Liberal reforms at the latest, the range of duties of Ministers in departments was beginning to be such that all but the most talented politicians were bound to be largely dependent on their advisers, who were increasingly likely to be generalists like themselves. However slow the process of reform actually was in what was to become the generalist side of the Civil Service, it was well under way before any comparable development regarding the specialists that the Service employed. While the Service lacked unity this was a constraint on the advance of the generalist; but, insofar as there was a ladder to the top it lay through the First Division – the forerunner of the Administrative Class. Ironically, the departmentalism that at least ensured some sustained specialization in administrative work, began to really break down only in the early years of the twentieth century, at the very time that the State began to take on a more purposive and almost more complex role.

II. THE MACHINERY OF GOVERNMENT AND ITS 'TRADITIONAL' FUNCTIONS

The 'traditional' functions of the State accounted for many of the main nineteenth century changes in governmental organization. However slow the overall process was, the changes represented a marked expansion in government, taking the century as a whole. This can be seen by examining the changes that took place in the organization for law and order, colonial management, defence, the conduct of foreign policy, and the raising of revenue.

(i) *Law and Order*

The nineteenth century witnessed the eventual establishment of effective police forces; the reform of the judicial system; and – from 1877 – the central administration of prisons through a Prison Commission.

The reform of the administration of justice, although long overdue at the start of the century in both England and Scotland, proceeded at a leisurely pace despite the urgings of Bentham, his writings and his followers. There were important changes such as the setting up of the Judicial Committee of the Privy Council in 1833. Nevertheless, the English local system was not effectively reorganized until a series of reforms between 1873 and 1880. The main legislation was the Supreme Court of Judicature Act of 1873. This Act which came into force in 1875 merged the medley of courts into a single Supreme Court of Judicature. This had two tiers: a High Court with divisions corresponding to the old courts; and a Court of Appeal. There was an accompanying rationalization of legal procedure. The Scottish system was gradually changed from 1825 onwards, while being said to leave sufficient scope for the Scottish love of litigation.[8]

The cursory arrangements for police persisted in many parts of Britain for much of the nineteenth century. Change began with the reforming Sir Robert Peel at the Home Office in the 1820s. The Metropolitan Police Act of 1829 set up a new police organization for the London area under the general supervision of the Home Office. Peel himself carefully supervised the initial superior appointments. He made clear his intention that the Metropolitan Police should serve as an example to be followed in other urban areas. As the old system of unprofessional, barely remunerated, part time peace officers seemed to be breaking down elsewhere – under the strains of increased population, and in the social climate of the Industrial Revolution – reform eventually occurred. The improved arrangements for policing London emphasized the defects of the provincial boroughs.

The Municipal Corporations Act of 1835, therefore, required every one of the 178 boroughs to which it applied to appoint a Watch Committee which would itself appoint sufficient police. The cost was to fall on the local rates, and the local authorities were entrusted with complete control. They had to report certain matters to the Home Secretary, but he had no power to inspect or interfere. A County Police Act followed in 1839, chiefly it seems because of fears of Chartist disorder. The years 1835 and 1839 did not witness sudden and fundamental changes in the policing of the counties and boroughs throughout the country. Police reform outside London was gradual, patchy and unspectacular. The 1839 Act was the more ineffectual. By 1856, police forces existed in 24 counties and in parts of 7 others, but in 20 counties no action had been taken.

The policing of the small and medium sized towns also left a lot to be desired. A major reform followed with the County and Borough Police Act of 1856, which required the Justices to establish a paid police force for the whole of each county. Crown Inspectors of Constabulary were to visit the county and borough forces and to report on their efficiency to the Home Secretary. The Government would provide one-quarter of the cost of the pay and clothing of every county and borough force which was certified by an Inspector to be efficient in numbers and discipline, except in the case of small boroughs. They could consolidate with the counties for police purposes or pay for their own forces. A similar Act was passed for Scotland in 1857. The subsequent experience did illustrate the effectiveness of two of the main administrative innovations of the nineteenth century: inspection and the Exchequer grant. The reforms of the 1850s eventually led to efficient police forces: those deemed not to be efficient on inspection fell from 120 in 1857 to nil in 1890.[9]

(ii) *Imperial Management*

'We seem . . . to have conquered and peopled half the world in a fit of absence of mind'. Thus runs one famous interpretation of the growth of the Second British Empire, which continued beyond 1815. Indeed, growth continued both during and beyond the middle quarters of the nineteenth century, an era supposedly dominated by 'anti-imperialism' and 'Little Englandism'. Imperial expansion seemed to have a momentum of its own. Some saw Britain as having a mission to civilize the world – the White Man's Burden. The more robust, such as Wellesley, simply believed that no greater blessing could be conferred on the native inhabitants of India than the extension of the British authority, influence and power.[10] As we have seen, he acted accordingly.

On what principles was the Second British Empire to be run? One was to be Free Trade, which was applied within the Empire from 1830 onwards. At first, colonial trade was thrown open to foreign countries on a reciprocal basis. Then, the Navigation legislation was repealed in 1849, and various imperial preferences were removed by 1860. The colonies were made part of the world trading system at large with no special advantage for Britain. Indeed, self governing colonies were allowed to impose protective tariffs against Britain, who continued to practise Free Trade down to 1932. Another principle was that of decentralization, itself aided by the demise of the Old Colonial System. Despite improvements in communication – most notably, the telegraph – that eventually made control from London easier, the Empire continued to be run on decentralized lines until the 1920s. There is no doubting the importance for the future development of the Empire that was subsequently given to Lord Durham's *Report on the Affairs of British North America* (1839), because of its advocacy of the eventual granting of responsible self government to colonies. J S Mill described the Report as marking the beginning of 'a new era in the colonial policy of nations'. The specific recommendations of the Durham Report were not closely followed even in Canada. The powers which Durham proposed should be given to colonies under self government were very limited.

What was important was that the principle of eventual self government was recognized. Colonies were presented with an alternative to the American method of advance by revolution. The ultimate destination remained uncertain. The First World War briefly revived dreams of imperial federation. What happened was an evolution in the direction of Dominion status helped by the consolidation of groups of colonial units into national states: Canada between 1867 and 1873, New Zealand in 1876, Australia in 1901, and South Africa in 1910. In the last case, the Boer War ensured that the evolution was not entirely peaceful. In South Africa before 1914, the imperial sentiments of common citizenship and equality before the law were already shown to have little practical meaning.[11]

What was good for the settlement colonies was not thought to be necessarily good for the others, including India. There, on the grandest scale, Britain proceeded to play out what seemed to be her imperial destiny. The East India Company was not abolished until 1858 – the year after the Indian Mutiny – a whole century since Robert Clive had first suggested that its dominion should be taken over by the Crown. However, the tone of British rule for some time had been increasingly non-commercial. The official had replaced the trader in British India, and the search for profit there was cast aside in the eagerness of many young Englishmen to join the Indian Civil Service and become District Officers and the like, shouldering the White Man's Burden of governing those deemed unfit to govern themselves. Macaulay's open competition for the Indian Civil Service came to attract much of the intellectual cream of the youth graduating from Oxford and Cambridge. The India Office in London – where a Secretary of State and a Council had replaced the Board and the Company – was not short of intellectual talent either. J S Mill – like his father before him – served there. Such was the prestige of the India Office that when Keynes finished second in the First Division open competition in 1906 he went there. During two sometimes frustrating years, Keynes later maintained that all he succeeded in achieving during that time was getting one pedigree bull shipped to Bombay.[12]

The pace of work in the contemporary Colonial Office seems to have been fairly amiable, according to John Anderson. Nevertheless, that the Office attracted the successful Anderson – top in the 1905 open competition – was evidence of its prestige. The Colonial Office did not formally exist as a separate entity until 1854. Between 1782 and 1801, the Home Office bore responsibility for colonial affairs. Then, this responsibility was transferred to the Secretary of State for War. He retained it until the pressures of the Crimean War led to its removal and the appointment of a Secretary of State for the Colonies. However, well before colonial affairs were formally separated, they were treated separately at least from 1812. One important part of the Colonial Office between 1840 and 1872 – when the emigration officers were transferred to the Board of Trade – was the Land and Emigration Commission. The emigration side of its work was multiplied by the effects of the Irish Famine.

The emigration officers concerned came to exercise powers of executive discretion more commonly associated with later administration. The general structure of the Colonial Office proved resistant to effective internal reallocation of duties, at least before 1907 when the Dominions Department was created. There were severely limited personal contacts between the Colonial Office and the colonies. The civil service of each dependency had a character of its own from the beginning. This was a reflection of the principle of autochthony in British colonial administration. In practice, the colonial service was overwhelmingly an African service, and secondly a South East Asian service. Only the highest offices such as Governor and Chief Justice were filled from outside.[13]

(iii) *Defence Organization*

In the century of the so-called Pax Britannica after 1815, Britain was usually at war somewhere, normally within or extending her Empire. Her involvement in the only general European war of the period – the Crimean War – led to changes in army organization. The Cardwell reforms and then the Boer War led to some more. Nevertheless, down to the early years of the twentieth century changes were much less noticeable than continuities in British organization for war, especially as regards naval administration.

That the Royal Navy should be particularly successful in resistance to organizational change was unsurprising. As Britannia ruled the waves anyway, why change? The reluctance of the transition from sail to steam power on the operational side was paralleled by a truly remarkable resistance to administrative change. This is not to say that some change did not occur. In 1832, the Navy Board and the Victualling Board were formally abolished, and all the administrative business of the Navy was for the first time concentrated under the Board of Admiralty. In practice, the Admiralty remained a network of departments, and it is difficult to establish the degree to which they were co-ordinated. Arthur Salter – fresh from the 1904 open competition – found himself entombed in the Admiralty's Transport Department it seemed for life. Oswyn Murray was thought to have ended his serious administrative career by transferring from the Admiralty Secretariat to the Victualling Department, but he survived to later become Permanent Secretary. The prospect of European war in general, and the reality of German naval competition eventually stirred the Admiralty up; but down to the Dreadnought era, naval administration from the top down to the dockyards seems often to have been ineffectual.[14]

Army administration at the outset of the Crimean War was much the same as it had been at the time of Waterloo. What the Crimean War accomplished in terms of military organization was not the revelation of unsuspected defects, but the creation of a political atmosphere in which decisions about change could no longer be postponed. On one view, between 1854 and 1871 the administration and command of the British army was completely revolutionized. A highly centralized organization was created under the Secretary of State for War to control and supervise the individual regiments down to the last details of military life. At the same time, the army became the instrument of parliamentary rather than monarchical government. Control of the army was taken from the Crown and given to the Cabinet and its civilian representative – the Secretary for War – who were, in turn representatives of Parliament.

Moreover, on this interpretation, the army itself was radically altered. With the abolition of purchase of commissions and the introduction of short service for private soldiers, subtle changes were introduced in the way of life, customs and traditions that had hitherto characterized the regiments. Ultimately, these changes are said to have transformed an essentially eighteenth century professional army into a modern machine of war. Certainly, there were changes in the period after the Crimean War. In 1855, the offices of Secretary of State for War and Secretary at War were amalgamated, and the latter was later abolished. A series of other amalgamations and rationalizations followed. These included the abolition of the Board of Ordnance, whose independence had lasted for four hundred years. By 1857 a War Office had been established; but it was one with no less than thirteen branches housed in three hundred rooms in Pall Mall.

The confusion resulting from doing business in this labyrinth is said to have led General Gordon to have resigned his staff appointment within a few days, declaring it was easier to find his way about Africa. Moreover, housed at the Horse Guards was a separate office under the Commander-in-Chief, who for thirty years was to be the Queen's first cousin, the Duke of Cambridge. This separation is said to have done much to foster antagonism between the military and civil administrations. The Cardwell reforms included a reorganization of the War Office with the Commander-in-Chief's office being brought under the same roof; an attempt to introduce career open to talent with the abolition of the purchase of commissions; and an attempted rationalization of the army in relation to its commitments. The results do not seem to have been dramatic. The Commander-in-Chief still proved to be a source of administrative confusion. The army remained similar in outlook. The Boer War, in fact, showed that, while Britain in 1899 was capable of calling more men to arms than had been possible in 1854, the old dilemma remained of an army initially too small, too poorly trained, and too lacking in inventiveness to achieve the military success a Great Power expected. Compared with the men and equipment of her European rivals, Britain was far from having a modern war machine.[15]

The period from the Boer War to 1914 did witness substantial changes at last in British organization for military conflict. A Committee of Imperial Defence was formed in 1903, developed from the defence committee of the Cabinet. It was given a full time Secretary following one of the recommendations of the Esher Committee in 1904. That Committee also successfully proposed the abolition of the post of Commander-in-Chief, which had even survived the Duke of Cambridge's retirement nine years before. A resulting rationalization of the War Office seemed to make for a more efficient organization. The Haldane reforms followed and an Imperial General Staff formed. The equivalent changes were not made in naval organization. Despite all that happened, Britain remained less well prepared than her enemies.[16]

(iv) *Conduct of Foreign Policy*

Political relations with other countries remained in the hands of the Foreign Office and the Diplomatic Service. The familiar aim of preventing one country from assuming a dominant position in continental Europe persisted. It could be said that Britain went to war in 1914 to prevent the German Empire achieving such dominance. The occasion for war was provided by a guarantee of Belgian neutrality made in 1831. This was an indication that Britain was not without such formal commitments in the nineteenth century, even if at the end of it she had no commitment that was really comparable with the Austro-German, the Triple or the Franco-Russian alliance. Then, Britain still enjoyed far more liberty of action in Europe than did any of the great continental powers. The supposed policy of 'splendid isolation' was not brought to an end by the Anglo-Japanese Alliance of 1902, although little was heard of it after that. The Liberal Foreign Secretary, Sir Edward Grey pronounced against European alliances in 1906, but the conversations between the War Office and the French military authorities that began then anticipated such involvements.

For all the aggression of Palmerston and the self conscious nationalism of Disraeli, British foreign policy was rarely just the naked pursuit of self interest. Gladstone's many and various pronouncements indicate a different outlook, if not always a different practice. There was detectable in British behaviour a humanitarian tradition. Evidence for it was the abolition of the slave trade in 1807, and of slavery in the British Empire in 1833, actions in which principles actually cost money.[17] Against this, as in the Opium Wars, some British behaviour in relation to China was reprehensible. Similarly complex was Britain's relationship with the United States. A brief war, threats of another, and mistrust characterized Britain's relations with America for much of the century. Against this, there then seemed to develop an overestimate in some parts of Britain's social élite of the community of interest between Britain and America.

That social élite was well represented in the Foreign Office. Its social prestige was one defence against outside critics. Its work also had the advantage of being directly derived from the royal prerogative, behind which the Office frequently sheltered in the face of parliamentary and other criticism. Trevelyan's reformism of the 1850s was decisively repulsed. His report on the Foreign Office remained unpublished. The Office's attitude was not simply obstructionist. The division of labour between intellectual and mechanical work was more easily adopted by administrative departments than by the Foreign Office, where the political work – the formulation of foreign policy – was still the most important function of the Cabinet. At that time, the Foreign Office really only required copying clerks for mechanical work, but employed established clerks because it was thought that State secrets should be known only to clerks whose family and social connections were similar to those of their political masters.

Although, before 1905, the Foreign Office did not take part in the open competition, its limited competition eventually attracted better entrants than earlier ones. One effect of recruiting people with talent only to employ them on routine copying was discontent and pressure for changes. The Foreign Office of the 1890s seems to have had a great deal in common with that of the 1780s. It was slightly larger, its work was a little more decentralized, but its spirit was the same. Substantial change then followed. On one view, the Lansdowne years (1900–5) were the crucial ones for change, at least regarding organization. On another, those years were transitional ones both in terms of policy and Foreign Office organization. The increasing volume of business and the personalities involved led to a situation in which, certainly after 1906, men who had been acting as clerks began acting as true advisers. The result was that whereas Lord Salisbury had ruled the Foreign Office, Lord Grey was to preside over it. While Salisbury's Foreign Office could still be discussed in terms of a Palmerstonian personal office, Grey's resembled its modern counterpart.[18]

The Diplomatic Service remained formally separate right down to 1918. Interchanges between the Service and the Foreign Office occurred, but they were not frequent. When limited competition was introduced, that for the Diplomatic Service included a property qualification. The absence of salaries in early career made private means essential. Royal Commissions and Select Committees nagged away for change but achieved little.[19] The diplomats themselves tended to be independent aristocrats of varying abilities. Their independence was said to be circumscribed by such developments as the electric telegraph.[20] The telegraph did change the time scale of diplomacy, enabling the Foreign Secretary to have earlier notice of events, and also, if necessary, to intervene more swiftly. Whether or not Ambassadors were more or less independent than before, the Diplomatic Service remained more or less separate. Only at the very highest levels did any tradition of transfer from the Foreign Office to the Diplomatic Service develop. After the turn of the century, as in other aspects of the Office's work, things changed, and exchanges became rather more common.[21]

(v) The Treasury and Finance

The power of the purse resided in the Treasury. On the face of it, that power was a pervasive one supported as it was by prevalent sentiments inimical to public expenditure both in Parliament and outside. The figure of Gladstone, so often at the Treasury as Chancellor and First Lord, begetter of no less than thirteen Budgets, seemed to be a guarantee of Victorian financial rectitude. To some extent, he was. Nevertheless, for all the persistence of radical and other pressure for low government expenditure, the path of financial reform proved to be a long one. For example, Sir James Graham's tightening up of the accountability of the Admiralty finances in 1832 was not extended to the War Office until 1846. It was not until 1861 that detailed accountability was extended to the revenue departments. The Exchequer and Audit Department Act of 1866 created for the first time an effective machinery for a retrospective annual audit of government expenditure. A Comptroller and Auditor General was appointed to 'send for persons, papers and records'. Usually a former Treasury man, he was to have the same security of tenure as a judge, and to report to the Public Accounts Committee, which the Commons had set up in 1861. The Treasury at last had the supportive mechanism with which to enforce the strictest standards of financial propriety. Gladstone's desired circle of control seemed to be complete.[22]

Treasury control, however, was essentially negative. As its Permanent Secretary told a Royal Commission in 1888, 'the Treasury simply watches and examines measures with a view to the maintenance of financial order'. Sir Reginald Welby went on to emphasize that 'the Treasury check is purely a financial check. There ends the Treasury power'. No matter how poorly organized or overmanned a department was, the Treasury had no power to interfere. Welby thought that the Treasury should have such power, but pointed out the difficulties: 'I think that it is essential that the Treasury should have · . . a voice in determining the pay and organization of the different departments. Unless the Treasury has such a voice in these particulars, the public can have no security that there is uniformity of organization in the public service, but I cannot say that the Treasury could order a department to be satisfied with a certain number of clerks, I am thinking of what is possible. I anticipate that such action of the Treasury, as applied to a department presided over by a Cabinet Minister, would lead at once to very great friction, and practically would end in making the exercise of a control in that form impossible'.[23]

In the raising of revenue, the Treasury could rely on its associated departments: the main ones taking the form of the Board of Inland Revenue from 1849 and the Board of Customs and Excise from 1909. In the control of expenditure, the Treasury had few departmental allies. The most prestigious of the other departments were the best able to resist the Treasury: the Foreign, Home, Colonial and India Offices. Policy grounds could be pleaded against the Treasury, especially by a forceful Minister. These grounds were also difficult to resist when they were based on specialized knowledge. Only the possession of such knowledge by Ralph Lingen – when Permanent Secretary before Welby – seems to have enabled the Treasury to have a real say in education policy in the 1870s and 1880s. In the case of the War Office and the Admiralty, professional and technical expertise could be pitted against the Treasury too.[24] Thus, Treasury control of finance in the nineteenth century was exerted, but was limited in its effects.

III. THE MACHINERY OF GOVERNMENT AND ITS ECONOMIC FUNCTIONS

The role of the State in the nineteenth century economy was a limited one. That economy was dominated by private enterprise. The ruling ideology for most of the century was that of the Classical Economists, which emphasized the virtues of the market economy. The eventual establishment of Free Trade was testimony to the dominance of such ideas. Britain's economic ascendancy seemed practical proof of their validity. Even when that ascendancy was successfully challenged, faith in the dictum that governments governed best when they intervened least in the economy persisted. So, to a large extent, did the resulting practice. Nonetheless, the State did come to perform regulatory functions in relation to public utilities and services even when they were privately owned. Government also undertook the regulation of working conditions in factories and mines. Capitalism was not unbridled, but was given substantial freedom. Its dominance was not seriously challenged at the time even by the growing public sector, which had begun to move beyond 'traditional' functions, and not only in the spheres of 'gas and water socialism'. Even as late as 1914, the State's role in the economy was severely circumscribed.

The nineteenth century State did not abstain from economic activity. However, down to the First World War, as far as central government was concerned, its economic functions were still mainly confined to the Post Office, dockyards and arsenals. Defence requirements also meant that the effects of government demand on the economy were not negligible. In 1914 itself, on

Winston Churchill's initiative as First Lord of the Admiralty, the State purchased a majority shareholding in what was then called the Anglo-Persian Oil Company (now British Petroleum). The motive was to try to secure for the Royal Navy an assured supply of oil at low prices.[25] The nineteenth century was characterized by a considerable expansion in economic activity by local government. Moreover of the activities of central government, the role of the Post Office had also expanded.

The Post Office, while still run as a conventional government department, and still largely treated as a source of revenue, gradually acquired wider responsibilities during the nineteenth century. In 1840, at the instigation of Rowland Hill, the uniform penny postage was introduced. The Post Office Savings Bank was established in 1861. The same decade saw the Post Office take over the electric telegraph. By the 1850s, Britain and the USA were alone in leaving the electric telegraph to private enterprise. Dissatisfaction with the cost and quality of the service provided by private companies, expressed not least by the Press, led to calls for the Post Office to operate the electric telegraph as a monopoly. This, following legislation in 1868 and 1869, it proceeded to do. The substantial compensation paid to the companies helped to ensure that the service had a subsequently poor financial record.

Another reason why this came to be so was, of course, the development of the telephone system. This was mainly left to a number of private companies (most importantly, the National Telephone Company) while the Post Office and some local authorities also tried to compete. The Treasury's attitude to Post Office telephone activities as late as 1898 was that 'the sound principle . . . is that the State, as regards all functions which are not by nature exclusively its own, should at most be ready to supplement, not endeavour to supersede, private enterprise'. Various regulative devices were attempted before finally at the end of 1911 the Post Office secured a monopoly of the telephone service in Britain, with the exception of Hull. In the sixty years down to 1914, the Post Office had grown considerably. In 1854, the Post Office was responsible only for the conveyance of mail and the issue of money orders. By 1914, it was not only operating those services on a vastly expanded scale, but it had added several other functions. Its Savings Bank had nine million depositors. It operated the telegraph service and almost all the telephone service. It supervised the development of wireless telegraphy. It acted as an agent for the issue of local taxation licenses and health and unemployment stamps, and for the payment of old age pensions. The staff grew from 21,574 in 1854 to 249,606 in 1914. Over that period, gross income rose from £2·69 millions to £30·8 millions, and expenditure from £1·41 millions to £6·2 millions. At a time when government intervention in private enterprise was limited, the Post Office had grown into an important public enterprise.[26]

Municipal trading was also an important area of increased government economic activity in the nineteenth century. Such trading was no novelty. In medieval times it was difficult to distinguish between the corporation governing the municipality and the craft and merchant guilds which conducted industry and commerce. The main forms of trading over subsequent centuries were water supply, the conduct of markets, and the management of docks and harbours. By the early part of the nineteenth century, with municipal organization in some disarray, bodies often known as Improvement Commissioners provided most of what services were made available. One example of such enterprise took place in Manchester. There, the local governing body known as the Police Commissioners began to manufacture gas on a small scale in 1807, at first in order to light the outside, and later the interior, of their offices. From 1817 onwards, in spite of the fact that they had no express legal authority to manufacture and supply gas as a public service, the Manchester Police Commissioners began to supply private consumers from a newly erected gasworks. Soon this undertaking – the first public gas undertaking – produced handsome profits, which helped to finance the numerous street improvements needed in the rapidly expanding Manchester of the early nineteenth century. Generally, however, in the first half of that century, it was not local authorities who took the lead in the gas industry.

The chief advances were made by private enterprise organizations such as the London Gas Light and Coke Company, established by royal charter in 1812. Municipal enterprise expanded markedly during the second half of the nineteenth century, although by no means on all fronts, and not always in traditional areas of activity. From gas, municipal trading moved naturally to electricity, and from electric supply to electric trams, during the short period in which they seemed to be without doubt the best means of urban transport. Some local authorities who owned electric tramways were later reluctant to license the early motor buses. Even at its zenith, municipal enterprise seems to have been limited in extent.

A return on municipal trading made by local authorities in 1909 showed that most of them reported on water, gas and electricity; many on tramways, markets, baths and working class dwellings; waterside places often on harbours, docks or ferries; a considerable number of places on cemeteries; and few on anything else. In retrospect, the creation of bodies on which local government was represented but did not run – such as the Mersey Docks and Harbour Board (1857), the Metropolitan Water Board (1904), and the Port of London Authority (1908) – pointed the way to what was to happen. At the time, however, 'gas and water socialism' seemed likely to form the main basis for later expansion of government economic activity, and it was, of course, to provide part of the base. Nevertheless, for all the controversy such 'socialism' caused among contemporaries, municipal ownership was almost entirely confined to industries tending to become monopolies; and industries, moreover, in which private enterprise continued to play a prominent part.[27]

The nineteenth century economy was dominated by private enterprise. The great industries of coal mining, iron and steel, cotton textiles, shipbuilding and engineering were all run by private interests. The period from the late eighteenth century down to the 1870s, when Britain was free from severe external competition, was the classic age of traditional capitalism. There is some danger of exaggerating the savage industrial individualism of the era if one concentrates attention on industries that underwent a relatively rapid metamorphosis, such as the cotton industry with the evolution of the factory system.

In several industries it is probable that, throughout the nineteenth century, there was a good deal of quiet price fixing; and that free and open competition was never perfectly attained or even universally and sincerely desired. Nevertheless, the tone of the nineteenth century economy remained remarkably individualistic in many sectors. This was so even after legislative changes made between 1825 and 1862 had provided a legal basis for big business in the form of the joint stock limited liability company. Trade associations developed in some industries from the 1880s onwards, although these associations seem to have had no real directing power. In the following twenty years, there was a combination movement in some parts of British industry. The resulting companies were not normally on the same scale as the American trusts and the German cartels that they had to compete with.

During and beyond the supposed Great Depression of 1873–96, doubts were expressed about the ability of Britain's industrial leadership to meet foreign challenges. It was one theme of the 'national efficiency' movement that was evident in governing circles between 1899 and 1914. Direct State action to improve industrial efficiency did not follow. Robert Lowe, as President of the Board of Trade, speaking in favour of the company legislation of the 1850s, expressed the prevailing sentiment of the nineteenth century and immediately after, when he described private companies as 'little republics' whom government left 'to manage their own affairs'.[28] Generally, the amount of freedom enjoyed by nineteenth century private enterprise was very substantial; but, as will be seen, in some areas of activity it was less than in others.

Such economic responsibilities as central government recognized outside its own small public sector were mainly exercised by the Board of Trade. Regulation of working conditions tended also to be the province of the Home Office. Commercial responsibilities were shared – and disputed – with the Foreign Office.

If the nineteenth century State had a department for trade and industry it was the Board of Trade, whose functions changed and expanded as the century progressed. The Board lost its responsibilities for the colonies to the nascent Colonial Office early in the century. In the 1840s with the victory of Free Trade – which some of its officials helped to promote – the Board lost its other leading hereditary duty. Yet, particularly from about 1830 onwards, the Board had begun to take on other functions. In one view, their performance meant that by 1855 the Board had been transformed from an advisory committee of the Privy Council into an administrative department of state. Whether transformed or not, the Board had become generally responsible for the regulation of the two great contemporary transport industries, merchant shipping and railways; and it had also been given a range of other duties that were regulative and supportive of private industry and commerce. [29]

The Board of Trade's regulative and supportive activities came to include the collection and publication of official statistics; the promotion of industrial arts and sciences; the imposition of uniform standards of weights and measures; the protection of trade marks, designs, and patents; bankruptcy administration; and the registration and regulation of joint stock companies. Not all these duties came to the Board at the same time, and not all were continuously exercised. For example, it was not until Joseph Chamberlain's Act of 1883 that the administrative functions relating to bankruptcy were transferred to the Board from the courts. Similarly, it was not until that year that patents administration became the Board's responsibility. It was only in 1883 also that the Board was given permanent administrative jurisdiction over designs – for which its responsibilities dated back to 1839 – and trade marks. The Board lost its functions in relation to the promotion of industrial arts and sciences in 1856 (to the Education Department of the Privy Council) and did not resume such responsibilities until 1899 when the National Physical Laboratory was established.

In its earlier years, the Laboratory was controlled by a Board representing the Royal Society and certain technical associations; but it received a State subsidy both in respect of capital and current expenditure, and the Permanent Secretary of the Board of Trade was made a member of the Executive Council. The Board's other duties had more continuity, although it was not until 1866 that it was definitely designated the custodian of Imperial Standards. The Board administered the legislation for joint stock enterprise from its inception, and it had a similar long standing responsibility for official statistics. This was made more serious from 1832 onwards with the formation of a Statistical Department headed by G R Porter, and regular publications eventually came to include the *Statistical Abstract of the United Kingdom*, the *Board of Trade Journal*, and the *Labour Gazette*. [30]

The nineteenth century Board of Trade also received important regulative functions in relation to various public utility and transport undertakings. Legislation in 1850 concentrated on the Board responsibilities for merchant shipping that had been previously scattered among a number of public authorities. It was the Board that administered the legislation, and the resulting statutory orders, relating to gas, water, and electricity undertakings. The Railway Department of the Board dated from the Railway Regulation Act of 1840, soon including an Inspector General of Railways. Various administrative devices were tried between then and 1851 after which date responsibility for government policy stayed with the Department within the Board. In the years after 1873, a judicial tribunal which came to be called the Railway and Canal Commission also intervened in railway matters. Governmental concern was perennially with company amalgamations, the regulation of charges and the safety of the travelling public; and later with the settlement of labour disputes. It may well be that by 1914, the railways were the most regulated form of economic activity in Britain. By that time over two hundred general acts had been passed relating to them. Sir Robert Peel caught a contemporary mood when he said in 1840 that, although 'no one was more adverse to any general interference with the employment of capital than he was ... it was impossible to deny that the railways were a practical monopoly.' As 'they had been established by the legislature' it was that body's duty to see that 'the public rights were not interfered with'.

Four years later, Gladstone, President of the Board of Trade in what was by then Peel's Government, proposed legislation which could have led to the eventual State purchase of new railway companies. The relevant Bill was emasculated in the House of Commons where the railway interest was well represented. They were aided by Cobden and Bright. The latter described State purchase as 'altogether a new principle in this country', and added that 'there was a wholesome absence of interference in this country in all those matters which experience showed might wisely be left to private individuals, stimulated by the love of gain, and the desire to administer to the wants and comforts of their fellow men'. The State, however, rarely left the railways alone in the nineteenth century. This was despite the fact that sea transport, for example, placed very real limits on the railways' ability to exploit their dominant position in inland transport. They had this inland dominance from about 1850 until electric trams and the motor car began to be important rivals for the steam locomotive in the years immediately before 1914.[31]

The regulation of railways was not accompanied by State provision of railway services; but, as was seen in the earlier discussion of 'gas and water socialism', in the case of some other actual or feared monopolies a mixture of government and private provision prevailed. The Board of Trade centrally administered the relevant restrictions. In the case of tramways and electricity supply the private companies were placed under restrictions from the outset. In that of gas and water, which were generally services developed earlier, there was some initial faith in the possibilities of benefits following from competition between private companies. Only after that, came firm regulation and municipal expansion. To consider water supply first, in 1845 there were only 10 municipalities out of about 190 which possessed waterworks. One explanation of this state of affairs was the absence of any General Act (like the Lighting and Watching Act of 1835) enabling local authorities to supply water if they chose.

More important was that the scale of expenditure involved was beyond what the authorities deemed as their capacity to meet. Although from 1822 onwards, it was the practice to limit the charges that private companies could make, until 1847 no conditions were imposed on them about the quantity or quality of the service provided. The increasingly onerous requirements of public health legislation, and the great willingness of local authorities to finance ventures by loans, led not only to improved services but also eventually to more local government involvement in the industry. By 1914, about two-thirds of the population was supplied with water by the local authorities. By the same date, only about one-third of the gas undertakings were under municipal control. Private gas companies had been made subject to some restrictions from 1918 onwards.

However, it was not until 1860 that a uniform system of regulation was imposed on the industry: with dividends limited to 10 per cent, a standard maximum price, quality controls, and

an obligation to supply. Gas and water companies usually held
perpetual concessions subject to meeting various statutory
requirements; but the Tramways Act of 1870 was based on a
different principle. This was that the local authorities could
compulsorily purchase the then novel means of transport by
tramways from the operating companies, after the lapsing of a
21 year period, or sooner if by agreement. The Act was
interpreted at first as meaning that local authorities were
prevented from operating tramways; but from the mid-1890s
onwards, local authorities rapidly took over tramways until by
1914 they owned about three-quarters of them. The example of
limiting company concessions to 21 years was followed in
legislation relating to the electricity supply industry passed in
1882, which also included price maxima; the term being
increased to 42 years in further legislation passed in 1888. By
the First World War about 60 per cent of the electricity supply
industry was under local government control. Some actual or
likely monopolies, then, came under State regulation in the
nineteenth century, and local government provision of public
utilities became increasingly prominent particularly from the
third quarter of the century onwards. Nevertheless, over most of
the nineteenth century, the extent of private activity in the
sphere of 'natural monopolies' was substantial.[32]

The Government largely stood aside from industrial relations
in the nineteenth century, particularly after the repeal of the
Combination Laws in 1824–5. It set some minimum conditions
and maximum hours of work. Besides this, its main presence in
industrial relations over most of the century was in the form of
judicial interpretations of law. The responsibilities that the
Board of Trade eventually came to have regarding industrial
relations began by way of statistical inquiry and publicity. From
1886, labour statistics were collected and published, and from
1893 a Labour Department was established. Subsequent
development followed from contemporary concern about the
persistence of unemployment, and the dislocation caused by
industrial disputes.

It was the latter concern which first led the Board of Trade to
take administrative action in labour matters. Britain was no
longer in such a strong position in relation to her international
competitors that the Government could disregard the effects of

industrial disputes. Following the Labour Department's unauthorized but successful interventions in the coal industry in 1893 and in the boot and shoe industry two years later, the Conciliation Act of 1896 was passed to regularize the Board of Trade's action, and to authorize further conciliatory activity on a voluntary basis. In 1911, the work was separated from the other functions of the Labour Department, and placed under a Chief Industrial Commissioner aided by an Industrial Council representing both employers and employed. Government arbitration was not made compulsory, which meant that British industrial relations were to consist of voluntary negotiations between employers and employed. Government did not regulate them, except insofar as it had already provided a special legal status for the trade unions.[33]

The Board of Trade's responsibilities in relation to the labour market were massively extended by the Trade Boards Act 1909, the Labour Exchanges Act 1909, and Part II (Unemployment Insurance) of the National Insurance Act 1911. That the Board of Trade secured these functions and not the Home Office or the Local Government Board is explained by a variety of factors. Some of them were to do with the political personalities in the Asquith Liberal Government. The Local Government Board had performed such previous responsibilities as central government had recognized regarding the unemployed; but its President, John Burns, was more of a figurehead for the trade union movement than an effective Minister. The Home Office had factory regulative functions, and Beatrice Webb had planned to expand it into a Ministry of Labour; but Herbert Gladstone had proved to be a very ordinary Home Secretary.

Winston Churchill having turned down the Local Government Board – not wishing 'to be shut up in a soup kitchen with Mrs Webb' – had become President of the Board of Trade instead in 1908. In this part of his career, Churchill was an ardent social reformer. He was the political author of unemployment insurance and Trade Boards legislation, as well as the Labour Exchanges Act which empowered the Board of Trade to establish a network of such exchanges throughout the country, and to collect information relating to unemployment. Beveridge, already an authority on unemployment problems, was made Director of Labour Exchanges. He had been brought into the

Board of Trade earlier by Churchill, urged on by the Webbs, and with the agreement of the reforming Permanent Secretary, Hubert Llewellyn Smith. In fact, the Board's new duties required massive external recruitment, and accounted for almost all the increase in its staff from 1,733 to 6,313 that took place between 1909–10 and 1914–15.[34]

The functions that the Board of Trade eventually gained in relation to industry and employment were, to some extent, offset by what it lost or had to share in the sphere of trade itself. For example, when Edward Cardwell became President of the Board at the end of 1852 he was to spend his two years or so there largely absorbed by the urgent problems of merchant shipping and railways. For Cardwell, commercial policy under Free Trade had become so simple a matter that there was no reason why the Foreign Office should consult the Board about it, or why an important branch of the Board should be occupied with the subject. Without tariff negotiations, the branch concerned – the Commercial Department – lost its main contact with commercial and industrial opinions and conditions. Deprived of any direct communication with British overseas representatives, the branch became increasingly diffident about offering advice on commercial questions to other government departments.

The Anglo-French Commercial Treaty of 1860, and the series of Cobdenite negotiations did bring new life to the Commercial Department. Under the direction of Louis Mallet, it became the headquarters for the new treaty negotiations. However, the revival of reciprocity treaties proved temporary. What proved to be more lasting was a confusion of responsibilities for overseas trade between the Board and the Foreign Office. Under pressure from interested parties such as the Chambers of Commerce, there was an attempted rationalization in 1872, which concentrated responsibilities on the Foreign Office. This lasted for ten years when the old dualism was revived, and persisted despite further outside commercial pressure for change.[35]

The complexity of government responsibilities for trade at home was matched in commercial representation abroad. There was in fact no one Consular Service in the nineteenth century, appointed for a single purpose and supplied with identical instructions. The Victorian Consular Service consisted of the General Service, the Far Eastern Service (China, and later Japan, Siam and Korea), and the Levant Service – though the latter was not formally separated from the General Service until 1877. The Levant Service was inherited by the British Government in 1825 (when the Levant Company ceased); and the Far Eastern Service followed in 1834 (when the East India Company's monopoly of trade with China expired). The Far Eastern Service developed at once into a specially recruited service with its own system of promotion and payment and its own code of instructions. The Levant Service eventually organized itself similarly, and by 1914 both Services were thought to be superior to the General Service in intellect and performance. The Consular Service was rationalized in 1903, but this did little to enhance the Service's low comparative status in relation to the Foreign Office to which it was directly linked in 1872. Trade was not thought to be a fit subject for a gentleman to concern himself. Such attitudes were bound to be present in bodies with the social composition of the Foreign Office and the Diplomatic Service. Even the obviousness of the challenge of foreign competition seems not to have greatly undermined this outlook.[36]

As the Board of Trade did not monopolize governmental responsibility for external trade, it is unsurprising that its role as the department for industry was also shared. When the Factories and Mines Inspectorates were established, they were placed in the Home Office. The first four Factory Inspectors were appointed in 1833. By 1878, there were thirty-nine of them headed by a Chief Inspector. The 1833 legislation had limited the Inspectors to textile mills; but gradually their purview was extended until in 1901 comprehensive factory and workshop legislation was on the statute book. The Inspectors themselves were one factor in the expansion of responsibility. One of the first four of them, Leonard Horner, was a notably determined reformer in the opening quarter of a century of the Inspectorate's existence. The first Mines Inspector, Seymour Tremenheere, was a colourful enough character too. A former Assistant Poor Law Commissioner, he was appointed under the 1842 legislation regulating coal mines. Tremenheere served for sixteen years without colleague or successor, and, set loose with only general instructions, he was practically independent of the Home Office. Tremenheere pressed with eventual success for a well staffed, scientifically trained Mines Inspectorate.[37]

Just as the nineteenth century State did not leave industry entirely alone, so it did not leave agriculture completely to its own devices, even after the repeal of the Corn Laws in 1846. However, it came very near to doing so. In the second quarter of the century, there were three government bodies dealing with land: the Tithe Commission (from 1836), the Copyhold Commission (from 1841), and the Inclosure Commission (from 1845). In 1851, these bodies were merged into one Commission. In 1882, this became the Land Commission. In 1889, it became the Land Department of the newly formed Board of Agriculture. One feature that these bodies had in common was the presence on them of James Caird, who finished a distinguished career in land administration by becoming Director of the Land Department. Caird not only had practical experience as a farmer. He was a prominent member of the Royal Agricultural Society, and of the Statistical Society, of which he became President in 1880. Indeed – although a firm advocate of individual enterprise – one duty that he thought that the State should recognize in relation to farming was the collection of agricultural statistics.

Despite his agitation, this function was not undertaken until an outbreak of cattle plague in 1865 forced action. The policy of slaughter and compensation by which the outbreak was combated, emphasized the importance of knowing the actual number of cattle on farms. Subsequently, the Inland Revenue collected the statistics, and the Board of Trade published them. The Cattle Plague Department of the Home Office, formed in 1865, was transferred to the Privy Council the next year, and a Veterinary Department was developed there from 1870 to deal with such subjects as the control of contagious diseases. In 1883, this became the Agricultural Department, also being made responsible for the publication of agricultural statistics. Then, in 1889, the Department and the Land Commission were merged in the Board of Agriculture, thus meeting a growing public demand that the now depressed farming industry should have a single department responsible for it. The Board was initially responsible for agriculture and forestry in Great Britain. Then in 1903, fisheries were transferred to it, and eight years later a separate Board of Agriculture for Scotland was established.[38]

IV. THE MACHINERY OF GOVERNMENT AND ITS SOCIAL POLICY FUNCTIONS

Changes in the role of the State in social provision came earlier than they did in the economic sphere, where private activity continued to dominate right down to the First World War. The Conservative and Liberal reforms of the final years of the nineteenth century and then the first decade or so of the twentieth century had made for substantial changes in the social policy responsibilities undertaken by government.

Previously, private philanthropy and voluntary action continued to be the dominant source of social provision. The Poor Law had continued to provide the main framework for such commitments as the State recognized in England. The reformed Poor Law of 1834 did not represent the triumph of *laissez-faire*, and it did not mean the radical decline of public responsibility for welfare. Public provision had always been inferior to that of private provision. The ideas of the Classical Economists were inconsistent regarding the Poor Law. The post-1834 arrangements in fact took a form that in some respects was inimical to the full working of the market philosophy. This is not to say that the liberal elements that came to power in the late eighteenth and early nineteenth century did not champion an industrial society based on individualistic principles. It is not to dispute either that, during the nineteenth century, the State only provided minimal public protection against economic insecurity at a time when such insecurity had greatly increased for large segments of the population. It is to say that such provision and protection had always been minimal in practice. Three main things were different now.

The overriding difference was that the scale of social problems posed by industrialization, urbanization, and rapid population growth was considerably greater than those experienced before. The second difference was that the dominant ideology of the Classical Economists was antipathetic to public expenditure. This is not to suggest that public expenditure was viewed favourably before, but it was not specifically and ideologically condemned. The third difference was that whereas previously private and voluntary provision had been dominant and localism had been the practice in such State provision as there was, this approach now received the general ideological blessing of such as John Stuart Mill. These attitudes sometimes conflicted, as when the local administration of the Poor Law was more generous than, or at least different from, the intentions of central reformers. Generally, though, they did not conflict.

For most of the nineteenth century, the prevailing individualist ideology meant that the response of the State to the massive social problems of the world's first industrialized society was a muted one. When the problems were recognized, the State left their solution partly to local government initiative, but mainly to private provision. Those in need looked first as always to family and friends. Those who had sufficient ability and resources organized themselves to avoid becoming dependent on the reformed Poor Law. People like Samuel Smiles treated Self Help as a virtue, but for many it was deemed a necessity. The 1834 Poor Law was designed to be exemplary in its harshness, and it has a punitive reputation. Yet, it was the case, for example, that the medical provisions of the nineteenth century Poor Law, while not intended as such, were one of the beginnings of the long and uncertain road to a National Health Service.

Similarly, the State's involvement in general educational provision in England proved to be permanent once the first grants to voluntary societies were made in 1833, even if direct provision outside the Poor Law had to wait until after 1870. Public health was also to be another area of important concern for the nineteenth century State.

It was not many years after the Charity Organization Society was formed in 1869 to rationalize the existing arrangements for social provision in the name of individualism that Green and Marshall undermined the intellectual ascendancy of the Classical Economists. The C.O.S. is sometimes said to have turned out to be a monument to a dying faith, or at least one which within two or three decades was mortally ailing. It has to be emphasized that the death was a lingering one. The individualist sentiments that the C.O.S. represented were still prominent in the 1930s. The C.O.S., however, was not the force that it had been even in 1914, and certainly not what it had been in the years after 1905 when confronting the Fabians on the Royal Commission on the Poor Laws. The middle class Fabians provided important intellectual opposition to individualism. They were involved, for example, in the 'national efficiency' movement, which was certainly a factor in increasing pressure for social reform, particularly after the Boer War had raised alarms about the military capabilities of British youth and the physical condition many of them were in.

Envious eyes were turned towards Germany and, for some, envy was directed towards the level of German social provision that was provided by government. Another factor that made for changes was that more information became available about the level of poverty that existing British social policy arrangements permitted: the inadequacy of the existing arrangements for social welfare were documented by Charles Booth and Seebohm Rowntree. A further factor was discontent among the working classes – and particularly organized labour – about the existing arrangements for social welfare. The Poor Law was especially hated. Both major parties of the time felt that they had to take the views of organized labour seriously. The Liberal Party searching for a radical identity felt this in particular. Ironically, the trade unions did not always approve of the social policy measures taken.[39]

(i) *The Poor Law*

The largest single item of civil expenditure in the nineteenth century was the Poor Law, through which government mainly exercised its commitments in relation to social provision. Indeed, such was the scale of expenditure that the Poor Law Amendment Act was passed in 1834 directed towards its diminution. This was explicit in the origins and creation of the New Poor Law, in its principles of uniformity, abolition of outdoor relief and less eligibility. Effective centralization was meant to be one of the chief ways of turning these principles into practice. The Webbs wrote of the 1834 Act: 'this revolutionary legislation not only gave a dogmatically uniform direction to English Poor Law policy, but also incidentally transformed the system of local government which had endured

for over three centuries, and established for the first time . . . the
principle of centralized executive control of local administration'. The 1834 arrangements were eventually a source of
important developments in English local government: central
supervision, central inspection, central audit, a professional
local government service controlled by elective bodies, and the
adjustment of areas to administrative exigencies.[40] However
important the Poor Law Amendment Act was in introducing
administrative principles, what was often to be lacking was their
effective nineteenth century practice.

The Poor Law Commissioners appointed in 1834 did not
represent an effective central authority. Edwin Chadwick – the
main author of the legislation – was made Secretary and not
one of the three Commissioners, who were Whig nominees.
Chadwick was privately promised that he would have the first
vacancy, and that in the meantime he would be able to act like
a fourth Commissioner. The other Commissioners resented
Chadwick's behaviour as Secretary, and he was not given the
succession. The situation was made for administrative conflict,
with the arrogantly talented Chadwick continually confronting
his formal superiors. The situation was made for political
conflict too. Chadwick had designed an administrative structure
entirely separate from the legislature. His model had been the
machinery for the regulation of the Friendly Societies, also
established in 1834. This worked quite well because the societies
were uncontroversial. The Poor Law was always controversial:
it could not be taken out of politics. The Commissioners in
general, and Chadwick in particular, were the subject of perennial parliamentary harassment. When the Home Secretary
defended the Commissioners, the House of Commons dismissed
him as a mouthpiece, and devised their own investigative
methods. As Chadwick himself said, the result was that the
central Poor Law authority was 'in a greater state of paralysis
and dependence on political movements than . . . any branch
of the business of the Home Office'.

What activated much of the political hostility towards the
Poor Law Commissioners was that they were thought to have
imposed a highly centralized system which meant the beginning
of the end of local self government. In fact, as they had no
coercive powers, the central Commissioners could not make the

local Boards of Guardians initiate anything. The demonaic Chadwick found the whole thing massively frustrating. He palliated his miseries with a series of inquiries whether or not they were wanted by his superiors. After the Conservatives came to office in 1841, he was more or less excluded from Poor Law work, which enabled him to concentrate his obsessions on public health. Chadwick had the satisfaction of helping to bring the Commissioners down over the Andover workhouse scandal. However, even when the Commissioners were replaced by a Poor Law Board (1847–71) and then a Local Government Board, each with a President with a seat in Parliament, it was still the case that the central Poor Law authority could propose, but it was a matter for local authority decision if it complied.[41]

Local administration of the Poor Law proved far more difficult to change than the reformers of the 1830s had imagined. They thought that the motley collection of 15,000 existing local authorities could be easily supplanted by identically constituted Boards of Guardians, with mechanically devised areas and a high rating qualification, to be elected by plural voting according to propriety, and diluted by the local Justices of the Peace as ex-officio members. In fact, the rationalization process took until 1868 to complete. Then, various excluded bodies – such as those formed under Gilbert's Act – were at last brought into the general framework of Poor Law Unions headed by Boards of Guardians. These Unions themselves were gradually brought into conformity with the reformed local government areas. What doomed the hopes of central dominance from the outset was the financial independence that the Boards of Guardians enjoyed, and the degree of administrative discretion accorded to them. For example, the central authority was not empowered to compel any Board of Guardians without their majority consent to erect or rebuild any workhouse involving capital expenditure exceeding £50, or one-tenth of the annual rates of the Union concerned.

It remained doubtful whether, even by making regulations for workhouses, the central authority could require the Guardians to appoint any definite number of salaried officers. To give another example, at different dates, the Poor Law Commissioners, the Poor Law Board, and the Local Government Board tried their utmost to induce Boards of Guardians to form combinations among themselves for particular purposes, such as the maintenance of asylums for the houseless poor, district schools, sick asylums, able bodied test workhouses and other specialized workhouses. Even as late as 1911, only a dozen such combinations had been formed. As the Webbs put it, the broad base of the administrative hierarchy of the Poor Law could only be moved with the greatest difficulty, at least on some matters. The Boards of Guardians, if they chose to be obstinate, remained substantially independent of the central authority.[42]

The Scottish arrangements were separate and different in some respects, although the roles of the central authorities concerned were remarkably similar by the end of the nineteenth century. In England, the Poor Law Commission claimed central powers from which it gradually retreated. In Scotland, when the Poor Law was reformed there in 1845, the Board of Supervision did not claim powers at the outset, but gradually accumulated centralized functions. Equally significant was the fact that, although the English system was avowedly uniform and the Scottish avowedly variable, they both had a similar range of variations in practice. Even the fundamental difference of Scotland having no workhouse test did not significantly alter the pattern of indoor relief. Nonetheless, there remained important differences. One was that the able bodied remained formally outside poor relief. Another was that the Scottish system formally defined a role for voluntarism which in England was left informal and implicit. The post-1845 Scottish system combined the ideology of Thomas Chalmers with traditional practice. It allowed parishes to preserve the voluntary system if they wanted to. The pressures on voluntarism – chiefly finance – gradually undermined this arrangement. So that, whereas in 1845 only 25 per cent of parishes had a formal assessment for a poor rate, by 1894 only 5 per cent did not need one.[43]

(ii) Public Health

The controversies that surround the Poor Law Commissioners were repeated when a General Board of Health was established in 1848 as the central authority for public health. The controversy again involved public antipathy towards what was seen as centralization. The controversy also centred around Edwin

Chadwick, once more connected with a governmental body only indirectly represented in Parliament, but this time as a Commissioner. The six years that Chadwick spent with the Board seem to have been the happiest of his official career. Obsessed with the 'sanitary idea', Chadwick was fulfilled in his daily toil of twelve to fourteen hours a day, whether drafting Bills or memoranda, advising Ministers, or sending his Inspectors to urge local authorities to install tubular sewerage and other good things. Chadwick also continued to try to promote sanitary reform in London, an area specifically excluded from the General Board's purview in the Public Health Act of 1848. Chadwick's mood as always was imperative but the Board's powers were as permissive as the legal commitments of the Local Health Boards that the Act had required to be set up in some areas but not in others. Nevertheless, the General Board had far too many powers in the eyes of anti-centralizers. In 1854, Chadwick was retired, and four years later the General Board was abolished. Its medical powers were transferred to the Privy Council (which had earlier had brief explicit responsibilities for public health in 1805–6 and 1831–4) and its work in town development devolved on a newly created Local Government Act Office in the Home Office.[44]

The demise of Chadwick and then of the General Board of Health did not mean the end of central intervention in public health. The problems were simply too pressing to be entirely disregarded, and a more effective reformer in John Simon was there to urge their solution. Simon had secured practical success in sanitary reform as Medical Officer of Health in the City of London between 1848 and becoming Medical Officer at the General Board in 1855. Simon flourished in the disparate administrative atmosphere of the Privy Council, and established his own Medical Department there in 1861. Under Simon and in the 1860s, central health administration in England is said to have become more exploratory and intrusive, more concerned with the intrinsic problems of health, more modern in outlook and method than ever before.

Among Simon's many achievements, he provided the main central administrative impetus behind vaccination. He was the effective author of the Sanitary Act of 1866 which made it the duty of local authorities among other things, to ensure that their areas had effective systems of water supply, sewage disposal and nuisance removal. Simon's biographer thought that this Act meant that the common health law of England thus became virtually universal and uniform in its application. This seems doubtful, given the existing condition of what passed for the system of local administration. The Public Health Act of 1875 consolidated the English sanitary code and set out the organization of local sanitary authorities in a clear, methodical and orderly manner. Town councils, Local Boards and Improvement Commissioners (the last named bodies dwindling in number year by year) were recognized as urban sanitary authorities for the administration of the 1875 Act; and Boards of Guardians served as rural sanitary authorities for the same purpose.[45]

The central responsibility for public health in England and Wales passed to a newly created Local Government Board in 1871. This was formed from three existing governmental bodies: the Medical Department of the Privy Council, the Local Government Act Department of the Home Office, and the Poor Law Board. The Local Government Board received powers to encourage local provision through grants-in-aid, and it was to develop a numerous and specialized Inspectorate. At the centre, however, it was dominated from the outset by its Poor Law work. Although Simon was made Medical Officer to the Board, he was denied personal access to the President, and he was excluded from policy discussion. Having previously had a relatively free hand, Simon resented his subordination, and resigned in 1876. The Medical Department was then broken up and the pieces relocated in the old branches of the Poor Law Board. For all its former powers, the Local Government Board proved to be an undistinguished department. In its defence, it has been said that the Board could not go faster than public opinion.[46] Yet, Simon had done so in the so called era of localism in the 1860s.

In Scotland, the Board of Supervision received public health powers in the 1860s. In 1894, it and its public health and Poor Law duties were taken over by a Local Government Board for Scotland.[47]

(iii) *Education*

Educational administration was slow to develop in the nine-

teenth century. No special machinery was established to administer the grants first made in 1833 to voluntary societies to
assist the building of elementary schools. The responsibility was
with the Treasury, but this failed to prevent administration of
the grants from being extremely loose. The need both to increase
the grant and to enforce more stringent conditions for its dis-
bursement led to the establishment of the Committee of the
Privy Council for Education in 1839. At first, the staff consisted
of only one Secretary, but soon two Inspectors were appointed.
By the mid-1850s, there were 41 staff in the Education Department. In 1856, the ministerial post of Vice President of the
Committee of the Privy Council on Education was established.
At the same time, the functions of the Science and Art Department were formally transferred across from the Board of Trade.
From its separate South Kensington base, this Department –
headed at first by Lyon Playfair – more or less independently
pursued its work of promoting scientific education and technical
instruction. In Whitehall, the Education Department, with its
responsibilities substantially extended from the Forster Act
onwards, and with other bodies such as a short lived Endowed
Schools Commission, and (from 1855) the long lived Charity
Commissioners involved in education too, by the end of the
nineteenth century some rationalization on central responsibility
for education was overdue. It came only in 1899 when the Board
of Education was established headed by a President, with the
important innovation of a Consultative Committee.[48]

The Board's early years proved to be stormy ones, with the
controversy that surrounded the Education Act of 1902 and
Robert Morant, that Act's administrative author and then the
Board's Permanent Secretary. Morant's rise to the top was
spectacular. He had begun his educational career as a private
tutor to the Crown Prince of Siam. He joined the Office of
Special Inquiries and Reports in the Education Department in
1895, being appointed by Michael Sadler, its Director, whom
he subsequently drove to resign. Within four years, he had
established himself in the Department's Secondary Schools
Branch. With educational reform on the political agenda, but
with his immediate political superiors blocking his way, Morant
persuaded Arthur Balfour to push through the Education Bill
that he had drafted. This Balfour did, despite Liberal opposition

that secured most of its emotive force from the prospect of Nonconformists having to pay local rates which could be used to subsidise Anglican schools. This religious controversy tended to hide the fact that the Act importantly widened the opportunities for secondary education, as well as rationalizing the arrangements for elementary education. The Act also importantly changed the local educational administrative arrangements when it abolished the separate School Boards established by Forster in 1870, and made the counties and county boroughs the local educational authorities. As for Morant himself, once he had reached the Permanent Secretaryship – which took him only seven years – he did not rest there. Before he moved on in 1911, teacher training, university reform, adult education, and nursery schooling all engaged his attention. He played a vital role in helping to establish school meals and the School Medical Service. [49]

Although the Scottish educational system was separate, its central administration was not, certainly before 1885. The Vice President of the Committee of the Privy Council on Education was effectively Minister of Education for Britain down to that date, despite the formation of what was called a Scottish Committee in 1872. In 1885, the appointment of a Secretary for Scotland rationalized this arrangement. [50]

(iv) *Pensions and National Insurance*

The Liberal social reforms, like workmen's compensation before them entailed surprisingly little formal organizational change. The Home Office had been given a general oversight of workmen's compensation. The Treasury and the Inland Revenue provided the administrative initiative for old age pensions and national insurance. The pensions were paid out at local post offices. Unemployment benefit was paid out at newly created labour exchanges, although the trade unions were permitted, in some circumstances, to handle the benefits. The health insurance structure established after 1911 was administratively more complex. The Treasury acted as a parent department for the Insurance Commissions set up for the four units of the United Kingdom, with a Joint Committee to co-ordinate practice. A local office organization was not deemed necessary.

The routine work of collecting contributions and making payments was delegated to Approved Societies: friendly societies, trade unions, medical aid societies and industrial assurance companies. The main Civil Service architect of the health insurance scheme was a Treasury man, W B Braithwaite, who had been despatched by Chancellor of the Exchequer, Lloyd George to Germany to study the Bismarckian scheme. Braithwaite performed the Herculean task of establishing the legislative and administrative basis of Lloyd George's scheme. The exhausted Braithwaite was then dropped by a political master as ruthless in dealing with subordinates as he was with opponents such as the British Medical Association. Lloyd George brought in Morant and a small but talented group of young Civil Servants. The overriding administrative importance of national insurance involved drawing talent from several government departments to ensure that the controversial legislation was passed.[51]

V. A NINETEENTH CENTURY REVOLUTION IN GOVERNMENT?

The nineteenth century witnessed substantial changes in the machinery of British government and administration. This is obvious when one contrasts its structure in the early years of the twentieth century with that of a hundred years before. The nineteenth century was characterized by major inventions in government machinery, some of which proved only too durable. Nevertheless, the process of their implementation was normally slow and not, as some historians have believed, revolutionary. If there had been revolutionary change, it would have been evident in the economic and social policy functions of government. Yet, it was not until the final years of the nineteenth century that there was substantial growth in the State's commitments even in social provision, while the role of government in the economy remained limited down to 1914.

The State's presence in the nineteenth century economy certainly was a modest one. As we have seen, the Post Office and naval and military establishments accounted for almost all the central government's direct economic activities down to 1914, when the half share in the Anglo-Persian Oil Company was taken. By that time, the Post Office's functions had been extended notably by its monopoly of the electric telegraph and near-monopoly of the telephone system. In the case of the telegraph, however, compared with all but one of the other leading industrial countries State control had come belatedly; and in the case of telephones it did not come until 1911.

At local government level, 'gas and water socialism' made substantial advances, and there was a pronounced movement in the direction of local authority ownership from the 1880s onwards; but what was also noteworthy for most of the nineteenth century was the widespread reliance placed on private provision in what often were cases of natural monopoly, and such provision was prominent as late as 1914. The regulation of public utilities and services even when privately owned was one of the duties that the nineteenth century State recognized. As we have seen, regulation of the railways eventually became fairly extensive. It has to be remembered, though, that even including the United States, Britain was the only country which left the financing and development of the railways entirely to private enterprise. Indeed, even when one takes account of factories and mines regulation, it can be seen that the nineteenth century British economy was dominated by private enterprise.

What the nineteenth century State made no attempt to regulate was the economy as a whole. Whether the country prospered or whether levels of employment were maintained were matters for private decisions only lightly affected by the State, as in the case of employment with measures such as the Poor Employment Act of 1817 and the Unemployed Workmen Act of 1905. Ideally, central government in particular was to be kept small in relation to the economy. The Budget was to be balanced. Taxation was to be kept low, and with it the level of public expenditure. The reduction of the National Debt was a priority. The name of Gladstone was associated with this outlook, but the sentiments came as easily to the lips of predecessors such as Pitt and successors down to Asquith. The seals of financial rectitude on the restrictionist model were kept in the Treasury. If the State was to intervene in the economy, if possible it was best done at local level. If not, and this was preferable, it should be done by a voluntary association: hence, the praise from John Stuart Mill for the nascent Co-operative Movement. Best of all, if at all practicable, economic activities were to be left to private enterprise. The banking system continued to be left in the hands of the Bank of England, a private institution.

The Bank Charter Act of 1844 ended any serious prospect of government intervention in the monetary system. Apart from the fiduciary issue rule, the State prescribed nothing about the Bank's behaviour in the manipulation of money and credit. The Gold Standard, although supposed to be automatic, was in fact quasi-organizational, being managed by the Bank of England. Except in times of crisis, the British Government was outside the process.[52] The extent to which the nineteenth century State was prepared to abstain from economic responsibilities was nowhere more marked than in the case of Free Trade. That far out-weighed in importance the other duties that the State took on.

Free Trade was an act of *laissez-faire* if ever there was one. It meant that the State was prepared to leave commerce, industry and agriculture to face world competition without safeguards comparable with those that other governments gave to their traders, businessmen and farmers.[53] Initially, it was perhaps only to be expected that the State should leave them to their own devices. Private enterprise had established Britain as the world's first industrial nation and dominant trader with limited help from the State. British farmers had also achieved an 'agricultural revolution' over the previous century or so also without substantial governmental promotion. What was remarkable was not only that the policy of Free Trade continued to be adhered to when other countries, even within the Empire, failed to follow in any sustained manner the example provided. The policy was also persisted with even when it was clear that Britain was not any longer equipped to deal with German and American competition on level terms. British capital was allowed to continue to develop Argentina or wherever the returns were thought to be higher, and the State took no steps to ensure the development of the British economy.

As what the State deemed to be its necessary role in the nineteenth century was not a minimalist one, in the sense that it could have done less (at least in theory), some may object to the term *laissez-faire* being used to describe it. Such definitional difficulties, however, need not be allowed to obscure the view that down to 1914, the State's role in the economy, particularly at central government level, was a restricted one. Compared with the ambitions of some former times, and with the contemporary practice of many of her economic rivals, the working of the British economy was to a very considerable extent left to private initiatives and market mechanisms.

The role of the State in social provision was more ambitious than in the economic sphere, and this was particularly marked in the period immediately before 1914. This was because of relatively recent legislation such as the Employers' Liability Act of 1880 and the Workmen's Compensation Acts of 1897, 1900 and 1906 relating to industrial injuries; the Housing Act of 1890; the Lunacy Act of 1890; the Education Act of 1902; the Education (Provision of School Meals) Act of 1906; the Education (Administrative Provisions) Act of 1907 which introduced compulsory medical inspection of school children; the Old Age Pensions Act of 1908; the Children Act of 1909; the Housing and Planning Act of 1909; the National Insurance Act of 1911; and the Mental Deficiency Act of 1913. This was a formidable array of measures extending government responsibilities. That parents of children who received free school meals and recipients of old age pensions were not disenfranchised were important breaches in the punitive philosophy of the Poor Law. Although, because of the Medical Relief Disqualification Act of 1885, they were not the first.

As the nineteenth century had proceeded, the State had taken on more and more responsibilities for social provision, notably in education and public health. The effectiveness of State intervention in public health has been exaggerated by accounts which rely on the existence of Royal Commissions and the passing of legislation as evidence of achievement. On that kind of interpretation, the Public Health Act of 1875 was supposed to have completed a process in which high standards of public health were established. In fact, there was no government machinery which could ensure this. Another, and more realistic, measure of progress is to look at it not in terms of legislation but in terms of the actual health of the public, that is the elimination of the causes of preventable mortality. In the middle period of the nineteenth century, the mortality that was most easily preventable was caused by a relatively small group of infectious diseases: typhus, typhoid, cholera, tuberculosis, scarlet and relapsing fever, measles, diarrhoea and smallpox.

Public health administration to be effective had to eliminate, as it virtually had done in mid-twentieth century Britain, mortality resulting from these diseases. In fact, in 1875, the death rate stood at almost exactly the same level as it had when civil registration began and Chadwick had first sent his Poor Law Medical investigators into the London slums. Infant mortality, the high level of which is commonly assumed to have accounted for the high general mortality in the early nineteenth century, scarcely began to fall before the end of the century.

There was very little real improvement in public health before the last quarter of the nineteenth century; and the most significant reductions to what may be regarded as mid-twentieth century standards of mortality – including particularly the reductions of infant mortality – were the work of the early twentieth century. So there was a substantial time lag between legislation and improvements in the mortality figures. Twentieth century medical standards required twentieth century medical developments, but the fact does remain that there was no necessary immediate connection between public health legislation and improvements in public health in the nineteenth century. The omissions of State activity need to be emphasized too. In the related sphere of housing, it was not until the Housing and Planning Act of 1909 that the principle of permanent local authority house ownership was established. Before that, housing was assumed to be the business of private enterprise, although philanthropic and other voluntary provision was also important.[54]

The State's major contribution to social provision over the nineteenth century as a whole remained the Poor Law, which, despite the predominance of outdoor relief, was associated with the workhouse. This was an institution which was 'neither school, infirmary, penitentiary, prison, place of shelter, or place of work, but something that comes of all of these put together'. This 'workhouse essence' pervaded the Poor Law. Practice did not always follow from principle, but the Poor Law rested on the assumption that 'where cases of real hardship occur, the remedy must be applied by individual charity, a virtue for which no system of compulsory relief can be or ought to be a substitute'.

The two systems were not totally separate. Those who sat as

Poor Law Guardians would very often be the same people who sat on the committees which controlled schools, hospitals and dispensaries, and the other forms of charitable organizations. They would also often be among those who took the lead in sponsoring local voluntary efforts in times of communal celebration or of disaster. In situations such as the Lancashire cotton famine of 1861–65, the help which the cotton operatives desperately needed had to come from private charity. Friendly societies and other organs of Self Help brought security to some; but the main burden of social provision for most of the nineteenth century was borne by private philanthropy.[55] It was only in the latter years of the century that it slowly but increasingly came to be more widely thought that State social provision was the only means of diminishing high and persistent levels of poverty, and of ensuring advance in other social spheres.

The functions of the State were not revolutionized during the nineteenth century, but was this also true of the machinery of government? No less than three major inventions in government machinery tend to be associated with the nineteenth century. One is the development of the ministerial department. Another is the creation of a classified Civil Service recruited by open academic competitive examination. A third is the elected multi-purpose local authority.[56] A fourth would be the use of central inspection both of private interests to see that they were complying with the law, and of local authorities to see that they were doing so too. Another would be the Exchequer grant as a central financial inducement to local authorities to do their duties. Nevertheless, while the nineteenth century did witness the growth of formal links between central and local government, the extent of central control over the largely financially independent local authorities remained limited. Moreover, reviewing the other nineteenth century inventions, one can see that the monopoly position of the ministerial department was short lived; the reformed Civil Service was an invention which could not be said to have been fully applied until well into the twentieth century; and that the process of change was slow even in local government, which was important because that was the dominant level of nineteenth century State activity.

The nineteenth century is commonly thought to be an era of

reforming change in local government. So it was in the sense that at the end of the century there was a discernible system of English local government whereas there had not been at the beginning; and that the Scottish arrangements had been changed too and made broadly similar. The Poor Law Amendment Act of 1834 and the Municipal Corporations Act of 1835 marked the beginning of the process of change. If the multi-purpose local authorities that covered England by the end of the nineteenth century had a specific model, it was that provided by the municipal corporations established under the 1835 Act. They were based on a ratepaying electorate, with audited accounts, a committee system of organization, and a separation of judicial from other administration. The appointment of a Town Clerk and a Treasurer was made obligatory. Nevertheless, the process of extending representative institutions of the municipal pattern to rural and urban districts generally took no less than two generations. It was not until 1882 that all boroughs were brought under the 1835 arrangements. It was not until 1888 that elected councils replaced Justices of the Peace as the administrative authorities in the counties. It was only then that London government was reformed, although the City of London still survived and metropolitan boroughs were not added until 1899.

In other major towns, county borough councils were established after 1888. An Act in 1894 created urban and rural districts from the bits left over from other jurisdictions, and finally abolished the remaining Improvement Commissioners, Turnpike Trusts and Local Boards of Health. School Boards were not abolished until 1902, and Boards of Guardians continued until 1929.[57] So, reform was a slow business even in the supposed heyday of local government. At most stages in the reform process as many areas and institutions were preserved as possible. Little attempt was made to relate the size and resources of local authorities to the functions to be performed.

That an area of local government should be appropriate to its functions was one of the three general principles of the Poor Law reform of 1834. The other principles were inherently conflictual with the developments that followed from the 1835 reform of the boroughs. For, a second Poor Law administrative principle was to use an elected ad hoc authority for a specific service, and a third was detailed central control. However, local autonomy was not just a sentiment that the muncipal reformers subscribed to. The Poor Law authorities – like the General Board of Health – found that it was a sentiment of the age. This is not to say that local responses to central initiatives were necessarily hostile or that the latter were necessarily ineffective. For example, as noted earlier, the combination of Exchequer grant and central inspection did eventually raise local police standards. Nevertheless, for most of the nineteenth century, local authorities had the freedom which financial independence supplies. It was not really until after the introduction of Goschen's system of assigned revenues in 1888 that central financial aid was generally important for local government. In 1868, municipal corporations seem to have found 95 per cent of their revenue from local rates.

Even in 1905–6, urban authorities provided 77 per cent of their finance. By then, the Local Government Board occupied a unique position among central departments in the amount of formal control it had over a local administration that was mainly paid for out of rates. While remarking on this, the Royal Commission on the Poor Laws reporting in 1909 recognized the negative nature of the Board's powers. A witness summed this up well when she said: 'the Local Government Board . . . although it can restrain them (the local authorities) from acting, is in practice . . . powerless to force them to act. It has no effective machinery indeed through which it can . . . force them to do anything they are determined not to do'.[58] Whether the Poor Law typically reflected the powers of the centre in relation to the localities is difficult to establish; but it does seem that even in the early years of the twentieth century the local authorities did enjoy considerable discretion in the manner in which they performed their centrally prescribed duties, and sometimes as to whether they did them at all.

Like local government, British central government machinery looked very different in 1914 compared with that of a century before. Some of the parts of the machinery were the same or nearly the same: Treasury, Privy Council Office, Home Office, Foreign Office, Colonial Office, India Office, Irish Office, War Office, Admiralty, Board of Trade, Post Office, Board of Inland Revenue, Board of Customs and Excise, and Public

Works Loans Board. The functions that these departments performed had in some cases changed considerably: for example, those of the Post Office and the Board of Trade. Other departments had broadly similar functions but were organized differently, such as the revenue departments. Some parts of central government machinery were new and not only in name. Although there was an Irish Office from 1801 onwards, a Scottish Office was not established until 1885.[59] By then, the Ecclesiastical Commission (1836), the Lunacy Commission (1845), the Board of Works (1851), the Charity Commission (1853), and the Civil Service Commission (1855) had established themselves. Some departments were mainly formed from pieces of existing machinery such as the Local Government Board (1871) and the Board of Agriculture (1889). The Local Government Board came to house several of the important Inspectorates, as the Home Office also continued to do. The Home Office was a parent to some departments, for example, donating functions to the Board of Agriculture. The Privy Council was a parent to others, including the Board of Education (1899).

Administrative boards not directly responsible to Parliament, such as the Poor Law Commission and the General Board of Health, not only went out of fashion but also out of existence, to be replaced by ministerial departments also confusingly called boards – the Poor Law Board and then the Local Government Board. Nevertheless, the early years of the twentieth century saw a partial return to administrative boards with the establishment of the Road Board and the Development Commission after the 1909 Budget, and the Port of London Authority the year before. The latter is sometimes called the first modern public corporation, but other candidates include the Metropolitan Water Board and also the Mersey Docks and Harbour Board. If the nineteenth century is to be credited with the political invention of the government department headed by a Minister responsible to Parliament, it has to be added that it was an organizational form that was not for long without its administrative challengers.

The foundations for the Permanent Civil Service could be said to have been mainly laid in the fifty years down to 1830. It was Permanent in the sense that posts were retained after a change of government. It was Civil in that it was distinct from the political or parliamentary service of the Crown. It was a Service because it consisted of full time salaried officers, systematically recruited, with clear lines of authority, and uniform rules on such questions as superannuation. As the monarchy rose above party, the Civil Service settled below party. Constitutional monarchy had as its counterpart what has since been called constitutional bureaucracy. Nevertheless, just as constitutional monarchy only evolved gradually, so did changes in the Civil Service. Trevelyan and Northcote certainly thought that there was a Permanent Civil Service in 1853, for that was in the title of their report on its organization.

However, it was not until after 1870 that recruitment to leading posts began to be conventionally made by open competition and not by patronage. Until the Civil Service was clearly separated from politics, Civil Servants could be treated as political animals. Thus, James Stephen was treated as if he was 'Mr Oversecretary' at the Colonial Office, and Edwin Chadwick was directly blamed for Poor Law and public health administration. Like Stephen, Chadwick complained about the situation, saying that attacks on Civil Servants like himself were like hitting a woman. Yet, as Chadwick and Stephen were publicly identifiable authorities on the subjects that they handled administratively, so they could not reasonably expect to escape direct criticism. The Board of Trade officials such as John McGregor and James Deacon Hume who campaigned for Free Trade in the 1830s were acting within the constitutional conventions of their time.[60] Robert Morant was probably not acting within those limits when he promoted the Education Act of 1902. A non-political bureaucracy was only slowly established.

Was constitutional bureaucracy a better instrument of government than the arrangements it gradually replaced? It seems plausible that it must have been. In place of haphazard patronage appointments, most of the leading posts came to be filled by the intellectual cream of the universities. Even if there was not always – indeed, for some time, not often – a real need for such talents at first, the latent strength of the First Division or Administrative Class seemed to be shown in the National Insurance adventure in 1911–12. Then, the First Division was treated as a whole for the first time. Arthur Salter was brought across from his unwilling apprenticeship at the Admiralty. John Anderson and Warren Fisher were brought in from their willing apprenticeships elsewhere. Morant moved from one area of administrative controversy to another. The administrative machine seemed to have conclusively shown that it could respond capably to new tasks. Yet was the new administrative dispensation entirely for the better? Looking back on a career that ended in 1938, H E Dale could not find a place among the four outstanding Civil Service administrators of his day for a conventional First Division entrant, and one of his four was clearly the unconventional Morant. Dale, however, was a lucid defender of the generalist administrator that the open competition was designed to recruit.

Such was the role of these permanent politicians as he described it that it raised a crucial question about the temporary politicians – the Ministers – who formally presided over them. Why did they need this type of support? Dale's answer was a working experience of running a bureaucracy in a parliamentary democracy.[61] However, this was to see the government departments as Ministers' private offices writ large, which was what they remained in theory, but not so much in practice as the duties of the State grew more complex. Such complexity demanded specialization, but the specialist increasingly became the subordinate of the generalist. Ironically, the unreformed Civil Service at its best had not been without its specialist talents including Simon and Chadwick whom we have mentioned, and some we have not such as Major Graham and William Farr at the General Register Office from 1836, and George Porter at the Board of Trade providing statistical intelligence. The creation of a career Civil Service independent of Ministers was not without its costs, not least the direct ones of the sometimes generous and almost always secure salaries of a Service which was beginning to be unionised from the bottom upwards well before 1914. Constitutional bureaucracy threatened not to be constitutional enough in the sense of who really guarded these increasingly numerous guardians?

The nineteenth century witnessed not revolutionary but usually slow and sometimes important administrative change. Government remained small even as late as 1891, when its employees accounted for less than 4 per cent of the working population. At central government level, the machinery was still almost entirely manned by soldiers and sailors, tax collectors and postmen. Although at local government level, the police, who had accounted for nearly 60 per cent of all local employees in the middle of the nineteenth century, represented no more than 30 per cent in 1891. This was because of the increased numbers employed in health and sanitation activities, and water supply and other utilities. The Conservative and Liberal reforms were one reason why the small totals of government employees had doubled by 1914, although defence remained numerically the most important source of central government employment.[62] The machinery of the State had been changed, but not transformed. In some important areas it was not made more effective for nineteenth century purposes. What happened too was that the century's administrative innovations proved only too durable in the changed situation to come.

Chapter 7

The Machinery and Functions of Twentieth Century Government 1914 - 1939

British government and administration was never the same again after the First World War. The particular combination of private enterprise and State activity that characterized the nineteenth century's economic arrangements proved unable to meet the relentless demands of the First World War. It was not possible for practice to match the contemporary slogan 'business as usual'. The attempt to wage war by the conventional processes of a liberal State was abandoned when Lloyd George was made Minister of Munitions in May 1915. Thereafter, and particularly after Lloyd George moved on to the Premiership at the end of 1916, the machinery of government grew remorselessly. The economy increasingly came to be dominated by the State. A substantial framework of economic controls was constructed, among others, in the fields of finance, mining, manufacturing, agriculture and transport, and sometimes involving international co-operative agencies. This framework of economic controls did not long survive the Armistice. 'Back to 1914' was the slogan by then, and this sentiment outlasted the post-war boom and persisted into the Depression and era of mass unemployment that followed. The return to the Gold Standard and the general continuance of Free Trade symbolised the craving that many had for Edwardian 'normalcy'. Going off gold and the advent of full Protection in the early 1930s marked the effective end of this sentimental backward journey.

The advent of the National Government ushered in a period that was to last down to the Second World War, which some contemporaries called one of planning and which was certainly one of widespread State intervention in the economy. The policies of the National Government were believed to be 'revolutionary' by one of its leading figures, Neville Chamberlain. Certainly, the growth of government, which extended too to the social services, was marked. What was lacking was a 'revolution' in the realm of ideas. Nineteenth century orthodoxies were too persistent for Chamberlain's description to be accurate. The financial experience of the First World War did not undermine the ideal of the Balanced Budget equated at low levels of taxation and expenditure, even if practice did not always follow suit. The wartime example of the State running an economy proved to be one it was not widely desired to follow in peacetime, even though the experience had coincided with the first ever period of full employment, in stark contrast with what followed. More influential was the belief that peacetime was different. As Churchill said of the Armistice in 1918, 'a new set of conditions began to rule from eleven o'clock onwards. The money cost, which had never been considered by us to be a factor capable of limiting the supply of the armies, asserted a claim to priority from the moment the fighting stopped'.[1]

What was needed for a 'revolution' in ideas in relation to practice was a situation in which the coming of peace made little difference to the belief that the money was always there to finance State activity. The Keynesian 'revolution' represented that kind of change. Although rooted in the inter-war experience, this occurred later. In the meantime, although T H Green's authority did not survive the First World War, the Marshallian School's did, even if the Treasury found some of its inspiration elsewhere, in Ricardo's teaching.

I. CROWN, CABINET, PARLIAMENT AND ADMINISTRATION

The continuities of British government were often as remarkable as the changes even in the period between the outbreak of the First World War and the beginning of the Second. The constitutional monarchy was as firmly established in 1939 as it had been in 1914, despite the drama of the Abdication crisis of 1936. The relationship between the two Houses of Parliament remained as laid down in 1911, not being really tested by a non-Conservative majority government in the Commons. Indeed, the tone of the political system had survived, despite the extension of the franchise in 1918 to all males of 21 years of age and over and most females, and then in 1928 to all adult females. The challenge to the political system posed by the trade union Triple Alliance in 1919 and then the General Strike in 1926 was also surmounted. Perhaps most remarkable of all, the mass slaughter of the First World War was simply accepted.

Change took place in the organization of the Cabinet. This broadly remained the body which could and did ask to review all major decisions and was collectively responsible for them. There was nothing resembling a well developed Cabinet committee system in the inter-war period. There was one important legacy of the War and of the excitements of the Lloyd George era in the permanent establishment of a Cabinet Secretariat. This owed its origins to the Secretariat of the Committee of Imperial Defence. Maurice Hankey, the Committee's Secretary, combined that role with the Cabinet Secretaryship until his retirement in 1938. Asquith had opposed the presence of an official at Cabinet meetings, believing this to be against established constitutional doctrine and practice.[2] It was certainly against constitutional practice. Asquith's objections, and those of others when the Secretariat was retained after the War, have been commonly dismissed as reactionary. The reason being that Hankey's presence made for the efficient despatch of Cabinet business. Ministers had Hankey's minutes to guide them, whereas before they could leave Cabinet meetings without knowing what had been decided. Nevertheless, decisions can be rendered in different ways. The so-called reactionaries had a point. It was that an official became part of the body which made government strategy, and that this was a task for politicians.

The political system did not survive the First World War unchanged in other respects. The Liberal Party did not continue for long as one of the two leading political parties. The supplanting of the Liberals by Labour as the main anti-Conservative political force was subsequently the subject of a variety of explanations. These explanations include the theses that the First World War killed the Liberal Party off as a leading party because it either undermined the Party's political principles or made them seem irrelevant; that the War merely speeded up an already evident process of Liberal decline; that the expansion of the electorate in 1918 ensured the rise of Labour and the consequent demise of the Liberals; and that Lloyd George killed the Party. Whatever its benefits for the prosecution of the war, Lloyd George's overthrow of Asquith in December 1916 was a disaster in Liberal Party terms. Moreover, Lloyd George fought the 1918 Election alongside the Conservatives who obtained a landslide victory. The independent Liberals were crushed, and the Party never fully recovered.[3]

What the Liberals had come to lack was an institutional power base. The trade unions would have done, and the Labour Party would have been without finance. The pre-1914 Liberals had failed to cement their links with the unions. Moreover, they had acted in electoral alliance with a Labour Party they should have tried to strangle at birth. As for Lloyd George, he was not of the big battalions of Capital and Labour, whom he seemed not to comprehend. He did not think of politics in institutional terms, otherwise he could not have behaved as he did to the Liberals in 1918. Lloyd George continued to be the most exciting politician of the inter-war period, long after the Conservatives had discarded him in 1922. Full of constructive ideas, he could not put them into practice because he did not have power. He could not attain power because he did not have an adequate power base. So, Lloyd George was left to fume on the political sidelines, while power was wielded by men he deemed pygmies compared with himself, but who had a big machine behind them.

The Conservative Party machine was particularly capably handled by Stanley Baldwin, its leader between 1923 and 1937, and thrice Prime Minister during that time. Baldwin dominated the inter-war political stage in Britain. He was conciliatory in the General Strike. He was adept at handling the Abdication. He reunited the Conservative Party after its flirtation with Lloyd George. Moreover, he kept it together despite divisions with its Press supporters over Empire Free Trade, with Churchill and Conservative Diehards over India, and with Churchill again over defence and foreign policy in the 1930s. The Governments that Baldwin headed or controlled were not gifted ones, although Neville Chamberlain was easily the ablest departmental minister of the period. Baldwin's Governments were cautious ones, at least after his relinquishing of office and a comfortable majority in 1923 in an unsuccessful dash to the polls to secure electoral endorsement of Protection. After that, Baldwin viewed the inexperienced electorate warily, despite the massive Conservative electoral victories of the 1930s.

His caution was particularly marked in his public handling of defence and foreign policy questions. 'You could lose a packet and still have a majority of 250', Sir Robert Vansittart said to Baldwin, urging him to rearm during the 1931 Parliament.[4] Baldwin thought that rearmament would lead to a dislocation of trade thus inhibiting economic recovery and the diminution of unemployment.[5] Unlike his nineteenth century predecessors, Baldwin had to try to carry a broadly based political democracy with him in support of his external policies. Unlike those predecessors too, both Baldwin and Neville Chamberlain – his successor as Prime Minister – had to take account of Britain's diminished strength, particularly economic strength. Britain had needed American intervention to win the first total war, and would certainly need it to win a second. Yet, they knew Britain was short of reliable friends, whereas she had a choice of potential enemies: Nazi Germany, Fascist Italy, Imperial Japan, and the Soviet Union. Britain's commitments were in excess of her resources. Thus the scene was set for at best near disaster.

While the advent of the Labour Party as their main electoral rivals had not made the lot of the Conservatives easier in defence and foreign policy matters, what was most distinctive about their newer party was its formal commitment to socialism. For such as Laski, the Liberals and the Conservatives had been like two wings of the same party. They had their differences over particular policies – sometimes bitter ones as over Ireland – but they had the underlying harmony that came from having the same social experiences. Above all, both the Liberals and the Conservatives remained convinced that the private ownership of the means of production could not be legitimately called into question. Laski's implication was that the rise of a Labour Party committed to socialism had called the private enterprise system into question.[6] The Conservatives' commitment to private ownership had in fact not prevented them from experiments with State control, and their preference for Protection was another indication of their ambivalence towards the free market.

However, a commitment to democratic socialism was something different. It was incumbent on those so committed to plan how such a socialist system would work or how a partly socialised one would, given that the goal might have to be approached in stages. This the Labour Party never did. That this was so was hidden by the colourful intellectual life of the Party, particularly in the 1930s. It was obscured too by the Party's more obvious failings in the defence and foreign policy sphere, in which the collective security of a League of Nations without armaments and American involvement impressed the Party faithful more than it deterred the German and Italian dictators or the Japanese. The apparent achievements of the Communist dictatorship in Russia deflected others. Certainly Herbert Morrison's derivative notions about public corporations did not amount to a socialist strategy, even if it was treated as one. So, the Labour Party was advocating a fundamental change in the role of the State without adequately preparing for the operation of the changed system.

The combative Laski, unhinged by the 1931 political crisis, seemed to think that the Civil Service might well be obstructive to a future Labour Government. Other Labour people, according to Beatrice Webb, idealized the salaried public servant, looking to them to save the world. The faith of the Webbs in rational administration was unbridled too, and their influence had pervaded that curious enterprise of the Reconstruction era, the Haldane Machinery of Government Committee. This body was appointed in July 1917 by the Ministry of Reconstruction 'to enquire into the responsibilities of the various Departments of the central executive Government, and to advise in what manner the exercise and distribution by the Government of its functions should be improved'. The Committee consisted of Lord Haldane; three MPs, including J H Thomas; two leading Civil Servants, Sir George Murray and Sir Robert Morant; and Mrs Webb. Even the indefatigable Mrs Webb found the subject matter 'immense', and she was left to wish that she was 'stronger brained' for the work involved. Nonetheless, her husband helped her with various memoranda. The whole business she found to be 'a pleasant sport. We sit twice a week over tea and muffins in Haldane's comfortable sitting room discussing the theory and practice of government. I tell them that I am discovering the land of Whitehall for the future Labour Cabinet'.

The questions raised, Mrs Webb believed, were 'vital to the success of the equalitarian State'. So they were, and she was able to say at the end of it all that 'the Report embodies all the right ideas and follows closely the lines laid down in the Webb document', meaning her own memorandum. She blamed 'Murray's vested interests' and 'Haldane's incurable delight in mental mistiness' for the fact that the Report's ideas appeared in 'nebulously phrased hesitating propositions'. However, the Webbs' intentions and their favoured structure of government was clear. The business of government was to be divided into: Finance; National Defence and External Affairs; Research and Information; Production, Transport and Commerce; Employment; Supplies; Education; Health and Justice. It was emphasized that it did not necessarily follow that there would be only one Minister for each of these branches. Some of them would undoubtedly require more than one.

The Cabinet, though, was to be 'small in number – preferably ten or, at most, twelve', and its wartime apparatus as was appropriate – such as the Cabinet Secretariat – would be retained. The Cabinet was to have the final determination of the policy to be submitted to Parliament; the supreme control of the national executive in accordance with the policy prescribed by Parliament; and the continuous co-ordination and delimitation of the activities of the several Departments of State. The problem that the Haldane Committee addressed itself to, as Mrs Webb said, was that of 'combining bureaucratic efficiency with democratic control'. As the definition of the functions of the Cabinet without mention of party suggested, the Webbs' solution was outside politics. [7] There was not much doubt whose disciples were meant to staff the Research and Information Department. No such Department was created. A few of the Haldane recommendations were followed, but the Report proved to be of little interest to practitioners.

The important changes which took place in Civil Service organization during and immediately after the First World War owed nothing to the Haldane Report. One was the introduction of Whitleyism. When in 1917, a Reconstruction committee advocated that joint consultation machinery should be set up in industry in the form of what came to be called Whitley Councils, the Coalition Governments could not really deny similar facilities to its own employees – although it did try. Ironically, Whitleyism only really took root in the public services. Its introduction into the Civil Service meant not only the full recognition of staff associations, but also their involvement, for example, in the reorganization of the generalist side of the Service that took place in 1920–21. A National Whitley Council Committee selected the favoured structure from the recommendations of a pre-war Royal Commission. The generalist structure was very broadly related to the existing educational ladder. A similar rationalization was not extended to the many specialist groups that the Civil Service had by this time. The dominance of the generalist in such departments as the Post Office led even the most mouse-like of Royal Commissions later to urge an inquiry. [8]

The cult of the generalist in the Civil Service reached the stage of refinement with Sir Warren Fisher's tenure of the Permanent Secretaryship to the Treasury between 1919 and 1939. Fisher persuaded Lloyd George to make him Head of the Civil Service with formal powers of advice to the Prime Minister regarding appointments to Permanent Secretary, Deputy Secretary, Principal Financial Officer, and Principal Establishments Officer in all other departments. As these powers extended to the Foreign Office, the complaints were long and hard from that source. Fisher's interventions in defence and foreign policy making were a source of controversy. This tended to distract from his forceful espousal of the view that a Civil Service administrator should be able to administer anything: he needed no training or knowledge of the subjects concerned. As the Civil Service over which Fisher presided was stagnant with promotion blocks, what he literally called 'musical chairs' may have been a useful way of keeping alive ambition, and giving the Service a sense of progress and, of course, Fisher opportunities for using his powers. However, there seems no reason to doubt that Fisher believed what he said about the general administrator. Under Fisher, the Civil Service at least obtained the unity Trevelyan had wanted for it, but not quite the administrative style. [9] Whatever the merits of that style for a State of limited tasks, the tone of ministerial departments was one of the factors which often decided even the cautious inter-war governments to look to other organizational forms when expanding the role of the State.

II. THE MACHINERY OF GOVERNMENT AND ITS 'TRADITIONAL' FUNCTIONS

The 'traditional' function of defence necessarily dominated the role of the State during the First World War. The repercussions of that total struggle changed Britain's position in the world for ever and for the worse. This was hidden for a time by finishing on the winning side in the war, and thus being able to take part in dictating terms to the vanquished Germany and her allies at the Versailles Peace Conference. An influential section of British opinion led by Keynes was consumed by guilt about the peace terms. Thus was sowed the seeds of the later appeasement of a totalitarian Germany and her new allies. The conduct of foreign policy was bedevilled by a widespread faith in the League of Nations as an international peace keeping body. Without American participation, the League was doomed from the outset to be little more than a British and French club, and no match for the Japanese in Manchuria, the Italians in Abyssinia, or the Germans nearer home in Spain. One result of the Versailles Settlement was that yet more territory was added to the British Empire. Some of it – the Palestine Mandate, for example – proved to be more trouble than it was worth. Even the promise of a Middle Eastern oil empire had to be shared. In fact, the British Empire reached its greatest extent in the immediate aftermath of the Great War; but with relative economic weaknesses evident and with Irish independence soon to point the way to eventual Imperial dismemberment.

(i) Law and Order

The violence in Ireland was later said to be one piece of evidence that Liberal Britain was tearing herself apart in the years 1910–1914. Widespread industrial unrest, the excesses of the suffragettes, and the intransigence of the House of Lords was supposed to be other evidence.[10] Yet, Asquith had already settled the House of Lords controversy, and a Government headed by Lloyd George was later to secure a settlement of a kind in Ireland. The industrial unrest, however, dragged on through the First World War and beyond. In 1919, there was even a police strike. The inability of the Triple Alliance of transport workers, railwaymen and coal miners to pursue their confrontation with the Government in 1921, only postponed the clash. When the General Strike finally came in 1926, the Government, well prepared organizationally for the unions' challenge, had sufficient popular support to win.

The administrative organizer of that victory was John Anderson, Permanent Secretary at the Home Office between 1922 and 1932. Anderson inherited a skeleton organization from the emergency preparations of the Lloyd George Government, and with others he made it a structure more adequate to its task. The country was divided into ten areas, with a separate scheme for Scotland, each with a Civil Commissioner, and supported by the necessary transport and supply organization. At the administrative centre for the whole of the General Strike was Anderson, not afraid at one point to tell the belligerent Churchill to stop talking nonsense.

The conciliatory Baldwin later acknowledged his debt to Anderson, who was perhaps the ablest of the new breed of Administrative Class Civil Servant. He certainly seemed to behave at times like a caricature of one. Nicknamed Jehovah by some of his staff, he often spoke like an official minute, and was reputed to read nothing but Blue Books in his leisure time. Even in ten years, Anderson left little imprint of his personality on the Home Office. Despite earlier links with Irish administration – which had now in its reduced form become a Home Office responsibility – he had no special interest in the department's subject matter, aside from its fundamental responsibility for law and order. Here, he did give his support to making the Home Office an effective centre of information and guidance in police affairs. Generally, though, Anderson was more interested in the art of administering than in the subjects administered.

His inclination was to administer efficiently and smoothly within the limits of existing policy.[11]

There were no major changes in the judicial system in the inter-war period, and few in the organization of the police which remained locally based. One change was an experiment in trying to recruit an officer class in the Metropolitan Police, which had relied almost entirely on promotion from below since the days of Peel. The Hendon Police College had a short five year life down to 1939, during which it was vigorously opposed by the Police Federation. The justification advanced for the Hendon experiment was the concern about the quality of the products of the traditional system. Perhaps also the authorities viewed the rank and file with some distrust after the 1919 strike. The police in the 1930s certainly faced grave problems of public order with the rise of Communist and Fascist groups prepared to take to the streets to advance their cause. The Public Order Act 1936 was particularly directed against the Fascists. Earlier, an Incitement to Disaffection Act had been passed in 1934. It was interesting that it was thought necessary to legislate for public order rather than largely rely as before directly on the judicial process.[12] Mainly outside that process too was a growing body of administrative law which reflected the enlarged role of the State. Some lawyers thought that the scale of administrative discretion given to Civil Servants without adequate parliamentary and judicial review threatened personal freedom, which it did. The lawyers' distrust of administrative tribunals, however, also followed from a desire to maintain their own monopolies.

(ii) *Imperial Management*

When it reached its fullest territorial extent in the years immediately after the First World War, the British Empire, including the United Kingdom itself, covered 14,272,782 square miles, or over one-quarter of the known land surface of the globe. Its estimated number of 445,388,500 inhabitants was thought to exceed one-quarter of the world's population. No less than 315,000,000 of the Empire's inhabitants, however, were concentrated in India and Burma, and the relaxation of the British grip on that sub-continent had already begun.

Britain still had a massive dependent Empire, but some of the Dominions – Canada, Australia and South Africa – were acting increasingly independently. Only New Zealand reacted positively to British appeals for support in the Chanak crisis in 1922. The establishment of the Irish Free State from 1921 onwards was a development very near to home that proved to be indicative of the future dismemberment of the Empire. For the present, the Balfour Declaration of 1926 seemed to satisfy the Dominions. It meant that internationally, they could act as one, or as separate nations. All who acknowledged the Crown as a common bond were to be 'equal in status', 'freely associated', 'in no way subordinate one to another' – including the United Kingdom. The Statute of Westminster of 1931 incorporated the essence of the Declaration into law, recording the achievement of *de facto* independence by the Dominions under the British Crown. Imperial matters loomed large in the discussions of the British Cabinet. Opinion in the Dominions was certainly a factor in the Abdication crisis, and in foreign policy in the 1930s. When war came in 1939, Australia, New Zealand and Canada declared war too. So did South Africa, although that country did not lack adherents of Nazi racialist theories. Eire stayed neutral. [13]

The changing nature of the British Empire was reflected in administrative organization when in 1925 a Dominions Office was established. Leopold Amery made the creation of a separate office to deal with the Dominions a condition of accepting the Colonial Secretaryship in the Baldwin Government of 1924–29. What happened was that the Colonial Office shed its Dominions Department – whose work had become essentially diplomatic – and concentrated on central adminis-tration of the dependent Empire. The change was obscured at first by Amery holding the two Secretaryships together, and the two Offices being in the same building. However, they soon came to function separately. The India Office remained, like India itself, an empire of its own. To those on the spot, the India Office back home seemed 'a place of cobwebbed and shady corridors, where life stirred only drowsily, like a hedgehog awakened from winter sleep, where the élan vital had given up all hope and men thought only in terms of files, reminders and reasons for inaction'.

This was an exaggerated picture, but the India Office did

seem to be over-legalistic in tone. The Indian Civil Service itself remained the cream of the cream, intellectually as well as socially. The paternalistic philosophy of the District Officer was shared, but the attributes of the Colonial Services were more obviously social. This was more or less ensured by the selection methods of Ralph Furse. Himself originally a patronage appointee at the Colonial Office, Furse survived several Secretaries of State and dominated overseas recruitment. A unified Colonial Administrative Service was established as late as 1932, and a collection of unified specialist services followed that. Amery was one Minister who tried to stir things up, insisting on Colonial Office staff serving time in the colonies, and trying to forge firmer links with Colonial Governors. Amery was an enthusiast for research into colonial development.[14] In practice, autochthony persisted. The Colonial Empire remained a disparate affair, like the British Empire – Commonwealth generally, run on a very loose rein. Whereas in India, the purpose of rule had become to prepare the Indians to govern themselves – if at a pace that Indian nationalists thought too slow – the purpose of the Colonial Empire seemed to have become governing almost as an end in itself.

(iii) *Defence Organization*

The demands of the First World War had stretched conventional military organization beyond its limits. The establishment of the Ministry of Munitions in May 1915 was a recognition of this, if a reluctant one. Lloyd George started the Ministry literally from nothing. The new Ministry was initially set up in a pleasant, old fashioned house just off Whitehall, owned by an art dealer. When Lloyd George arrived there with his mistress Frances Stevenson, and his other secretary, J T Davies, they found virtually no office furniture. The Office of Works tried to take away what little they had; but Lloyd George prevailed upon them to leave him with a table and a chair. It was an encounter with what he called the departmental bindweed of red tape, which he was determined to defeat. Lloyd George had to get results, not least because his Ministry usurped part of the role of the War Office under the immensely popular Lord

Kitchener. The new Ministry was to be a business organization. Finance was subordinated to policy and costs were not to be allowed to interfere with programmes of production. Businessmen such as Sir Eric Geddes were called in to run the Ministry's activities. With such support, Lloyd George succeeded in delivering the 'mountain of shells' for which he had called, and the Ministry's activities represented a decisive step in the transition from a peacetime to a wartime economy.[15]

Lloyd George's methods were unconventional and disrespectful of military advice. When Kitchener recommended that four machine guns for each battalion would be enough, Lloyd George responded by squaring the figure, multiplying it by two, and then doubling it for good luck. When Kitchener died in June 1916, Lloyd George became Secretary of State for War. The Ministry of Munitions was by now a thriving concern. Lloyd George had less success with the War Office, a traditional Civil Service department. One of his few achievements was to get the railways behind the lines in France in working order so that the supply of ammunition to the front lines would not be impeded. The problem seemed beyond the comprehension of the British Commander-in-Chief, Sir Douglas Haig. Lloyd George wanted the job entrusted to Geddes, but Haig was reluctant to have a civilian in charge of the work. Lloyd George had Geddes made a Major General. Geddes swiftly constructed the essential light railway network.[16]

When Lloyd George became Prime Minister in December 1916, the arrangements at Downing Street were made a characteristic mixture of the bizarre and the practical. As noted above, the former Secretariat of the Committee of Imperial Defence became the Secretariat of the War Cabinet. However, literally in the garden of his official residence, the Prime Minister also established his personal staff in 'Lloyd George's Garden Suburb'. Lloyd George's direction of the war was vigorous, and continued to include the harrying of bureaucrats and service advisers. Enemies of those forms of human life have many times recalled how Lloyd George forced the Admiralty to adopt the convoy system. In April 1917, the Germans' unrestricted submarine campaign was so successful that one in four of the ships leaving port was being sunk. There was the real threat of the British merchant fleet being decimated, and, therefore, of defeat in the war. The convoy system was a possible answer, but Admiralty statistics suggested that the number of merchant vessels made its widespread application impractical. This convinced the Admirals, and even the powerful First Lord, Sir Edward Carson, but not the Prime Minister. Otherwise briefed, Lloyd George descended on the Admiralty, and undermined the credibility of the statistics.[17] The convoy system was introduced. It was a dramatic success.

Lloyd George was the supreme energiser of the scarcely irresistible British war machine. Traditionally, he is portrayed as the dynamic innovator, and the military leaders as strategic nihilists. Lloyd George did manage to get rid of Sir William Robertson, despite the support for him from George V, and, more importantly, the Press and the Conservative backbenchers. He never actually took Haig on. Presumably, he could have found a successor, a man eager for advancement who would have conducted the war as the Prime Minister wanted: but did Lloyd George have any strategic innovations to offer?

Given existing techniques, the Western Front had to be a war of attrition, unless neutral countries such as Holland or Denmark were either brought in or invaded to stretch the front and German resources. Churchill deserves credit for introducing the tank, but it could only travel at five miles an hour. This was too slow to enable a bridgehead to be established, although at Cambrai it was touch and go. In the end, Haig won through, punching away, sustaining his troops remarkably. Despite Lloyd George's contempt for his advisers – 'epauletted egotism impenetrable to ideas'[18] it is unclear what military ideas of value he had himself. Lloyd George's contribution was to provide a sense of urgency and dynamism as he did at Munitions and over convoys. He also played a vital part in keeping the allies together. He excelled in the conference situation. He excelled at brokerage functions. Lloyd George contemplated a negotiated peace but never defeat. At the time of Ludendorff's spring offensive in 1918, he was swift to draft reserves into the battle. He used the occasion to appeal to President Woodrow Wilson for the immediate use of American troops, whose entry made victory certain.

Defence organization was never quite the same again after the First World War except for the Admiralty which had never even relinquished its supply functions. Plans for a permanent Ministry of Supply were abandoned. The Ministry of Munitions was wound up. However, to the Admiralty and the War Office was added a third Service department – the Air Ministry. The battle for a separate Royal Air Force and a separate Ministry was fought with a ferocity that might have been admired at Ypres. The posts of Secretary of State for War and Air were jointly held at first by Churchill. Lloyd George gave his bellicose colleague the War Office in the hope that immediately after a World War even Churchill would not find further hostilities to take part in.

Yet, Lloyd George later complained, Churchill took his maps with him everywhere, and Britain was involved first in Russia and then in the Chanak crisis. Churchill's appointment did mean that he bore collective responsibility for the Ten Year Rule introduced in relation to defence expenditure in 1919. This stated that the Service departments had to frame their estimates on the assumption that 'the British Empire will not be engaged in any great war during the next ten years, and that no Expeditionary Force will be required'. When he returned to office in 1924 as Chancellor of the Exchequer, Churchill had responsibility for continuing the Rule. In 1928, he proposed that the Service estimates should continue to be based on the Ten Year Rule, but that it should be reviewed every year by the Committee of Imperial Defence. The Rule was not abandoned until 1932.

Churchill later wrote 'Up till the time when I left office in 1929 I felt so hopeful that the peace of the world could be maintained that I saw no reason to take any new decision; nor in the event was I proved wrong. War did not break out till the autumn of 1939'. The damage done to the munitions industry was not as easily reversed as Churchill's attitude to armaments in the 1930s. Then, he plagued the National Government with demands that they should rearm in the face of the menace of Nazi Germany. From the Defence White Paper of 1935 onwards, the Government slowly did so. Behind the scenes, Baldwin did encourage radar research, and the development of the Spitfire and Hurricane aircraft. Publicly, if unfairly, the appointment of Sir Thomas Inskip as Minister for the Coordination of Defence in 1936 made Baldwin seem lacking in

seriousness on the subject.[19] Rearmament was under way
properly in 1937. The introduction of conscription for the first
time in peacetime in 1939 – despite Labour opposition – and
of a Ministry of Supply was evidence of seriousness. The
Hore-Belisha reforms had made for army reorganization, and
in 1939 Britain's defence policy was related not just to empire
but to a newly developed continental commitment. The Expeditionary Force sent to France was highly mechanised and
tactically relevant. It was also too small. Britain was ill prepared for total war in 1939.[20]

(iv) Conduct of Foreign Policy

Britain never again had the independence of action internationally that she had enjoyed for much of the century down to 1914.
The First World War had only been won in the end with
American money and with the aid of American troops. American support was needed if the League of Nations was to be
effective. Even when this was not forthcoming, the Americans
had to be cultivated. The Japanese alliance was abandoned
after American insistence at the time of the Washington
Conference of 1921–22; but without any guarantee of American
support in the Far East in the event of Japanese aggression.
When the Japanese attacked Manchuria in 1931, the Americans
showed no sign of intervening. Urging a further alliance with
Japan in 1934, Neville Chamberlain wrote: 'we ought to know
by this time that the USA will give us no undertaking to resist
by force any action by Japan, short of an attack on Hawaii or
Honolulu'. Negotiations were unsuccessful. As Chamberlain
feared, Britain faced a war on two fronts. Fascist Italy posed a
further threat. When she intervened in Abyssinia, Britain was
urged to stand up to her; but as Warren Fisher said to Baldwin:
'if Italy persists in her present policy, is England really prepared
not merely to threaten, but also to use force, and is she in a
position to do this successfully?'. Fisher and Vansittart advocated keeping Mussolini's Italy and Hitler's Germany separate,
regarding the latter as the real enemy and urging rearmament to
deter her. The National Government stayed out of the Spanish
Civil War and stood aside while Germany annexed territories
and Austria. The Munich Agreement was signed in September

1938 rather than go to war to save parts of Czechoslovakia from German aggression. War was declared in September 1939 rather than see Poland annexed too. Churchill had said of Munich that it was 'a total and unmitigated defeat'.[21] With only the divided French for allies, Britain faced such a defeat in war, unless and until the Americans intervened, which they did in their own time and only after the Japanese aggression that Chamberlain had anticipated. Britain had the responsibilities of a Great Power but not the means to match the role. She could no more successfully defend her Empire than she could hope to ensure that, even if Nazi Germany was to be defeated, another totalitarian regime, the Soviet Union, would not cast its dominant shadow over Europe.

The inter-war Foreign Office had to operate in a much changed world. Sir Robert Cecil told the House of Commons in 1918 that 'diplomacy, once a question between Court and Court had now become a question between People and People'. There was widespread discontent at least among the politically interested with the 'old diplomacy' – meaning secret negotiations conducted by an irresponsible self selected élite. How a 'new' or 'open diplomacy' would work was less clear, but changes in the Foreign Office seemed to be needed. Changes of a kind were forthcoming. In 1918, the Foreign Office and the Diplomatic Service were formally merged and changes were made in recruitment procedures. The latter were aimed at greater democratization, but still included interviews to exclude the socially undesirable.

The merger foundered as early as 1920 with the abandonment of joint seniority lists above the lowest two grades of leading posts. Full interchangeability was blocked, and the Treasury denied Foreign Office moves for parity with its staff.[22] The treatment of the Foreign Office as part of the Home Civil Service, and thus subject to Warren Fisher's purview, was a running sore in the inter-war period. Fisher was even blamed for the policy of appeasing Germany, despite the fact that – like Vansittart at the head of the Foreign Office – he was if anything obsessed with the need to prepare for war with Hitler.[23] Diplomatic and Foreign Office advice did reach the Cabinet. This was so whether the despatches from the Ambassador at Berlin were unfavourable to the Nazi régime – as with Sir

Horace Rumbold and Sir Eric Phipps – or favourable, as with Sir Nevile Henderson. It does seem to have been the case that the Cabinet tired of Vansittart's memoranda.

The Foreign Office had learnt in the days of 'Lloyd George's Garden Suburb' and at Versailles that it was only one source of foreign policy advice. The Government, moreover, had to take account of popular sentiment. Both Baldwin and Neville Chamberlain must have been aware of a popular reluctance to fight another war; a reluctance that seems to have lasted down to 1940. The National Government leaders were well aware too of Britain's economic weakness in relation to her responsibilities, and how this impinged on her military capabilities. If, in this situation, Chamberlain preferred the foreign policy advice of his fellow appeaser, Sir Horace Wilson, to that of Fisher, Vansittart and others in the Foreign Office, that was his responsibility. His reputation suffered for it.

(v) *The Treasury and Finance*

Warren Fisher's arrival at the Treasury coincided with a reorganization there which left him as Permanent Secretary in a position that was 'deliciously vague, floating somewhere rather Olympian'. From 1919 to 1932, the Treasury was in practice divided into three departments – Finance, Supply Services, and and Establishments – each with a Controller of Second Secretary rank (equivalent to Permanent Secretary elsewhere). Fisher later told the Public Accounts Committee that he did his best to work the scheme, but 'it was an extremely unwieldy . . . and unsatisfactory arrangement'. In 1932, the Treasury reverted to a divisional form of organization with a Permanent Secretary, a Second Secretary, and three Under Secretaries in charge of the divisions. Fisher himself concentrated on his role as Head of the Civil Service, seeing the Treasury as a clearing house; and even recruiting his younger staff not from the Administrative Class open competition, but from those deemed more promising in other government departments. One innovation Fisher did introduce in relation to finance was to insist that Permanent Secretaries should normally be Accounting Officers for their departments.[24]

Whatever its lack of grip during the First World War, the

inter-war years Treasury seems in retrospect to have been the soul of financial rectitude. Even a typist could not be appointed in a government department without Treasury approval. The Treasury itself was understaffed in relation to its functions, perhaps as an example. The Treasury was better at the containment of public expenditure than the promotion of better organization and methods of work. One interesting feature of the Geddes Reports on National Expenditure of 1922 was that they did represent an attempt, however crude, at assessing the cost effectiveness of government expenditure. The need to appoint the Geddes Committee at all was seen by some as an indictment of the Treasury's failure to control finance. Whether this was so or not, the Geddes Committee did its job well. No subsequent inquiry – not even the May Committee in 1931 – was able to suggest substantial economies in administration. The numbers in the Civil Service fell steadily until 1934. Total expenditure on administration was very little different in 1929 in relation to public spending from what it had been in 1922. Until the rearmament years, the Civil Service grew little, despite the additional duties that, for example, the National Government's economic policies involved.[25]

III THE MACHINERY OF GOVERNMENT AND ITS ECONOMIC
AND SOCIAL POLICY FUNCTIONS

Despite the attentions of the Geddes Axe, the economic and social welfare machinery of the State did not return to what it had been in 1914. Before the Axe had even been wielded, wartime creations such as the Ministries of Munitions, Shipping, Blockade, Food and Reconstruction had been abolished. The Department of Scientific and Industrial Research (1916), the Ministry of Labour (1916), the Ministry of Pensions (1916), the Ministry of Health (1919), and the Ministry of Transport (1919) were governmental growths which survived the economy campaign. As the Ministry of Health at least partly represented an administrative rationalization, its survival had its logic even in the context of a cut back in public spending. The Ministries of Transport and of Labour could be presented as being little more than the hiving off of parts of the Board of Trade. Moreover, even if, for example, the Ministry of Labour had been abolished, the scale of inter-war unemployment at the very least would have ensured the survival of its labour exchanges system. The level of unemployment was taken as one indicator that the British economy was ailing. Whether it was or not, that economy was now plainly insufficiently strong for the State to be unconcerned about its performance and to take no action, even if it was not until the era of the National Government that this was almost universally accepted.

(i) *The Economic Departments*

If the Government had to have an economic policy, which department was to be the main source of official advice? The Treasury qualified, if only by default. In importance, particularly before 1931, it was matched by the Bank of England, although that was still a private institution. It was Montagu Norman, the Governor of the Bank from 1920, with whom Keynes had to do battle over economic policy, as well as the Controllers of Finance at the Treasury, Sir Otto Niemeyer and then Sir Richard Hopkins. Keynes and the Chancellor, Churchill, lost over the return to the Gold Standard in 1925. When Keynes met Hopkins in intellectual combat over the 'Treasury view' before the Macmillan Committee, the Chairman declared it a 'drawn battle'. Keynes, in fact, won on points, but he needed a knockout victory to change economic policy. Keynes's presence on the Economic Advisory Council that the desperate MacDonald Labour Government set up in 1930 made little difference. Advisory meant what it said. The Council had no executive powers. Neville Chamberlain's long tenure of the Chancellorship in the 1930s is said to have seen a strengthening of the Treasury's position in relation to the Bank of England. This it may have done, but the victory was incomplete. It was still unclear, for example, whether the Bank had ceased to act independently over the Bank Rate even in 1939.[26]

What the Bank and the Treasury had in common was an adherence to 'sound finance' that was inhibitive of attempts to promote inter-war economic recovery. This did not mean that policy was necessarily imposed on Ministers, despite the frustration of Churchill's wish to be a renegade over the Gold Standard. The views of Philip Snowden, the Chancellor of the

N

Exchequer in both MacDonald Labour Governments, were in harmony with those of his advisers. Churchill observed, 'We must imagine with what joy Mr Snowden was welcomed at the Treasury by the permanent officials. All British Chancellors of the Exchequer have yielded themselves, some spontaneously, some unconsciously, some reluctantly to that compulsive intellectual atmosphere. But here was the High Priest entering the sanctuary. The Treasury mind and the Snowden mind embraced each other with the fervour of two long separated kindred lizards, and the reign of joy began'.

The joy was very much confined for those who looked to the second Labour Government to fulfil its pledge to cure unemployment. J H Thomas, as Lord Privy Seal, was specifically charged with fulfilling that pledge. Leopold Amery warned him of his fate. When Thomas was vague about the extent to which the Treasury was under his control, Amery said: 'Jimmy, you are starting your job with a noose round your neck and the other end of the rope in Snowden's hands'. Thomas's year as 'Minister for Unemployment' proved to be one of tragi-comedy. When he was moved to the haven of the Dominions Office, unemployment policy became the responsibility of a small Cabinet committee headed by MacDonald himself. It made no difference.[27]

The scale of unemployment was one reason why the Ministry of Labour failed to live up to the high hopes some reformers had of it at its formation in 1916. The atmosphere of hostility in labour relations was another. Industrial Courts legislation in 1920 increased the Ministry's powers of intervention in trade disputes, and provided a mechanism for conciliation that, for example, Ernest Bevin eloquently used. The range of Trade Boards was extended too. Nevertheless, the inter-war Ministry of Labour was dominated by the problem of unemployment. It became a Ministry for Unemployment, as three times a week the large, slowly moving queues of jobless shuffled through the doors of its Labour Exchanges, unlikeliest of all to be offered employment in the areas most in need of it. When Special Areas legislation was passed in 1934, the Commissioners concerned were made partly responsible to the Ministry of Labour. They were also responsible to an Unemployment Assistance Board. That body was set up in 1935 partly in a vain attempt to take the relief of the unemployed out of politics. It was more successful in fulfilling Neville Chamberlain's hopes of greater central control of unemployment assistance.[28]

The loss of its Labour Department to form the Ministry of Labour was only one of a series of changes which affected the Board of Trade from 1916 onwards. That very year saw the establishment of the Department of Scientific and Industrial Research under the Privy Council, to which the Board transferred its responsibilities in the field, notably for the National Physical Laboratory. The creation of a Ministry of Transport in 1919 saw the Board lose its responsibilities for railways, canals and docks. The new Ministry also absorbed the Road Board. The Board of Trade itself absorbed the Mines Department of the Home Office in 1920. The long standing dispute between the Board of Trade and the Foreign Office over jurisdiction in relation to commercial policy was resolved by establishing a Department of Overseas Trade jointly responsible to both of them. This Department was given delegated power to collect and disseminate commercial intelligence and assist traders in Britain, and also to administer the commercial services abroad. The Consular Services also changed. Unification of recruitment in 1919 made for an improvement in quality.

This eventually resulted in the General Service reversing its pre-1914 position of inferiority compared with the other Consular Services, although not in relation to the Foreign Office and the Diplomatic Service. An amalgamated Consular Service – with the exception of China – was established in 1934. The new Department also included an Export Credits Office, which from 1919 administered on behalf of the Board of Trade legislation under which the State guaranteed bills drawn by British exporters. This took the State into the world of commercial insurance. The Board of Trade itself was given additional responsibilities from time to time, such as the administration of the subsidies given by the National Government to shipping from 1935 onwards. Nevertheless, the Board seemed to lose more in direct jurisdiction than it gained. This was so even after the full return to Protection in 1932. The Board of Trade was involved in the implementation of the National Government's policy of industrial reconstruction and tariff making; but the responsibility for the tariff was actually given to the Treasury, importantly aided by an Import Duties Advisory Committee, which the Board did not displace until 1939.[29]

The return to Protection also related to food, and signified a renewed State participation in agriculture on a substantial scale. In the 1920s, the Ministry of Agriculture – as it had been renamed in 1919 – had remained a small and comparatively static department. It had even lost statutory responsibilities in 1919 when a Forestry Commission had been established. From 1932 onwards, tariffs were imposed on a wide range of fruits, vegetables and other horticultural produce. The tariffs were the responsibility of the Import Duties Advisory Committee; but the Ministry was concerned both in supplying the Committee with information and in discussion with the Treasury and other departments on implementing the Committee's reports. The Ministry was more directly involved in the imposition of quota restrictions on imports of bacon, ham and other meat, and subsidies or price insurance schemes for wheat, cattle, milk manufactured into butter and cheese, and later for sheep. The Ministry also became involved in statutory bodies such as the Sugar, Wheat and Livestock Commissions which were set up to administer other subsidies. The agricultural Marketing Acts of 1931 and 1933 enabled producers to control the marketing of their produce through statutory marketing boards. Such boards were established for hops, milk, pigs, bacon and potatoes.[30] Even the National Government hoped to stay at arm's length from the problems of agriculture.

(ii) *The Public Corporations*

One result of the greater involvement of the State in economic affairs was the creation of a small group of public corporations. Running State enterprises as conventional government departments like the Post Office did not seem to appeal to the Governments of the period.[31] Local government either was or was deemed to be inappropriate to administer the public services concerned. The Forestry Commission (1919), the Electricity Commissioners (1919), the Central Electricity Board (1926), the British Broadcasting Corporation (1926), the Coal Mines Reorganization Commission (1931), the London Passenger Transport Board (1933), the Coal Commission (1938), and the

British Overseas Airways Corporation (1939) were among the public corporations created.

The establishment of the Central Electricity Board was the most important development. The demands of the First World War had emphasized the deficiencies of the electricity supply industry. Several government committees called for the industry's reorganization. The Lloyd George Coalition Government responded by creating the Electricity Commissioners in 1919. They were made responsible to the Ministry of Transport, whose control was thought to be relevant because of the imminent development of railway electrification. The relevant legislation was emasculated in the House of Lords. Whereas the Government had wanted the Commissioners to have powers to compel undertakings to be reorganized and amalgamated, they were left as a supervising body with advisory powers. The Commissioners could check and control, but not initiate.[32]

The problems of the electricity supply industry, however, could not be shelved for ever. At the beginning of 1925, the Baldwin Government appointed a committee under the prominent Scottish industrialist, Lord Weir, 'to review the national problem of electrical energy'. Weir – who had previously rejected an offer from Baldwin of becoming Minister of Transport – warned the Prime Minister that he would interpret his terms of reference to produce a new policy, and that both courage and heavy expenditure would be needed to put it into practice. Baldwin agreed, and Weir pushed ahead with such enthusiasm that he completed the Report in about four months. The main proposals were in favour of a Central Electricity Board, which alone would sell electricity to all the local areas. Thus, 438 separate generating stations – with surplus capacity, individual frequencies, and different voltages – were to be unified. Moreover, they would be unified not merely in a monopoly; but a State monopoly, financed half by government guaranteed stock and half by local undertakings.

Baldwin referred the Report to a Cabinet committee and ensured that it was embodied almost unchanged in legislation. Many of the Cabinet were opposed, and most Conservative backbenchers. The Minister of Transport, Wilfred Ashley, very much a second choice for the job, was not the man to drive through controversial legislation. Baldwin had more or less to make the case for the Bill himself. Its most notable Conservative opponent denounced the Bill as embodying 'the socialist principles of State control and State management'. Equally predictably, the Labour Opposition criticized the Bill for not being socialist enough. They wanted 'the principle of public ownership' to 'run right down through the system from the top to the bottom', and include distribution as well as generation and main transmission. The Labour Party, however, were pragmatic enough to accept the Government's proposals as better than nothing. Indeed, without Labour support, it seems doubtful if the Bill could have got through the committee stage, except in tatters. Important amendments were made, but the Electricity (Supply) Act 1926 was passed much along the lines Weir had indicated and Baldwin had argued for. The Central Electricity Board became the heart of the contemporary British electricity supply industry. The resulting establishment of the national electricity grid made for the rationalization of electricity supply and for impressive growth. The number of consumers rose from 750,000 in 1920 to 9,000,000 in 1938. The 1926 Act may well have been the most important single Act passed between the Wars.[33] The impressive record of the Central Electricity Board was itself seen as a recommendation for the public corporation form of organization.

The Central Electricity Board is often said to be the original prototype of the modern national industrial public corporation. One important difference was that the Minister's powers were less than under the post-1945 legislation. The Board's Chairman and seven members seemed to be under closer control in the 1930s from the Electricity Commissioners than the Minister. The philosophy of the times was that Ministers should not interfere. This was well put by the National Government's Minister of Transport, Leslie Hore-Belisha in 1934; 'It is surely inherent in the philosophy of instituting great public boards to administer public utilities that we should give those boards something approximating to the business latitude which is allowed to ordinary boards in conducting private business. If every step that they take, is to be looked on with lack of confidence, and if it is to be suggested that their day-to-day transactions are to be closely scrutinized . . . their capacity to bring about the public good for which we look to them will be severely hampered. The Central Electricity Board is not a profit making concern. It has a single minded purpose and a sole duty of guarding the common interest'.[34]

The Conservatives were later taunted by Herbert Morrison for their 'socialistic legislation', not only creating the Central Electricity Board in 1926, but also turning the British Broadcasting Company into a public corporation the same year. What Baldwin had in mind in 1926 was not socialism, but the establishment of 'such an authority as the Mersey Docks and Harbour Board or the Port of London' to run the electricity supply industry. The creating of the British Broadcasting Corporation simply followed from the proposal in the Crawford Report the year before that, in the sphere of radio broadcasting, a public corporation was needed 'to act as a Trustee for the national interest'. The Liberals—having themselves founded the Port of London Authority in 1908—developed some enthusiasm for the public corporation. The famous Yellow Book stated in 1928 that 'for the administrative and executive management of public concerns, the *ad hoc* Public Board points to the right line of evolution'. Labour spokesmen were initially unenthusiastic about the BBC; but Morrison, during his spell as Minister of Transport in the second MacDonald Government, was impressed by 'how successfully the Central Electricity Board was working'. It had influenced him in favour of a publicly controlled 'business board' to run London Transport.

Morrison also revealed that he had been influenced by the ideas of the Liberal Yellow Book of 1928, as well as 'modern socialist thought and my own municipal experience'. Morrison developed his and other people's ideas in *Socialization and Transport*, as the Labour Party languished in the political wilderness in the 1930s. Meanwhile, the National Government established the London Passenger Transport Board in 1933, which took over all the London passenger transport services previously run by municipalities and private companies. One of the last pieces of legislation passed before the Second World War was an Act to merge two private but State subsidized airlines (British Airways and Imperial Airways) into a British Overseas Airways Corporation. The year before, the Coal Mines Reorganization Commission set up by Labour and doing little actual reorganization, was replaced by a Coal Commission. Mining royalties were nationalized, but the Chamberlain Government did not anticipate going farther.[35]

The inter-war enthusiasm for public corporations is difficult to explain. Ministers and officials may have been sympathetic to a form of organization that minimized parliamentary control over them. Labour suspicions of the Civil Service perhaps led them to favour independent boards. The Conservatives possibly thought that if State activity had to be extended, public corporations were more acceptable because they were at least similar in appearance to private enterprise undertakings. Moreover, their expenditure did not count as supply expenditure, the level of which was a sensitive political indicator. So was the number of Civil Servants, and—apart from the Forestry Commission— the corporations' staffs did not count as such.[36] Whatever the reasons, the record of the Central Electricity Board in particular did lead many to think that a large public sector could be successfully run too. They were wrong.

(iii) *The Public Social Services*

There were changes in the organizational means chosen by the State to meet its commitments in social provision, although not major ones, for example, in education. Some changes were controversial, such as the establishment of the Unemployment Assistance Board. Other changes were administrative rationalizations. The establishment of the Ministry of Health and a Scottish counterpart in 1919 (called the Department of Health for Scotland from 1929) witnessed the abolition of the Local Government Boards, the Insurance Commissions, and the Joint Committee.[37]

There were high hopes in some quarters that the Ministry of Health would be an instrument of social reform. These are commonly thought to have died with the Ministry's Permanent Secretary, Morant, in 1920. Nevertheless, the Ministry did establish itself as the main central government department for health, housing and relations with local government. The commitment to State provision of housing was sustained. The Ministry attracted its fair share of political talent. John Wheatley's record there was one of the few positive features of the Labour Government of 1924. His immediate Conservative successor, Neville Chamberlain, was remarkably successful. Within a few days of taking office, he had set the Ministry to work on a four year reform programme. Within three weeks, he had laid before the Baldwin Cabinet a list of twenty-five measures which he wanted passed. Of these, twenty-one became law before he left office in 1929. The remainder were incorporated in later legislation. Finding the statute law relating to his Ministry's responsibilities in a scandalous condition, Chamberlain pushed through important consolidating measures.

His other major pieces of legislation included the Widows, Orphans, and Old Age Pensions Act of 1925 and the Local Government Act of 1929. While he owed a good deal to the advice of his Permanent Secretary, Arthur Robinson, and his Principal Medical Officer, George Newman, Chamberlain's strategy was very much his own. In local government, for example, there were few gaps in his experience. He could brief his Bills better than his experts. He could explain to the Commons the technicalities of complex rating measures with an enviable lucidity. Chamberlain's powers of work seemed to be boundless. As he said, 'my pleasure is in administration rather than in the game of politics'.

This did not mean that Chamberlain lacked political combativeness, as he showed over Poplarism. The Labour controlled Poplar Guardians, led by George Lansbury, treated their local unemployed better than the regulations allowed, and publicized the fact. Other authorities did the same, but made less fuss about it. Chamberlain eventually regularized the Poplar situation, without conceding the status of martyrdom that Lansbury and his allies were seeking.[38] One feature of Chamberlain's Local Government Act of 1929 was the abolition of the Boards of Guardians. Their function passed to public assistance committees, which were made compulsory for the counties and county boroughs to establish.

IV. THE CHANGING ROLE OF THE STATE

The machinery of the State was more complex in 1939 than it had been in 1914, and it tried to do more. The Treasury and the other established government departments were still there, except, for obvious reasons, the Irish Office. Some new ones had made a permanent appearance. The creation of an Air Ministry reflected changing means of warfare. The establishment of the Department of Scientific and Industrial Research marked a firmer State involvement in science. A range of research establishments was subsequently established, with the Privy Council acting as an umbrella department, as it also did for the separate Medical Research Council established in 1920. The Board of Trade spawned the new Ministries of Labour and of Transport. The establishment of the Ministry of Health represented a consolidation of government activity, and there were important rationalizations in Scottish administrative arrangements. Consolidation and rationalization would seem to be the hallmarks of the period, once the upsets of the First World War were over. Yet the period was also one of experiment. When the State explicitly recognized new responsibilities, it often tried to do them at one remove from Parliament. Thus when aid to universities was increased, a semi-independent University Grants Committee was established in 1919.[39] The Unemployment Assistance Board was another example. The public corporations were very important examples, and ones that were to be imitated.

The experiments with government machinery, like the functions that machinery performed, were reflective of an era in which nineteenth century attitudes towards the role of the State, especially in the economic sphere, had been only undermined, not overthrown. With the Armistice, the business and financial communities understandably wished to turn the clock 'back to 1914'.[40] For traditionalists, unprecedented levels of government expenditure and of direct taxation, and a vastly increased National Debt, made the situation in 1918 one of impending disaster. A swift return to normality – meaning, of course, a restricted role for the State in the economy – was believed to be the way to avoid this. Pigou was later to write that 'with a less impetuous abandonment' of the State's wartime controls over the economy 'the Government would have had the power – though not necessarily the will – to enforce some evening out of industrial activity during the three years that followed the Armistice; and so might have rendered the distresses of the great post-war depression less serious than they were'.[41] In fact, once the post-war boom had collapsed in the latter part of 1920, the Government was under greater pressure to speed the return to what was seen as normality.

The swift dismantling of the wartime controls and the wielding of the Geddes Axe and other reassertions of 'sound finance', however, did not mean that the State's role in the economy reverted 'back to 1914'. The State loomed much larger in the inter-war economy than it normally had in peacetime conditions in the nineteenth century, and there were several indications of its increased prominence. Even by the latter part of the 1920s the standard rate of income tax was still about three and a half times what it had been in 1913–14. Whereas in that financial year, only some 6 to 8 per cent of the net national income was raised in national taxation, in 1925–26 the comparable figure was some 17 to 19 per cent. Government expenditure in the 1920s never accounted for less than 24 per cent of the Gross National Product, whereas in 1913 the figure had been 12 per cent.[42]

For all the force of the arguments that it should be, the State's role in the economy was never cut back to its pre-war level. The Railways Act of 1921, which amalgamated the railways into four large privately controlled groups, is sometimes seen as almost the only working legacy of the State's system of wartime economic controls. Yet, State activity which had no precedent before the war included the subsidizing of Imperial Airways in 1924; the work of the Forestry Commission and the Export Credit Guarantees Department; as well as the nationalization of electricity generation in 1926. That the State's economic boundaries were much more extensive even after 1921 than they had been before 1914, and that in some cases they continued to expand, did not, of course, mean that 'back to 1914' sentiments were not powerful. More, that they were not always successfully translated into practice in an economic climate which, as the 1920s progressed, became one that was obviously different from that of pre-war and full of severe problems. The persistence of high unemployment after 1921 was a continual reminder that the economic system was not working as well as it was thought to have done before the war. With the exception of the depressed years 1921–22 and 1931–33, national unemployment rates for most of the inter-war period, in fact, may not have been much worse than the national average rates which prevailed before 1914. The First World War may have been either the first period, or at least a rare one, in which industrial Britain had enjoyed very low unemployment.

Nevertheless, the unemployment of the inter-war era was different from that of earlier periods, in that it was officially documented in the National Insurance statistics. Hence, the publicized figures which showed that from 1921 onwards, the national average annual percentage of insured workers unemployed was never less than 9·7 per cent (the figure foi 1927), and that it was normally rather more, sometimes very substantially more. For example, in the years 1931, 1932, and 1933, the relevant figures were 21·3, 22·1, and 19·9 per cent respectively. What was also different about the inter-war unemployment was the extent to which it was structural and regionalized. The hard core of unemployed workers were mostly to be found in industries such as coal, iron and steel, cotton textiles and shipbuilding, in whose activities large areas of the country had specialized. It is not surprising that the problem of unemployment dominated the politics of the inter-war years, and obscured the economic progress that also characterized them. [43]

The ambition to go 'back to 1914' did not square with the economic realities of the 1920s. Nevertheless, in debates on the economy, victory usually went to the adherents of nineteenth century values. This was certainly so over Free Trade and the Gold Standard. Nineteenth century attitudes that government should keep its distance from industry persisted too, despite the instances of State involvement already given. At least once the economic depression was under way, the governmental preference for detachment was not always desired by private industry. Through bodies like the Federation of British Industries, formed in 1916, industry had organized itself in relation to government as well as in relation to employees, represented as they were by the long established Trades Union Congress. Although the Ministry of Labour had been one survivor of the immediate post-war purge of the State's wartime economic paraphernalia, this did not mean any sustained attempt by the State to organize the labour market. [44] Industry was largely expected to put its own house in order.

One way that private industry tried to do this was by

amalgamations, the most prominent of which saw the formation of Imperial Chemical Industries and of Unilever. The solution to industrial ills was also sought in 'rationalization', which in practice meant a variety of behaviour ranging from an emphasis on an industry needing to concentrate on its most productive areas or activities, to a wish for restriction of output and an abatement of 'wasteful' competition. The various Governments of the 1920s normally stood aside from such activities. The Baldwin Government, for example, even declined to become involved in the creation of Vickers-Armstrong in 1927, despite its defence implications, leaving the matter to the Bank of England.[45] The behaviour of the Baldwin Government of 1924–29, at one time partially nationalizing the electricity supply industry, at another refusing to become closely involved even in the plight of the 'basic' industries, was indicative of contemporary uncertainty about what in practical circumstances the State's role in the economy was supposed to be.

Such uncertainty did not extend to the dominant body of opinion in the Treasury. Their views on budgetary policy, or the value of public works, and the general ability of governments through expenditure to create employment, remained governed by the precepts of 'sound finance'. They were urged upon usually willing Chancellors of the Exchequer. The 'Treasury view' on public works prevailed, even though it was contrary to the current orthodoxy of the Marshallian School in arguing that (besides undermining confidence both at home and abroad), such expenditure could result in no net increase in employment. It is not surprising that, as heavy unemployment persisted, the approach that it typified came under increasing criticism. The Treasury, together with other government departments, was in fact required by the Baldwin Government to reply to the critique contained in the Liberal Yellow Book.[46] The setting up of an Economic Advisory Council in 1930 was an attempt by the second Labour Government to widen the range of economic advice available to it. The Council was the first body at the centre of government consisting mainly of economists and concerned exclusively with economic advice. The actual economic policy of the ill fated Labour Government of 1929–31 remained dominated by Chancellor Snowden.[47]

The period of the National Government of the 1930s was one

of considerable change in the role of the State in the economy. The National Government saw itself as adventurous, was as made clear by Neville Chamberlain, its Chancellor of the Exchequer between November 1931 and May 1937, and Prime Minister thereafter. He believed that the National Government was not a 'safety first government destitute of new ideas', but one which was 'continually introducing changes of a really revolutionary character'.[48] Going off the Gold Standard was certainly to break with past economic beliefs, although not with what the actual practice had been between 1914 and 1925. Moreover, the action was forced upon the Government.

More deliberate, and a break with past ideas and practice, was the introduction of comprehensive Protection with the Import Duties Act of 1932. The National Government's intervention in agriculture was in dramatic contrast with the period since 1846, aside from the years of the First World War. With that exception too, the State was more involved in the workings of private industry than it was in the nineteenth century. After 1931, the old certainties about the State's place in the economy were much modified. Evidence for this was the National Government's essays into public ownership such as the establishment of the London Passenger Transport Board; and the passing of measures like the Petroleum (Production) Act of 1934, which vested in the Crown the property in petroleum and natural gas in the UK. In the eyes of some contemporaries, what was being initiated in the inter-war years, and particularly under the National Government, was an 'age of planning' or an 'era of planning'. Even if it was not one on such a grand scale as Roosevelt's New Deal in the USA, or Mussolini's Corporate State in Italy, or the 'experiments' in the Soviet Union and Nazi Germany.[49]

In Britain, the National Government's 'planning' in fact stopped at the door of 'sound finance'. The emphasis of the National Government's financial policy remained on balancing the Budget and on keeping down public expenditure. It was, above all, in its budgetary approach that the National Government's internal recovery policy was remarkable for its orthodoxy. This may well have been promotive of domestic business confidence; and also, very importantly, of international confidence at a time when Britain was in too vulnerable and dependent a position in the world economy to disregard external opinion. The adherence to 'sound finance', however, necessarily made it difficult for the National Government to make such measures as the Special Areas Act of 1934 more than a minimal contribution to alleviating unemployment. Given the structural and heavily regionalized nature of contemporary unemployment, whether Keynesian measures would have been more than ameliorative is at least doubtful.

As it was, the National Government took some important steps in the direction of the Managed Economy, most obviously, but not exclusively, in the sphere of external economic policy. Whether this made the National Government a 'revolutionary' government depends on the definition that one attaches to that adjective. It seems to me that Government was important in the development of the Managed Economy, but not 'revolutionary'. This is because it did not feel able to take up ideas on the overall management of the economy of the kind that Keynes expressed both in print, and in his famous debate with Sir Richard Hopkins before the Macmillan Committee.

In the sphere of social policy, established attitudes were slow to change too, although by 1939 the State in Britain provided a range of social services which were probably as extensive as those of any country. The Social Service State was mainly the creation of the Conservative and, particularly, Liberal Governments of the years immediately before the First World War. The relevant legislation was importantly supplemented by later Governments before 1939. Rent restriction dated from the First World War itself, but it was the Lloyd George Coalition Government afterwards which brought the State into house-building effectively for the first time.[50] That Government also importantly extended unemployment insurance, and introduced the first of what were to be a series of types of additional unemployment assistance. The brave Reconstruction plans of the latter years of the First World War largely vanished in the depressed economic climate that soon followed; the conventional reaction to which was to cut back on governmental commitments where possible. The more imaginative schemes to extend State social provision were ignored.

This was the case with the Dawson Report of a Ministry of Health consultative committee advocating a unified Health

Service in 1920; and the individualistic Eleanor Rathbone's perennial campaign for family allowances. Social policy was almost submerged by the dominant inter-war problem of mass unemployment. Nonetheless, by the centenary of the famous Poor Law Amendment Act of 1834, the measures passed to alleviate some of the effects of that unemployment had led – like the earlier social insurance schemes – to the development of a national system of governmental social provision that was undermining of the localized Poor Law. The Poor Law, in fact, on one estimate, only accounted for about 12 per cent of total expenditure on what by the mid-1930s were widely called the public social services.[51]

Private philanthropy too had a diminished place in social provision by the 1930s compared with the 1890s, and even with 1914. However, it was still an important place, as, to give one example, the prominence of the voluntary hospitals testified. A system of combined statutory and voluntary services unique to Britain had been established: 'the new philanthropy'.[52] The establishment of the Social Service State had certainly seen some novel governmental commitments in social provision. That the commitments did not go farther partly followed from persistent attitudes in favour of the need for 'economy' in government expenditure. Such attitudes were shared by the Labour Party, which some looked to as the main vehicle for social reform after Lloyd George's fall. The need to outbid the Labour Party in social reform did not normally exercise the Conservative controlled Governments of the inter-war period. An exception was the Contributory Pensions legislation in 1925, a measure which was viewed all the more favourably because it could be introduced at little immediate cost.[53] It had been the cost as well as the doctrine of unripe time that had stopped Neville Chamberlain from implementing other Conservative plans for 'all in insurance' in the 1920s, which to a large extent would have anticipated Beveridge.[54] What was needed to translate the Social Service State into the Welfare State was a fundamental change in the dominant view of the value of the relatively less well off to the community. It was the Second World War that brought about such a change, and – together with Keynesian ideas – the necessary change in attitudes towards the role of public expenditure.

The role of the State in the economy and in social provision had been changed but not revolutionized in the years between 1914 and 1939, and the same was true of the machinery of government. At its core that machinery remained an essentially nineteenth century structure, with the uneasy addition of a handful of public corporations. It was optimistic to expect such a machinery, even one much extended, to perform successfully a vastly more ambitious role than that required of it by 1939: but when peace returned that is what government was committed to.

Chapter 8

The Machinery and Functions of Twentieth Century Government from 1939

The establishment of the Managed Economy Welfare State during and immediately after the Second World War represented a sea change in the role of government in the economy and in social provision. Of the years 1939–45, the official historian wrote: 'by the end of the Second World War the Government had, through the agency of newly established or existing services, assumed and developed a measure of direct concern for the health and well being of the population which, by contrast with the role of government in the 1930s, was little short of remarkable'. The feeling that the resources had been available before the War to abolish want if there had been the will to do it was part of the contemporary mood in 1942 when the Beveridge Report on Social Insurance and Allied Services appeared. So, indeed, was the belief that the resources would have to be forthcoming in future.

Beveridge caught this mood, and made 'the abolition of want after this War' the aim of his Report and of the Plan for Social Security that it contained. The Beveridge Report advocated a comprehensive insurance scheme which covered unemployment, industrial injuries, sickness and old age. In what Beveridge expected to be the limited number of cases of need not covered by social insurance, national assistance, subject to a uniform means test, was to be available. The Report further recommended the establishment of a National Health Service. Beveridge's scheme was the same as Lloyd George's in that it retained the contributory principle of sharing the cost of security between the three parties – the insured person, his employer (unless self employed), and the State. It retained and extended the principle that compulsory insurance should provide a flat rate of benefit, irrespective of earnings, in return for a flat contribution from all. The only really novel feature of the scheme – family allowances financed by taxation – was the only one which attracted Conservatives, who were worried by the overall cost of the Beveridge Plan. The Labour Party's outlook was different. Popular enthusiasm was such that the wartime Coalition made the necessary commitments in 1944 in what Beveridge himself called 'a White Paper Chase'.[1]

The provisions of the Beveridge Report were implemented by the Churchill wartime Coalition Government, his Caretaker Government, and then by the Attlee Labour Government. A host of other social policy measures were also passed during and immediately after the War. They included the Education Act 1944, the Town and Country Planning Act 1947, the Children Act 1948, and the Housing Act 1949. The role of the State in social provision was substantially extended in the decade after 1939. Underwritten by the Keynesian governmental commitment to full employment, and a changed attitude to public expenditure, the basic framework of the Welfare State established then proved sufficiently durable to survive the demise of the atmosphere of social unity in which it was constructed.

The Managed Economy really began with the Budget of 1941. Then, Sir Kingsley Wood, the Chancellor of the Exchequer in Churchill's Coalition Government, decided the amount of new taxation required by reference not to government accounts alone, but to the estimates of the threatened inflationary gap between total money demand and the prospective supply of goods at current prices. Keynesian economics had come to be the new orthodoxy. Such came to be the faith in it that the Coalition Government, in its Employment Policy White Paper published in 1944, not only expressed the belief that its peacetime successors would be able to maintain 'a high and stable level of employment without sacrificing the essential liberties of a free society'; it committed them to doing so. The prevailing mood, as the Treasury remarked at the time, was to anticipate a Brave New World and not a Cruel Real World. The Government was to regulate total output to ensure full employment: but it looked to voluntary moderation to secure stability in wages and prices. There was optimism too about the likely results of the post-war economic settlement. Britain, like the USA, thought in terms of a short period of readjustment after which the world would return to 'normal'.[2] The Second World War in fact left Britain in a dreadfully weakened political and economic position, which being on the winning side only helped to obscure. The peacetime Managed Economy was launched when the British economy was less independent than ever before. It came to be associated with a continuation of the decline of the British economy relative to that of her major international competitors. Yet, although the economic prosperity in the Real World remained precarious the peacetime Managed Economy was also to be associated with a quarter of a century of full employment, even if it was accompanied by inflation.

The Second World War left an indelible mark on the British economy. In 1945, Britain had a massive balance of payments deficit, substantial sterling liabilities, and she had sustained considerable losses of shipping, overseas investments and export markets. She was the world's largest debtor. Even before the actual surrender of the Japanese, the Americans, allies who had prospered mightily in the war, cut off their main form of aid to Britain, Lend-Lease. Keynes – having helped to set up the International Monetary Fund at Bretton Woods in 1944 – was confident that Britain could negotiate a generous American loan. Hugh Dalton, the first post-war Chancellor of the Exchequer, described Keynes setting out for Washington as Britain's representative. The great economist was 'almost starry eyed' about the prospects of the Americans granting Britain a free gift or, at worst, an interest free loan. The Americans had no such intention.

Dalton recorded that 'as the talks went on, we retreated, slowly and with a bad grace and with increasing irritation, from a free gift to an interest free loan, and from this again to a loan bearing interest; from a larger to a smaller total of aid; and from the prospect of loose strings, some of which would be only general declarations of intention, to the most unwilling acceptance of strings so tight that they might strangle our trade and, indeed, our whole economic life'. As a commercial proposition, the terms of the American loan were generous.[3] What Britain was looking for were special favours for having been the only country to have fought the Second World War from start to finish as an adversary of Nazi Germany and her allies. Such special favours were not forthcoming. The generosity of Marshall Aid, which was later to help with the recovery of the British economy, was shared with other Western European countries similarly thought to be threatened by Russian imperialism.

Britain found that American opinion, expressed through the International Monetary Fund, that the pound sterling should be devalued was a major factor in that devaluation actually taking place in September 1949. The American Government's involvement in the Korean War, and her stockpiling of raw materials in anticipation of a wider conflict with the Soviet Union, fostered a world wide inflation, and made for trading difficulties that Britain was powerless to do more than adjust to. In the Anglo-Iranian Oil Dispute in 1951, the British hold on Middle Eastern oil, the most obvious economic benefit of her Empire, began to be eroded. In the subsequent settlement, the Americans improved their position. The Second World War had severely undermined Britain's political and economic independence. She was to prove less able even than the leading powers that she had helped to defeat when it came to trying to re-establish her position.

If Britain's position in the world political economy had been changed for ever by the Second World War, so had the British political economy. It was not just that the State had been committed by the Coalition Government to the Managed Economy. It was also that relationships within the economy to be managed had been permanently altered. The Agriculture Act of 1947, for example, underlined that the State would continue the substantial subsidization of farming undertaken during the war. The general relationship between government and private enterprise was changed by the war. The influence of the Federation of British Industries on the National Government seems to have been inconsiderable; but the war brought business and government closer together. In the immediate post-war period, with direct controls over the economy retained, this was partly because raw materials and labour allocations, building, investment and import licences were all obtained through a departmental sponsor.

What persisted beyond this was a system in which there was no field of economic activity not covered by a definite Ministry, versed in its problems and performing statutory functions with regard to it. If departmental sponsorship of industries became a usage of the unwritten British economic constitution as a result of the war, so did the involvement of the trade union movement in the upper reaches of government. This was signalled by the appointment of the General Secretary of the Transport and General Workers Union, Ernest Bevin, as Minister of Labour in May 1940. Almost exactly fourteen years before, he had helped to lead the General Strike. Previous trade union leaders in government had often been passengers in the Cabinet. Bevin's abilities were such that he swiftly became an important figure in the War Cabinet. He saw himself not just as the spokesman of the Government to organized labour, but also as the representative of the trade unions and the working class in the Cabinet. [4]

Bevin took care to involve the trade union movement in the policy making process. Its leaders were not for long to be absent from the process again, even if consultation was at times imposed on the Government of the day. The development of a much more integrated economy, together with full employment, enhanced the bargaining power of the trade unions. Nevertheless, the unions retained the rights and legal privileges of their era of relative weakness. They also still had their close association with what had become one of the two great political parties of the State, the Labour Party.

What had changed most about the machinery of government after 1939 was its scale and its range of functions; and that, even in peacetime, it operated in a context in which, following Keynes, public expenditure had become respectable. Public expenditure was supposed to be the insurance of full employment, an obsessive aim after the experience of the 1930s. The main forms that the machinery of government took continued to be the ministerial department, the multi-purpose local authority, and the public corporation. The structure used for the National

Health Service was more novel, although, like previous struc-
tures in the health field, it was one dictated by the interests of the
doctors.

The advent of the Managed Economy Welfare State or
Positive State was not preceded by much effective preparation
in terms of machinery of government. General plans for peacetime had been made by a committee chaired by Sir John
Anderson, and wartime machinery was handed on to its Labour
successors by the Churchill Coalition Government. The ability
of the machinery of government to meet the ambitions of the
Positive State was not a prominent question until the second
half of the 1950s. From then on, economic difficulties in relation
to an obviously reduced place in the world forced what passed
for a national reappraisal. For many years afterwards, changing
the machinery of government in often superficial ways was
preferred to examining the assumptions of the Positive State
and the Keynesian theory on which it rested.

I. CROWN, CABINET, PARLIAMENT AND ADMINISTRATION

The prestige of British political institutions in 1945 was immense. It reflected Britain's record in fighting the Axis powers
for all the six years of the Second World War. Even in 1958,
when constructing the institutions of the Fifth French Republic,
it was Britain to whom Charles de Gaulle looked for an
example of how to secure political stability. Ten years later,
when the Republic was almost toppled by the French mani-
festation of the political unrest that surged through Europe and
America, the British political system survived unscathed. The
popular monarchy, the House of Commons, and the House of
Lords were still there. So was Cabinet Government.

Nevertheless, persistent economic failure was a major factor
which disturbed the complacency to which the British system
was prone. Electoral volatility was marked from the early
1960s onwards, destroying Conservative and Labour Governments in turn. There was more than one Liberal revival. Celtic
nationalism flared up again, and not just with the resurgence
of the Irish problem in 1968. Scottish and Welsh Nationalists
won parliamentary seats. By the mid-1970s, it was not fanciful

to wonder if the United Kingdom would not follow the British Empire into dissolution. Moreover, by that time, the coal miners' strikes of 1972 and 1974 – which had the impact of General Strikes – had been successful. British parliamentary democracy survived, but it was not without its serious challenges.

The politics of wartime and then the 1945 Election destroyed the consensus on which the Conservatives had governed right down to 1940. Had there been an Election then or in 1939, the Conservatives would probably have won yet again. Their victory in 1935 was more handsome in terms of seats and percentage of the poll than any subsequent electoral victory of the next forty years. So, the Labour triumph in 1945 was a remarkable one. The egalitarianism of total war may have undone the Conservatives, undermining popular support for the attitudes towards restricted public expenditure and social responsibility of which they had become the main guardians. The Conservatives showed their reluctance to associate themselves with the Brave New World many expected when peace returned, and which Labour was only too keen to promise. The Conservatives may simply have paid the electoral price for being in government for so long during an era of high unemployment, and for leading the country into war less than ideally prepared. The irony of an electoral victory on this basis going to a Labour Party under whose second Government unemployment had more than doubled, and which had resolutely opposed rearmament, was probably clear to the defeated Conservatives.

Nevertheless, the 1945 Election did not inaugurate thirty years of Labour rule as some expected. The Labour Party was in office for six years, and altogether for less than half of the period down to 1975. Its leaders having served their political apprenticeship under Churchill during the war, the Attlee Labour Government was a distinguished one. It got more credit than it deserved for implementing Beveridge and for practising Keynes, but it also got more blame than it deserved for the austerity of the immediate post-war period. Nationalization proved both less popular and effective than expected. Although Labour lost office surprisingly quickly after 1945, it was a serious contender for office during the thirteen years of Conservative rule from 1951, narrowly obtaining it under Harold

Wilson's leadership in 1964. The closeness of the battle between the major parties was inhibitive of thought about change from the Managed Economy Welfare State, although the latter plainly could not meet the demands made upon it, not least in terms of economic growth. The only government elected with a programme to change the system – the Heath Conservative Government of 1970 – soon abandoned the implementation of its manifesto in the face of opposition from the trade union movement, and fears of electoral suicide from the unemployment involved.

The palliative sought for the problems of the Managed Economy Welfare State was change in the machinery of government. Few would dispute that if there had to be more government, then there had better be more efficient machinery. This was easier said than done, as can be seen at the very centre of the political system – the Cabinet. The period of the Second World War and immediately afterwards witnessed the development of a complex Cabinet committee system serviced by the Cabinet Office. The problem of co-ordination was such that, when he returned to office in 1951, Churchill introduced a short lived experiment with supervising Ministers or Overlords. The Anderson Committee had earlier recognized what its Chairman had called 'the importance of adequate machinery for making a reality of collective responsibility'. Nevertheless, judging by the results, despite the supportive mechanisms that were tried from time to time (such as the Economic Section), asserting this responsibility and obtaining a strategic overview and grip on policy eluded successive Governments.

When the Heath Government established the Central Policy Review Staff in 1971, it consciously made it a non-political body, although it was doing work which, ideally, the Cabinet was supposed to do. That the a-political Higher Civil Service was increasingly usurping the role of Ministers, and that consequently, the convention of Ministerial responsibility had become a fiction, was a familiar observation about British government from the 1950s onwards, if one not always substantiated. The Crichel Down case of 1954, thought at the time to confirm the convention because it led to a ministerial resignation, eventually proved to be the turning point, after which the British Constitution was never to be quite the same again. [5]

When complacency about British government eventually dissolved – as it did by the 1960s – institutional change came to be widely seen almost as a panacea for arresting national decline. Such activity was certainly easier – as both the Wilson and Heath Governments found – than tackling the trade union movement or trying to ensure that the private sector thrived. So few political institutions escaped change or proposals for change. This was true of the House of Lords. Its delaying power had been reduced to one year after it had delayed the Attlee Government's iron and steel legislation for two years. Changes in its composition made it less hereditary in basis and less Conservative. A more fundamental reform failed in 1969. The House of Commons subjected itself to a variety of changes in procedure and organization in an attempt to assert itself in relation to the executive.

The appointment of a Parliamentary Commissioner for Administration was an admission that conventional means of examining the use of administrative discretion were not enough. The office of Commissioner was a constitutional innovation of considerable potential, although it remained to be seen how its holders developed it. The specialized committees that the Commons established – from 1971 mainly under the umbrella of a Select Committee on Expenditure – could also eventually develop into important investigative instruments. However, this was unlikely while performance in such committees was unimportant for political advancement. Politicians still made more of a mark in the debating chamber itself: but did debating skills necessarily have much to do with being a Minister in modern conditions of often large, often complex government departments? This was a crucial question. Yet, when the Fulton Committee of 1966–68 reviewed the Civil Service, the role of Ministers was precluded from it, thus minimizing the utility of its Report.[6]

As review after review was undertaken, published and either ignored or expensively implemented, it became clearer that the problems of the Managed Economy Welfare State were beyond institutional tinkering. The Plowden Committee, reporting in 1961 on the control of public expenditure, attributed the failure of Treasury control to the absence since 1939 of a strong body of critical opinion, which before had served as a check on public spending. The post-Plowden system failed dismally too in the absence of such support. A major change in public attitudes towards the role of the State was a condition for positive change.

II. THE MACHINERY OF GOVERNMENT AND ITS 'TRADITIONAL' FUNCTIONS

The burden on public spending placed by defence and the other 'traditional' functions of the State became less onerous as the post-1945 period progressed. During the years 1939–45, of course, the waging of war was of paramount importance. The dependent relationship with the Americans established then persisted into the post-war world, a feature of which was Russian imperialism. As for British imperialism, it was dead within thirty years of the declaration of the Second World War. An alternative commitment to Europe was not confirmed until thirty years after the end of that war. The pace of change was swift by the standards of the past. The resulting adjustments were often reluctant ones.

(i) Law and Order

The maintenance of law and order was a 'traditional' function of the State, which became increasingly difficult to perform. There was little new in the failure to solve the Irish problem when it surfaced again. A solution had eluded the confident Victorians. What had diminished in Britain itself was a willingness to respect the law. Hence, the trade union movement's behaviour in successfully undermining the legal framework imposed on them by the Industrial Relations Act of 1971. The Heath Conservative Government learned the truth of the maxim that in a liberal democracy laws are binding because they are accepted, at least when they affect groups with the powers of British trade unions. Whether liberal democracy could survive the unfettered use of such powers was a question that was seriously raised by the miners' strike of 1972. Then, the miners' union forced the Heath Government to submit to its demands in seven weeks, whereas in 1926 it had battled on for seven months after the General Strike without success. The ill advised Heath Government made none of the preparations that Anderson had made for Baldwin. With a modern, relatively sophisticated and integrated economy – importantly integrated following Baldwin's own Electricity Act of 1926 – the Heath Government's task was vastly more difficult. The forces of law and order were humiliated in 1972. Britain was not ungovernable; but it was immensely more difficult to govern than before.

The number of changes made in organization for law and order were small. The Home Office remained at the political centre. The Prison Commission became part of it in 1963, without the deleterious consequences some feared. The Scottish arrangements remained separate, being the responsibility of a Home Department from 1939 and Home and Health Department from 1962. The police force remained locally organized, and its higher posts were once more mainly filled from the ranks. Localized police did have the advantage of closer links with communities. Arguments for a National Police Force tended to be met by fears about its use as a vehicle for the introduction of totalitarian rule. The real safeguards against this were not organizational, but lay in the democratic sentiments of the police themselves and the community from whom they were drawn. The Courts Act of 1971 did represent the most important change in formal judicial machinery for a century. [7] However, despite the advent of legal aid in 1949, the legal system remained largely closed to the willing participation of the mass of the population. Meanwhile, the mainly separate system of administrative tribunals continued to grow with the role of the State, threatening to eventually leave the judicial system on one side in an expensive and restricted corner.

(ii) *Imperial Management*

The tasks of imperial management, which loomed so large in the affairs of British government before the Second World War, were a very small part of its activities within a quarter of a century of the defeat of Japan. Victories by the Japanese in the Far East during the war – especially the capture of Singapore in 1942 – were testimony to the collapse of British power. The lesson was not lost on the more ambitious of Britain's colonial subjects. Moreover, the main victors in the Second World War were hostile to British imperialism. The Americans, once subject to it themselves, primarily wanted to own the world not to govern it. (They forgot that sensible maxim in Vietnam.) The Russians wanted to win the world for themselves, in the name of Communism. That they themselves retained – and retain – a territorial empire was evidence of their political skill. With friend and foe against her, Britain had to concede to the pressure for the end of her rule in Asia and then Africa. From Indian independence in 1947 to the cession of Aden took only twenty years.

The only serious bid to halt the tide was in the Middle East where the prize was oil; but the Suez expedition was a fiasco. After it, the end of Empire was pursued at breakneck speed. The advent of a multi-racial Commonwealth to replace Empire disguised the change for some; but the bonds of British popular affection were only with the Old Dominions, the former settlement colonies. From the early 1960s, the tradition of free entry to Britain from the Commonwealth – a sustainable policy only when the offer was not taken up more than minimally – was progressively diminished. Britain, however, had already imported a racial problem. There was little dignity in the decline of the British Empire.

The speed of the demise of the British Empire was not administratively anticipated in 1945, or even after Indian independence. That critical event meant the end of the India Office and the Indian Civil Service. The Dominions Office was renamed the Commonwealth Relations Office in 1947. The Colonial Office carried on much as before. Until his retirement in 1948, Ralph Furse implemented his plans for a more numerous and better trained Colonial Service, but one run on the old lines. His successor followed suit. The only difference that the Attlee Government made was to slow selection down for a time in a vain attempt to exclude candidates whose qualifications were merely social. The tone of the Colonial Service remained one of autocratic paternalism. It provided a mixture of authoritarian spirit and machinery plus democratic ideals, not a set of democratic ideals and institutions. The succeeding regimes reflected this. As independence followed in colony after colony, the Overseas Civil Service – as it was called from 1954 – was gradually disbanded. The central government arrangements were reluctantly changed too. A merger between the Colonial and Commonwealth Relations Office was finally effected in 1966, and a Foreign and Commonwealth Office established two years later.[8] The loss of Empire meant that the State had for once given up an established function.

(iii) *Defence Organization*

If defence organization in the First World War came to revolve around the exotic figure of Lloyd George, in the Second it had the romantic character of Churchill at its centre. Unlike his predecessor, Churchill had military ideas of his own. Sometimes they were wrong, as with his initial inclination to commit fighters to France in 1940. Sometimes they were right, such as his gamble on an initiative in North Africa. Sometimes they consisted of the only offensive course open to him, as with the heavy bomber assault on Nazi Germany at a time when invasion of continental Europe was thought impractical. For good or ill, Churchill, as Prime Minister and Minister of Defence, was supreme in the British conduct of the war. It was around him that the War Cabinet revolved. He was the energizer of the British war machine. Yet, once the Russians had been attacked by their German ally and had changed sides, and once the United States had been attacked by Japan, the role of Britain and Churchill was a diminished one. Churchill was President Roosevelt's 'lieutenant' and Britain America's dependent ally. From 1941 onwards, Britain could make no more than a contribution to Western defence. She could not hope to make war without American support or acquiescence. This lesson was cruelly learnt in the Suez episode in 1956, when the Americans deemed their interests not to be at risk. Britain had to hope that Western Europe did represent a sphere of interest to the Americans, and that even after their humiliation in Vietnam they would use their nuclear weapons to defend Western Europe against Russian aggression. There was no guarantee of this. Britain needed the United States, but the United States did not need Britain.

Having disarmed precipitously after the First World War, Britain did not do the same after the Second. The Soviet Union was an obvious potential enemy. Down to the 1957 Defence White Paper, Britain maintained both conscription and nuclear weaponry. Then, in the aftermath of Suez, she abandoned the former to rely on the latter. As Britain's economic condition was one reason for cutting down on defence, a nuclear strategy was unconvincing, as keeping up with the various weapons developments was bound to be costly. Perhaps with Britain's level of dependence on the unreliable Americans, any strategy would have been costly. Reluctantly, Britain drew in her military horns.

Once Ministries such as those for Production and Economic Warfare had been wound up in 1945, and a Ministry of Defence had been established in 1946, further organizational change was slow in coming in the defence sphere. The Ministry of Supply survived down to 1959, and even then a Ministry of Aviation continued to perform some of its functions. The separate Service Ministries had survived the establishment of the Ministry of Defence, which they matched in prestige and excelled in organizational resources. Harold Macmillan's experiences as Minister of Defence under Churchill led him to favour a rationalization of defence organization, which he made one of his ambitions as Prime Minister. Economic pressures and a series of costly failures in defence procurement were among the factors which favoured change. Macmillan needed the aid of Lord Mountbatten's authority to push through reforms; but, eventually, in 1964, the separate Service Ministries were finally absorbed into a unified Ministry of Defence. Even then, it was not until 1972 that the old Ministry of Supply functions were fully brought within the Ministry of Defence with the establishment of a Defence Procurement Executive. These various changes made for more than mere administrative neatness.[9] However, the fact remained that the State had defence commitments without the economic resources to sustain them and perhaps not even the political will.

(iv) *Conduct of Foreign Policy*

Britain's diminished position in the world was hidden by the prestige of her performance in the Second World War. It was hidden too by the international prestige of Churchill himself, in or out of office. His Fulton Speech heralding the Cold War was delivered when he was Leader of the Opposition. Yet, the world listened. Churchill's view of Britain as the overlapping area in three international circles – the Commonwealth, the Atlantic Community (effectively, the USA), and Europe – dominated British foreign policy into the 1960s. British prestige did not long survive Churchill's resignation in 1955 and Suez in 1956. After that, it was obvious that if Britain was a Great Power, the USA and the Soviet Union were something more. Britain could still play a useful lesser, mediating role – as Harold Macmillan did over the Test Ban Treaty finally signed in 1964 – if the Super Powers agreed to that role being performed. Britain played an important private role in the Cuban missile crisis of 1962, but no public one. By that time, Britain's options in foreign policy had closed considerably with the changing nature of the relationships with the Commonwealth and the USA. Britain had to make a choice between the circles of influence. After twelve years of intermittent and frustrated negotiation with suspicious Europeans, she joined the European Economic Community at the beginning of 1973.

The question of what sort of external relations arrangements a middle rank power really needed – especially in an age in which Prime Ministers and Foreign Secretaries could travel more easily – was only reluctantly faced. It was understandably not on the agenda at the time of the Eden reforms of 1943. One of the authors of the reforms, Frank Ashton-Gwatkin, compared the existing arrangements with 'one of those old country mansions that had grown together over a long period of time, full of corners and corridors and waste spaces and staircases and attics, the complete plan of which was known only to a few old retainers. It was rather picturesque and full of tradition and family ghosts, but it was inconvenient and insanitary'. Others thought that the arrangements smelt for other reasons, but Ashton-Gwatkin made his reply clear: 'a good deal of nonsense has been talked and written about democratization of diplomacy and abolition of the old school tie. The real object of Mr Eden's reforms is to create order out of confusion, and to provide the country with a businesslike machine'.

Among the reforms was the merger of the Foreign Office, the Diplomatic Service, and the Consular Services. The reshaped Foreign Office certainly worked well with Ernest Bevin in one of the more purposive Minister-Civil Servant relationships of the post-1945 period. Whether it worked as well as it did because the Office shared Bevin's enthusiasms, as for the North Atlantic Treaty Organization defence arrangements, or his prejudices over Palestine, is difficult to establish. After Eden's advent to the Prime Ministership, Foreign Secretaries no longer had the freedom even Eden himself enjoyed during Churchill's premiership between 1951 and 1955. After Suez, and with relationships with the Commonwealth changing, further alteration in the arrangements for external relations machinery seemed only a matter of time.

Change gradually took place in the 1960s. The Plowden Committee on Representational Services Overseas recommended in 1964 that the overseas staff attached to the Commonwealth Relations Office were merged with the Diplomatic Service. As noted before, the CRO was not itself merged with the Foreign Office until 1968. That year also saw another review, this time by the Duncan Committee. This report published in 1969, had no illusions about Britain having a world role. British foreign policy was to be concentrated on Western Europe and the North Atlantic Alliance. Outside that 'area of concentration' British concerns were largely commercial.[10] This was an interpretation in keeping with Britain's diminished status, but against the tradition of her overseas representation.

(v) *The Treasury and Finance*

The Treasury's position in relation to the control of public expenditure and as the governing department of the Civil Service proved to be as controversial as its handling of its new powers of economic management. Churchill's experience at the Treasury in the 1920s, and the presence there at its head of the arch-appeaser Horace Wilson ensured the department's relative demise during the Second World War. Wilson, like Fisher before him, had made the role of Head of the Civil Service controversial. When Sir Edward Bridges succeeded to the post in 1945, he tended to play down the trappings of the role, while retaining the powers of advice about senior appointments.[11] The Eden reforms had separated the Foreign Service from such central control, which removed one source of conflict. The undesirability of the Treasury continuing to act as the central department for the Civil Service was a perennial theme of staff association agitation. The associations were not just content with the benefits of Whitleyism and comparable pay with outsiders. In 1968 – following the Fulton Report – the Establishments side of the Treasury was made into a Civil Service Department, the Permanent Secretary of which was made Head of the Service.

The Treasury's inability to effectively control public expenditure – an important part of which was Civil Service pay – was a continuing problem. Changes in Treasury organization in 1956 left it essentially with its 1930s structure intact, except at the highest levels. A further reorganization in 1962 was more fundamental: the Treasury was divided into a Management side and an Economic and Financial side instead of the previous 'mixed' arrangements. This second reorganization was a consequence of the Plowden Report on the Control of Public Expenditure published in 1961. The Report gently suggested that Treasury control did not work. The cash approach on an annual basis had to be replaced by one of 'real' resources on a rolling five year basis. An apparatus was devised including a Public Expenditure Survey Committee of leading officials, centred on the Treasury, and a vetting of public spending proposals. The process which was supplemented by others, became complicated and its activities were couched in specialized language of impressive difficulty. What this system had in common with the old was that it did not work. One reason for this was inflation, which undermined the public acceptability of the 'real' resources approach. A second reason was the difficulty in containing local government expenditure, in which central government grants had come to be the largest single element. The crucial reason why public spending could not be kept under control was the lack of effective political sentiment in favour of such control. In 1976, the failure of the post-Plowden system was acknowledged by a return to attempting to contain public expenditure by cash limits.[12]

III. THE MACHINERY OF GOVERNMENT AND ITS ECONOMIC AND SOCIAL POLICY FUNCTIONS

The Churchill Coalition Government's commitments to a

Managed Economy Welfare State made for subsequent changes in and a subsequent expansion of the machinery of government. A special structure had to be devised for the National Health Service. Other social welfare functions were performed by ministerial departments, a successor to the Unemployment Assistance Board, and the local authorities. The responsibility for management of the economy came to normally reside with the Treasury, although there were short lived attempts to locate it elsewhere. Other ministerial departments – subject to a spate of mergers, renamings and occasional innovations – were responsible for several of the government's other economic functions. A National Economic Development Council – which some thought a precursor of a Corporate State – proved more durable than the various bodies which were set up to regulate prices and incomes. In addition, the nationalization measures of the Attlee Government left behind a range of public corporations, later to be added to and constituting a substantial State presence in the economy.

(i) *Management of the Economy*

During the Second World War, economic machinery had tended to develop outside the Treasury. The main decisions centred on the allocation of specific scarce resources: manpower, materials and also shipping. Financial decisions, although important, were secondary. The machinery was essentially inter-departmental, with the Lord President of the Council – as chairman of the main committees – playing a role somewhere between overlord and senior co-ordinator. In this he was served by the Cabinet Secretariat, with an Economic Section in effect part of his staff. The system was retained under the Attlee Government, with Dalton as Chancellor, Morrison as Lord President, and Cripps at the Board of Trade. There was, therefore, a division of responsibility for economic policy. Financial and budgetary policy was the province of the Treasury: 'physical' planning was for the most part outside it. With the return to peace and the renewed importance of finance, the Treasury gradually reasserted its position.

Even before that it was where Keynes was housed, and essentially where the conversion to his ideas had to take place and did. Morrison was in some doubt about the extent to which the Treasury was subject to the rest of the machinery for economic co-ordination. The difficulties of the Attlee Government in 1947 including Morrison's illness, led to further changes. Cripps temporarily took on Morrison's duties as well as the Board of Trade. It was announced that a Central Economic Planning Staff was to be established. Sir Edwin Plowden – of the future Plowden Reports – was made Chief Planning Officer. In September 1947, Cripps moved from the Board of Trade to the new post of Minister of Economic Affairs. He inherited the economic responsibilities of the Lord President. He was to give 'undivided attention' to Britain's 'economic problems at home and abroad'. Six weeks later, on Dalton's resignation, Cripps became Chancellor and took to the Treasury his various powers, thus re-establishing his new department's supremacy in economic policy making within the government machine.[13]

The Treasury never really lost the position that it secured in November 1947, even if it had to be shared with a Bank of England that – although nationalized – continued to act as a spokesman for the interests of the City of London. The economic planning machinery under Plowden, which became mainly bound up with Marshall Aid requirements, was located in the Treasury and was absorbed into it in 1953. That year also saw the Treasury take over the Economic Section of the Cabinet Secretariat. The Treasury had by then seen off an attempt to curb it by the Conservatives, who had established a Treasury Ministerial Advisory Committee to supervise it. This was a creature of continued Churchillian distrust of the Treasury and also of the Chancellor, R A Butler, a former appeaser. The Committee of four was eventually absorbed into the Cabinet's ordinary Economic Policy Committee. Butler's authority derived from the general success with which his economic policies were associated.

The Conservatives had returned to office in 1951 with decided views about economic policy, and ones that emphasized the virtues of the market. This emphasis did not extend to floating the pound sterling, although the Robot scheme devised by Treasury and Bank officials in 1952, and supported by Butler, did propose this. The Churchill Cabinet preferred the less adventurous course of adhering to the fixed parity to which

Cripps had devalued in 1949. Otherwise, in the context of particularly favourable external trading circumstances, and a neutral trade union movement, Butler was able to take the lead in dismantling the closely regulated economy that he had inherited. The Conservative approach ran into difficulties not long after their electoral victory of 1955. Balance of payments difficulties led to the brakes being applied to economic expansion. However adventurous they had been three years before, the Treasury and the Bank put sterling first, an approach which, when persisted with, was to be widely blamed for Britain's subsequent economic difficulties.

After Butler left the Chancellorship in 1955, the Tories searched for an overall strategy which would bring economic success. Despite the resignation of the entire Treasury ministerial team in 1958, the Macmillan Government rejected the temptation of moving back in the direction of Neville Chamberlain. Instead in 1961, the Conservatives embraced an economic planning approach to economic management, when they established the National Economic Development Council. This survived to provide a useful forum for government, industry and the trade unions to meet. The NEDC drew up a plan for economic expansion; and the last Conservative Chancellor of the period, Reginald Maudling, certainly pursued expansionary policies. In fact, the thirteen years of Conservative Government between 1951 and 1964 were characterized by rates of economic growth which compared very favourably with past periods of British economic history. The trouble was that Britain's main rivals tended to do better.[14]

The Wilson Labour Government elected in 1964 certainly believed in economic planning. It made the production of a National Plan the centre-piece of its economic policy. The Plan was made the special responsibility of a Department of Economic Affairs. The establishment of this department was supposed to introduce competition into economic policy making. The DEA had responsibility for long term policy, while the Treasury retained powers for the short term. This was a formula for confusion, except about the eventual result. As the political and economic situation primarily concerned the short term, the DEA was bound to be cast in the role of bodies like the Economic Advisory Council of the 1930s. It could propose, but others disposed. The Labour Government did not command sufficient international confidence to maintain the economic expansion that it had inherited, together with a balance of payments deficit. The sterling crisis of July 1966 destroyed the National Plan. The DEA was put to one side to return in 1969 to being that part of the Treasury it had been five years before.[15] Not that from 1969 onwards, the Treasury could be seriously said to be managing the economy as opposed to presiding over it. The Treasury's economic advice had been based on assumptions about relationships between inflation and unemployment that could be seen no longer to hold. The underpinning of Keynsian macroeconomic managing theory had gone.

(ii) *Industry, Agriculture, Trade and Employment*

The institutional arrangements relating to State intervention in the economy were fairly stable down to 1964, once the upsets of wartime and the nationalization measures were over. The Board of Trade remained the leading department for private industry and commerce. The other departments still included the Ministries of Labour, Transport and Agriculture. Newer departments included the Ministry of Fuel and Power (from 1957, Power) and Aviation. The last two Ministries were eventually absorbed into the Wilson Government's creation, the Ministry of Technology. In addition, connected with these departments and sometimes others were various regulative, investigatory and promotive bodies.

The Board of Trade recovered its control over the promotion of overseas trade when the Department of Overseas Trade was abolished in 1946. The Board's Export Credit Guarantee Department continued to be responsible for the promotion of exports. The Board retained regulative functions in relation to business practice. The Monopolies Commission was attached to the Board from 1948, as was the Office of the Registrar of Restrictive Trading Agreements from 1956. From 1945 onwards, the Board of Trade was given the main responsibility for location of industry policy, which was pursued more extensively than before. In addition, the Board maintained its traditional statistical activities, its administration of tariffs and an umbrella role in relation to private enterprise. It also shared – with the

Ministries of Transport, Power and Aviation – responsibilities for public enterprise. Towards the end of the Conservatives' long period of office, the wider role of the Board of Trade received formal recognition when its President in 1963–64, Edward Heath, also received the title of Secretary of State for Industry, Trade and Regional Development.

The view that the Board of Trade was insufficiently dynamic for its promotive role was present in Labour circles in 1964. The incoming Prime Minister, Harold Wilson, a former President of the Board, had long felt that Britain needed 'a ministry to discharge two functions which existing departments were inadequate to perform. It was to be a "Ministry of Industry", starting with a relatively small number of industries, but taking on a wider and wider sponsorship, with a very direct responsibility for increasing productivity and efficiency, particularly within those industries in urgent need of restructuring or modernization'. The ministry's second task would be 'to speed the application of new scientific methods to industrial production'. The Ministry of Technology was given these functions.

In addition, the DEA was given responsibilities for industry too, which involved the setting up of a range of interventionist agencies that seemed to duplicate the supportive framework of the NEDC. Initially, the DEA also had responsibility for the Industrial Reorganization Corporation. This latter institution had been seen by Wilson as one which would take British private industry 'by the scruff of the neck and drag it kicking and screaming into the twentieth century'. The IRC saw itself as 'a prod not a prop', and its principal purpose was to bring about industrial mergers that would not otherwise have taken place. When the DEA was abolished, the Ministry of Technology took over the IRC. It also absorbed the Ministry of Aviation in 1967 and the Ministry of Power in 1969. In 1970 the Heath Conservative Government abolished the IRC and merged the Ministry of Technology and the Board of Trade into a Department of Trade and Industry, with a supposedly strategic overview of its subject matters.[16] The Heath administration itself felt obliged to establish a Department of Energy in 1974, and its Labour successor proceeded to split the remainder of the Department of Trade and Industry into three more departments.

These various essays in institutional change were not accompanied by any marked improvement in Britain's industrial and trading performance.

The State's responsibilities in the labour market continued to be exercised separately. The Ministry of Labour – which at last took over the Factory Inspectorate in 1940 – acted as a ministry of industrial relations and welfare, and of employment and manpower. The Ministry tried to escape from its association with the mass unemployment era. It was partly successful, given that its local offices could now more easily be employment exchanges as there was full employment. The Ministry provided industrial training to the extent that finance and trade union restrictive practices permitted. The Ministry was also associated with Wages Councils – the former Trade Boards – which continued to attempt to relatively improve wages and conditions where labour was poorly organized. The Ministry was the main official source of conciliation and arbitration machinery in relation to organized labour.

This worked well in terms of securing amiable, usually mildly inflationary settlements, until the more aggressive trade unionism of the 1960s. Then, various mechanisms were tried in an attempt to curb inflation. The most important was the National Board for Prices and Incomes. The DEA at first had responsibility for incomes policy. When that passed to the Ministry of Labour in 1968, that department's name was changed to Employment and Productivity. Its name was changed again to Employment in 1970.[17] Whatever the advantages of these name changes, predictably, they did not ensure the better performance of departmental functions, especially in industrial relations.

The Ministry of Agriculture survived both in name and fact as the State's main organ of government in relation to the farming industry, and fisheries. It became the Ministry of Agriculture, Fisheries and Food in 1955, absorbing the Ministry of Food, a wartime survival. The Food functions were performed for Britain as a whole, but there also continued to be a Department of Agriculture for Scotland. The Ministry of Agriculture essentially became a client department in relation to the National Farmers Union, administering a collection of extensive State subsidies. Although particular schemes have come and gone since 1939, agricultural marketing boards remained a feature of relations between the State and farming.

(iii) The Public Corporations

The Baldwinian or Morrisonian public corporation was the means chosen by the Attlee Government to fulfil its nationalization commitments. There seems to have been no real consideration of the British Petroleum approach. Ideas for the State, for example, to take over the railway track structure and leave the track to the companies were disregarded.[18] The act of nationalization itself was supposed to lead to large scale economies. It certainly led to large scale bureaucracies. The National Coal Board, the Central Electricity Authority, the National Gas Council, the Transport Commission, the British Overseas Airways Corporation and British European Airways were among the leading nationalized bureaucracies created. Many had supporting regional organizations. Indeed, the gas industry was regionalized rather than nationalized.

The first nationalization measures of the 1945 Government led to the Bank of England being made a public corporation. That a private institution should act as a central bank was thought to be an anomaly. It was desired to emphasize the Bank's subordination to government economic policy. It was also an aim to expunge the memory of the Governorship of Montagu Norman who had retired in splendid misery in 1944. Dalton pushed the measure through with zest, noting with delight Churchill's personal unwillingness to oppose him, doubtless remembering Norman and the Gold Standard.[19] Nevertheless, nationalization seemed to make more difference to the Bank's formal status than to its role. The Governor remained by no means the Government's creature. The Bank continued to act as a representative of the interests of the financial world generally and of the City of London in particular. If it was Dalton's design to change this, his legislation was inadequate for the task.

Inadequacy was certainly a characteristic of the preparation that the Labour Party had made for the running of nationalized industries. The Labour Minister of Fuel and Power in 1945, Emmanuel Shinwell, had an unexpectedly free rein when he 'immediately took up the task of preparing the legislation for nationalization of the mines'. Shinwell confessed that he had believed that 'in the Party archives a blue print was ready. Now, as Minister of Fuel and Power, I found that nothing practical and tangible existed. There were some pamphlets, some memoranda produced for private circulation, and nothing else. I had to start on a clear desk'.[20]

Despite this, the Coal Industry Nationalization Act 1946 swiftly made its appearance. It included some constitutional novelties in the relationship indicated between the Minister and the National Coal Board. Hugh Gaitskell, Shinwell's Parliamentary Secretary, explained the Government's thinking: 'As soon as it is decided to set up a great public corporation of this kind one is faced, of course, with a number of alternatives. This is not the first corporation of the kind in existence in our country. We have, for example, the Post Office. There we have a trading organization; but it is entirely financed by the State, and is completely controlled by a Minister of the Crown responsible to Parliament for all its details, and its employees are Civil Servants. That is one extreme.

'At the other extreme we have an organization such as the London Passenger Transport Board, where the finance is not State finance. The Board has finance of its own, not backed by State credit. The Minister has not even the power of appointment to the Board, and Parliamentary control is remote in the extreme, and scarcely arises at all, except when the Board happens to have come to Parliament for fresh powers'. In the case of the National Coal Board, Gaitskell said that the Government was taking 'the middle way' between these extremes: 'We do not think there should be a Minister in charge of the day to day business of this great organization. On the other hand, we do not think that the National Coal Board can or should be independent, entirely remote from control. We say that the Minister must have powers of general direction'. A Conservative critic complained that it would be difficult to tell whether a particular decision had been taken by the Board on industrial grounds, or by the Minister on political grounds. The Minister would be able to use the Board as a facade, behind which he could retire when convenient.

Herbert Morrison – defending what some thought to be his

brainchild – argued that Parliament would 'find a way' of properly examining the industry. He said that in a high proportion of cases the use of general direction would not be necessary at all. What did this mean? Would matters be settled less openly? Morrison believed that the establishment of public corporations meant that 'we shall get the best of both worlds. We shall get business management, public accountability, but not meticulous political control'. In practice, Ministers came to indulge in comfortable back seat driving.[21] One Fabian enthusiast had to complain as early as 1952: 'Ministers cannot be permitted to remain in the twilight zone in which some of them love to dwell, flitting happily from one private meeting to another, talking things over with the Chairman at lunch, in the club, in the House of Commons, in the department, without disclosing either to the public or to Parliament the real extent of their intervention'.

The same enthusiast saw similar behaviour by Conservative Ministers in the 1950s as 'a transformation, if not a travesty, of the relationship which was intended to be established between a Minister and a public corporation under the post-war legislation'. Yet, there was nothing new in Governments trying to get what they wanted without being publicly responsible for it.[22] What was defective was a theory which assumed that a clear practical division could be made between the Boards' responsibility for management and the Ministers' ultimate responsibility for policy.

The imprecision in the legislation about how the public corporations should conduct their activities was soon reflected in their economic performance. The legislation gave little practical guidance as to how the nationalized industries were to be run. The National Coal Board, for instance, was required to use its monopoly to secure 'the efficient development of the coal industry'. The Board was charged with 'making supplies of coal available, of such qualities and sizes, in such quantities and at such prices, as may seem to them best calculated to further the public interest in all respects'. What the latter phrase actually meant was unclear. The Board was also subject to the 'break even rule'. This stated that 'the revenues of the Board shall not be less than sufficient for meeting all their outgoings properly chargeable to revenue account . . . on an average of good and bad years'. The Central Electricity Authority had to balance its accounts 'taking one year with another'. Contemporary discussion indicated that some comparatively short period was intended. The main stress was on accounts being balanced annually. Gaitskell talked of losses being made when 'there was a heavy slump and a lot of unemployment'.[23] Yet, in practice, the formula of 'one year with another' proved an inadequate guide to financial discipline.

The experience of having a large public sector of industry was an unhappy one. Among the reasons was the indecision about what role the public corporations should actually play. 'What are we?' asked one Chairman of the National Coal Board. 'We are not flesh, fish or good red herring. We are not a commercial undertaking; we are not a public service; we are a bit of each'. The public corporations were a double compromise. On the one hand between a government department and a private concern as regards the extent of political control. On the other between a social service and a commercial concern as regards its actual operations. Once the Conservatives, on their return to office in 1951, had ruled out more than partial denationalization, means were looked for to improve the performance of the public industries. For a time this took the form of a search for better organizational forms. Regional decentralization was supposed to be the answer. However, the Fleck Report on the National Coal Board reported in 1955 that its structure was too decentralized already.

The Herbert Committee on the Electricity Supply Industry, reporting a year later, indicated a different approach. Its view was 'without any qualification that the governing factor in the minds of those running the Boards should be that it is their duty to run them as economic concerns and to make them pay'. The Committee bluntly stated that, 'If it is thought in the national interest that some course other than a purely economic course should be followed, it is in our opinion the responsibility of the Minister acting on behalf of the Government to require that course to be adopted ... It is not for the persons running the industry to undertake uneconomic schemes of expansion, whether in rural or urban areas in the supposed national interest, if the effect is to subsidize one particular body of consumers out of the pockets of others'. The message was clear.

If the Government wanted the public corporations to act against their commercial interests, then the corporations should be explicitly subsidized for doing so. It was a message that by the late 1960s had become orthodoxy.

In 1968, for instance, the Select Committee on Nationalized Industries was certain that 'where extra social or wider public interest obligations are imposed on or undertaken by the industries, they should be publicly identified, quantified and appropriately financed by the Ministers concerned'. Practice followed precept in the Coal Industry Act 1967, which reimbursed the National Coal Board for postponing pit closures, and the gas and electricity industries for using uneconomical coal. The Transport Act 1968 made provision for keeping open unremunerative railway lines on social grounds. As for the main economic activities of the public corporations, the White Papers of 1961 and 1967 on their objectives were in harmony with the Herbert philosophy. Indeed, the latter White Paper endorsed the adoption of the latest methods of investment appraisal and the use of marginal cost pricing.[24]

The desire to improve the grim economic record of the nationalized industries was understandable, especially as the public sector had been extended yet again with the establishment of the British Steel Corporation in 1967. In 1969, the Post Office was made into a public corporation,[25] an administrative rationalization that did little to make it a more effective organization, but which diminished direct governmental responsibility. For, the public corporations remained at one remove from the Government in theory, and when this was politically preferred. When it was not, the rules of the kind indicated in the 1967 White Paper could be swept aside. So they were when the Heath Government tried to contain inflation from 1970 onwards, using the nationalized industries as examples of price stability.

Moreover, the niceties of the constitutional position of the public corporations were not respected by the trade unions. They recognized that the ultimate power to settle wage claims lay elsewhere. As early as 1955, a Court of Inquiry had preached 'fair wages' for railwaymen, irrespective of the British Transport Commission's ability to pay them.[26] The variously named successors to the Commission faced the same problem. The public corporation form of organization was not characterized by good labour relations. Indeed, as the period after 1945 went on, it was as difficult to see what advantages the modern public corporation had brought as it was to devise viable alternatives.

(iv) *The Social Services*

The social services continued to be organized in a variety of bureaucratic forms. Ministerial departments were prominent among them. At various times their ranks included Ministries or Departments of Education, Education and Science, Health, Pensions, National Insurance, Pensions and National Insurance, Housing and Local Government, Social Security, and Health and Social Security. In addition, there was an Unemployment Assistance Board which was changed to an Assistance Board in 1940, to a National Assistance Board in 1948, and a Supplementary Benefits Commission in 1966. Local authorities also provided a range of statutory personal social services. There was also a separate National Health Service structure.

Were these various organizations effective for their tasks? When the Conservatives wanted to reach their housebuilding targets in the 1950s, the Ministry of Housing and Local Government seemed to be effective enough. Bevan as Minister of Health is sometimes said to have taken his responsibilities for housing and local government fairly lightly. He told Dalton – and, hence, the world – 'I never spent more than a hour a week on housing. Housing runs itself'.[27] Understandably, Bevan's main energies were taken up with the establishment of the National Health Service. The Ministry of Health was later a less formidable department to run when it became in effect the Ministry for the National Health Service and little else. With a smaller range of responsibilities than Bevan had, Macmillan could tackle housing with zest. He ran the Ministry of Housing and Local Government like a wartime department in order to reach the politically crucial housing targets. One reason he could do so was the financial freedom he was given. Other Ministries in this and related fields were given less financial scope.

That the central organization for social administration was fragmented reflected the lack of a coherent set of social policies. Decisions about priorities were not thought out in any broad context. For example, huge sums of money were spent on keeping old people in hospitals. The old could have been sustained more cheaply and pleasantly by means of local authority community services, but such services were financed separately, and it proved difficult to substitute them. To give another example, racial and urban problems attracted a collection of little policies – the setting up of education priority areas, urban development areas and housing improvement or action areas – usually requiring local initiatives. Yet, the communities most in need were the ones least likely to have the leadership necessary, so there was no guarantee that they would be the ones helped. Local welfare services – child care, mental health, services for the disabled and elderly – were difficult to monitor except on crude terms (such as numbers of social workers per group).

There were a succession of attempts in the 1960s and 1970s to rationalize government machinery. The Seebohm rationalization of local authority personal social services in 1970 was the best received among the interested public.[28] Yet, the actual reorganization was troubled by in-fighting among the various professional groups. At the end of the day, probation was still left out of the local Social Services Departments. At the centre, a Department of Education and Science was formed in 1964, the inclusion of science indicating the British preference that it should be impractical. Local education authorities continued to bear formal responsibility for the actual working of the State education system, but central government provided most of the policies.

At the centre also, the Ministry of Housing and Local Government was absorbed into the Department of the Environment in 1970, an administrative creation that also took in Transport and what had come to be called the Ministry of Public Building and Works.[29] Similarly, another rationalization, the creation of the Department of Health and Social Security in 1968 did not make for administrative coherence: the subject matters were too diverse for this. The establishment of the Supplementary Benefits Commission in 1966 had the argument for it that it ended the clear distinction between contributory and supplementary social security, which might make it easier for those in need to apply for assistance. Whether this desired result followed is difficult to establish.[30]

The structure of the National Health Service proved most resistant of all to change. If there was a logical place for its administration, then it was in local government changing the financial arrangements there to accommodate it. With the change in emphasis in medical care from infectious to degenerative diseases, the social impact of illness was greater. Medical care was likely only to ameliorate rather than cure patients. Hence, the advantage of closely linking medical services and social aid in, for example, the care of the disabled and of the elderly. However, there was little or no likelihood of the National Health Service being placed in local government. It might be said that the local government system in 1948 was unable to accommodate the Service, but this was not the main reason why a separate system of Regional Hospital Boards and Management Committees was set up. When local government was reformed in 1972, the most that could be done was to try to equate the Area and District health authorities with the new local authority areas.

The reason was the opposition of the medical profession to any closer link with local government. They thought such a link would inhibit their clinical freedom, and – in the absence of control by price – their sole right to decide medical need. So, the structure of the National Health Service was changed around the doctors. The main beneficiaries of the new structure seemed likely to be the administrators. As for the majority of doctors, their relationship to State medicine remained that of independent contractors, what it had been from 1911.

IV. THE MACHINERY OF GOVERNMENT AND THE MANAGED ECONOMY WELFARE STATE

The commitments to the Managed Economy and the Welfare State were made in the atmosphere of optimism of the 1940s, with the problems of the 1930s in mind. Tawney caught one mood of the times when he expressed the belief that a Social Democratic Britain would provide the world with an envied alternative to Soviet Communism on the one hand, and American capitalism on the other.[31] He was to be disappointed. For, while the British Managed Economy Welfare State came to possess an effective means for redistributing income, what it lacked was a means of making wealth at a pace comparable with that of Britain's competitors.

The Managed Economy had failed to halt the decline of the British economy relative to that of the other leading Western economies. Britain's economic performance was not helped by the country's slowness in accepting her reduced political position in the world and her unwillingness to act accordingly. However, even when that reduced position had been reluctantly accepted, the economy did not prosper. While it was by then too late to seize on missed past opportunities, the continued relative failure of the economy suggested that it was characterized by deep-seated problems. Whatever the reasons, British private enterprise, which had been in difficulties before 1939, proved unable to prosper in a sustained manner under the post-1945 dispensation.

One result of this was that Britain, a trading nation, displayed a persistent lack of success in competition with her major economic rivals. Consequently, she was more vulnerable to international economic pressures than she would have been otherwise. Internally, the development of a large public sector, and extensive government intervention beyond that, had proved to be no guarantee of economic efficiency. The tone of the British economy was uncompetitive. Among other things, this was reflective of full employment not being defined in terms of full productive employment. In the end, this was bound to undermine the aim. In the meantime, the artificially created overall shortage of labour greatly strengthened the bargaining position of the trade union movement, the most effectively organized sections of which were able to impose inflationary wage settlements. As the 1970s wore on, the words of one of Keynes's critics, Jacob Viner, reviewing the *General Theory* seemed prophetic: 'in a world organized in accordance with Keynes's specifications there would be a constant race between the printing press and . . . the trade unions, with the problem of unemployment largely solved if the printing press could maintain a constant lead and if only volume of employment, irrespective of quality, is considered important'.[32]

The Welfare State had reached a critical juncture in its development by the 1970s. The Beveridge Report and the legislation of the 1940s was believed at the time to have intro-

duced a comprehensive system of State social provision second
to none. Certainly, private philanthropy and voluntary action
assumed a relatively much diminished role in social care compared with 1939. The family, of course, remained crucial to the
operation even of the vast panoply of State services that were
established. Together with friends, the family, as before, provided the first line of social defence. This did not diminish the
notion of the State as universal provider. Indeed, government
was looked to for more and more social provision. Once
poverty on the Rowntree definition had been abolished, poverty
was re-defined in terms of relative deprivation. This meant that
the poor were always with us. Although it was a corrective to
complacency, this approach was also an invitation to endless
public commitments. Ugly gaps remained in the Welfare State,
especially in the care of the elderly, the handicapped, and the
mentally ill.

The necessity of concentrating resources on those most in
need was recognized, as was the need to rationalize the tax
and social security systems. The problem was how to do it.
The cost of the Welfare State had risen – and continued to rise –
remorselessly. Many of its beneficiaries seemed to be masses of
government employees, not just Civil Servants and their
bureaucratic counterparts, but armies of teachers and social
workers of various kinds. The public thought that the State
could and should meet most human needs; but, at the same
time, the scale of public expenditure involved was moving
beyond the willingness of the community to pay for it.

The many changes in the machinery of government that were
made in the 1960s and 1970s represented one approach to the
problems evident by then. Their solution was looked for in a
changed Civil Service, larger local government authorities, and
a revised structure for the National Health Service, among other
institutional ventures. At the end of this institutional tinkering,
and as a result of further expansion of State activity in 1974
approximately 27 per cent of the working population were
government employees,[33] and public expenditure accounted
for about 50 per cent of the Gross National Product.[34] Whether,
in the long run, this scale of government activity, and the
machinery it required, was compatible with an Open Society
was a question which was faced only with reluctance. Extensive

government intervention necessarily means more control over people's freedom, their money and information about them – and their whole personal lives. If people's control over their incomes is taken away, how can they be expected to be responsible in the use that they make of services and in the expectations that they have of more services?

Greater government activity has brought costs as well as benefits, in the problems of controlling the bureaucracy and the limitations on personal choice, as well as the level of public expenditure and taxation involved. Nevertheless, recent experience has been that once the State steps in – at least domestically[35] – it rarely steps out again. The growth of government has shown little sign of abating. It has survived the obvious undermining of the Keynesian theory of economic management. It survived too the knowledge that the State was not a universal provider. The historical evidence in this book indicates that there is nothing new in the State not being able to perform the role preferred for it. What is different with the Managed Economy Welfare State is the scale of responsibilities. For experience so far has shown that the State cannot – as it is now supposed to do – perennially increase real incomes, attain price stability, sustain full employment, and continually expand the social services. Yet, such a role for government has become an integral part of Britain's liberal democracy.

References

In these references only the short titles of books that appear in the Select Bibliography are given. When consistent with clarity, all the references in a paragraph of the text have been grouped together.

Chapter 1: The Growth of Government

1. Liberalism has been called the English ideology by George Watson, but it seems more appropriate to call it the British ideology. Adam Smith was very much part of the Scottish Enlightenment.
2. Harris, *William Beveridge*, pp 2, 30–2, 57, 62, 85–107, 198, 209, 217, 247–52, 290–303, 311–33, 364–5, 370, 429–34, 440–8.
3. J Veverka, 'The Growth of Government Expenditure in the United Kingdom since 1790' in Peacock and Robertson eds., *Public Expenditure. Appraisal and Control*, pp 111–27; Peacock and Wiseman, *Growth of Public Expenditure*, pp 150–209; Abramowitz and Eliasberg, *Growth of Public Employment*, pp 16–19, 24–32.
4. Keynes, *General Theory*, p 383.
5. Harrod, *Life of Keynes*, p 462.
6. For example, O MacDonagh, 'The Nineteenth Century Revolution in Government', *Historical Journal*, 1 (1958), pp 52–67; and also Elton's thesis on Tudor Government noted later.

Chapter 2: The Classical Economists and Government

1. Smith, *Wealth of Nations*, 1, pp 416–17.
2. J D Gould, 'The Trade Crisis of the early 1620s and English Economic Thought', *Journal of Economic History*, 15 (1955), pp 121–33; Blaug, *Economic Theory in Retrospect*, p 12; Grampp, *Economic Liberalism*, 1, pp 48–9; J J Spender, 'Mercantilist and Physiocratic Growth Theory' in Hoselitz ed., *Theories of Economic Growth*, p 17. Viner described the bulk of mercantilist literature as open or disguised pleas for special interests (*Studies in the Theory of International Trade*, p 115).
3. This is to follow the definition of who the Classical Economists were given by Robbins, *Theory of Economic Policy*, pp 2–3.
4. Samuels, *Classical Theory of Economic Policy*, p 3, This reference is deliberately taken from a book which presents the most developed account of the position of the Classical Economists as yet available, perhaps possible.

5. Smith, *Wealth of Nations*, 2, p 160; 1, pp 250, 130; 2, pp 129, 159, 365; 1, p 4.

6. Ibid., 1, pp 323, 419, 421.

7. Ibid., 2, pp 184–5.

8. Ibid., 2, p 186; 1, p 429; 2, p 23; 1, p 429, 427.

9. Ibid., 2, p 202; Smith, *Lectures*, p 154; Smith, *Wealth of Nations*, 2, p 395; Ibid., 1, p 307.

10. Ibid., 1, pp 214–15, 217, 303, 269, 270, 272–3, 267–68; Smith, *Lectures*, p 154; Smith, *Wealth of Nations*, 2, p 272; Ibid., 1, p 137.

11. Ibid., 2, pp 310–11, 327, 300–1, 410–11.

12. Ibid., 1, p 436; 2, pp 367, 152, 41, 245; 1, p 435, pp 338–9.

13. Manning, *Mind of Bentham*, p 88; Everett, *Bentham*, p 87; Mack, *Bentham*, pp 69, 298; T W Hutchison, 'Bentham as an Economist', *Economic Journal*, 66 (1956), pp 301–2.

14. Bentham, *Works*, 3, p 311; Bentham, *Economic Writings*, 3, pp 311–12.

15. Ibid, pp 324, 333–34, 341.

16. Ibid., p 337; 1, p 211; 3, pp 339–41.

17. Ibid., p 338; Bentham, *Works*, 10, p 85; Bentham, *Economic Writings*, 3, pp 337–8; Ibid., 2, pp 134–6; 3, p 361; Bentham, *Works*, 4, pp 39–40; Ibid, 11, pp 96–7.

18. Ibid., 7, 389; Poynter, *Society and Pauperism*, p 144; Bentham, *Works*, 9, p 13.

19. Ibid., pp 204, 428–52, 273–93.

20. Ibid., pp 95, 160, 438–9; 5, p 17; 9, pp 640, 625–6, 232–3, 257.

21. Ibid., pp 1, 112, 110; Mack, *Bentham*, p 288; Bentham, *Economic Writings*, 3, pp 363, 367, 482; Ibid., 1, pp 247–8; Ibid., 3, p 427; Ibid., 1, pp 188–90, 292, 94; Ibid., 3, p 443; Bentham, *Principles of Morals and Legislation*, p 125; Bentham, *Economic Writings*, 2, p 312.

22. Ibid., pp 335, 52, 41. Bentham's attitude towards public expenditure changed from generosity towards frugality from about 1789, including a proposal to abolish official salaries (Mack, *Bentham*, pp 418–19).

23. Keynes, *Essays in Biography*, p 144.

24. Bluag, *Economic Theory in Retrospect*, pp 139–40.

25. Ricardo, *Works and Correspondence*, 1, pp 292, 185; 5, p 32; 7, p 116.

26. Ibid., 2, p 449; Malthus, *Principles*, p 326; Corry, *Money, Savings and Investment*, p 161; P Sraffa, 'Malthus on Public Works', *Economic Journal*, 65 (1955), p 543; Keynes, *General Theory*, p 32.

27. Schumpeter, *History of Economic Analysis*, pp 472–3.

28. Ricardo, *Works and Correspondence*, 4, pp 71–3, 271–300; R S Sayers, 'Ricardo's Views on Monetary Questions' in Ashton and Sayers eds., *Papers in English Monetary History*, pp 92–3.

29. Malthus, *Essays on Population*, p 71.

30. Blaug, *Economic Theory in Retrospect*, p 73.

31. Malthus, *Essays on Population*, pp 143, 101, 98–9, 100, 102–3.

32. Ibid., pp 101–2.

33. Ibid., (1826 ed.), pp 413–15.

34. Bowley, *Nassau Senior*, pp 237–38.

35. Ibid., p 242; Levy ed., *Industrial Efficiency and Social Economy*, 2, p 302.

36. Bowley, *Nassau Senior*, pp 247, 244–5, 266–8, 290, 283, 271.

37. Ibid., p 242; Levy ed., *Industrial Efficiency and Social Economy*, 1, pp 107–8.

38. Bowley, *Nassau Senior*, p 247.

39. R D C Black, 'The Classical Economists and the Irish Problem', *Oxford Economic Affairs*, N. S., 5 (1953), p 39.

40. J Viner, 'Bentham and J S Mill: the Utilitarian Background', *American Economic Review*, 39 (1949), p 373.

41. Mill, *Principles*, pp 957, 950.

42. Ibid., pp 941, 957–8.

43. Ibid., pp 956, 954, 955–6.

44. Ibid., pp 968–9.

45. Ibid., pp 800. 975–6, 969–70.

46. Ibid., p 977.

47. Ibid., pp 962, 899–903, 962–3.

48. Mill, *Representative Government*, pp 207, 217-8; Mill, *On Liberty*, pp 290, 287; Mill, *Representative Government*, pp 281–2.

49. Ibid., pp 355, 346, 354, 355, 356.

50. Ibid., pp 357–58, 355. On what he himself called 'the fundamental question of centralization', Mill came under Alexis de Tocqueville's localist influence at the time of Poor Law Reform, which led him to resolve to be more open minded about inherited pro-centralization attitudes than before (Mill, *Autobiography*, pp 192–4).

51. Mill, *On Liberty*, pp 150–1; Mill, *Principles*, pp 581, 856, 922, 791.

52. Ibid., p 808; Mill, *On Liberty*, pp 164–5; Mill, *Principles*, pp 942–3.

53. H S Gordon, 'Laissez–Faire' in D L Sills ed., *International Encyclopaedia of the Social Sciences*, 8 (1968), pp 546–7; and his article, 'The London *Economist* and the High Tide of *Laissez-Faire*', *Journal of Political Economy*, 62 (1955), pp 461–88. Robbins associated extreme *laissez-faire* with the Physiocrats, Frédéric Bastiat, Spencer and the Manchester School (*Theory of Economic Policy*, pp 3, 34–7).

54. For example, Grampp, *Economic Liberalism*, 2, p 75. Robbins's thesis in his *Theory of Economic Policy* was that Classical Economists did not even advocate *laissez-faire* in principle. This is only sustainable on a very narrow definition of *laissez-faire*. Yet, Robbins's interpretation has since come to dominate the literature.

55. O'Brien. *J R McCulloch*, p 249.

56. Ricardo, *Works and Correspondence*, 1, p 106; 7, p 248.

57. Blaug, *Ricardian Economics*, p 199. McCulloch's own remedy for over-population was assisted emigration (O'Brien, *J R McCulloch*, pp 324–31), a policy which Malthus dabbled with, but which he generally opposed (Winch, *Classical Political Economy and Colonies*, pp 56–60).

58. M Blaug, 'The Classical Economists and the Factory Acts—a Re-examination', *Quarterly Journal of Economics*, 72 (1958), p 224.

59. J S Mill believed that the classing together of women and children

for the purposes of the Factory Acts was indefensible because 'women are as capable as men of appreciating and managing their own concerns', and because such legislation closed some of the few independent openings for female industrial employment (*Principles*, p 959).

60. As Robbins reported they have been described (*Theory of Economic Policy*, p 5).

61. Ibid. Smith, far from being an advocate of subsistence wages, thought that high wages were conducive to family life (*Wealth of Nations*, 1, p 81). One reason why J S Mill found the Malthusian approach to population so attractive was because it seemed to be the 'sole means' available of 'securing full employment at high wages to the whole labouring population' (*Autobiography*, p 105). The Ricardians' attitude towards wages particularly at first, was influenced by Malthusian beliefs, and never by any adherence to a Wages Fund theory designed to combat trade union pressure by showing wages as being at their practical maximum (Blaug, *Ricardian Economics*, pp 120–27). McCulloch, the economist most closely, and, in the above sense, wrongly associated with the Wages Fund, was in fact a leading figure in securing the repeal of the Combination Laws. He saw 'a positive role' for the trade unions 'in redressing the balance of bargaining power' (O'Brien, *J R McCulloch*, pp 366–67, 369–70).

62. Bowley, *Nassau Senior*, pp 280–81. J S Mill's sympathy for the trade unions was qualified by his belief that they were a passing phenomenon, a common radical misconception of the time (Schwartz, *New Political Economy of J S Mill*, p 77).

63. Mill, *Principles*, p 934.

64. Smith, *Wealth of Nations*, 2, p 246.

65. O'Brien, *J R McCulloch*, pp 290–91.

66. Blaug, *Ricardian Economics*, p. 242.

67. O'Brien, *J R McCulloch*, pp 284–85.

68. As recorded by Robbins, *Theory of Economic Policy*, pp 34–7. Thomas Carlyle's famous phrase 'anarchy plus the constable' uttered in his Inaugural Address as Rector at Edinburgh in 1866 (*Critical and Miscellaneous Essays*, 6, p 329) was not a direct reference to the Classical Economists.

69. Smith, *Wealth of Nations*, 1, p 328.

70. Samuels, *Classical Theory of Economic Policy*, p 173.

71. However, Senior and McCulloch did not hold this view. Malthus saw a need for industrial progress to be accompanied by 'a proper proportion of unproductive expenditure' (Ricardo, *Works and Correspondence*, 9, p 11). The notion of government expenditure being unproductive originated, among the Classical Economists, with David Hume. Nevertheless, he recognized the need for a community to have a 'certain proportion' between 'the laborious and the idle part of it' (Rotwein ed., *David Hume*, p 97). The elder Mill simply treated government expenditure as 'unproductive consumption' (Winch ed., *James Mill*, p 337).

72. Robbins, *Theory of Economic Policy*, pp 17, 19.

73. Cairnes, *Essays in Political Economy*, pp 250–51.

74. On Free Trade, besides the various reservations of Malthus and the concessions of Smith and J S Mill, it can be noted that Torrens (a minor figure among the Classical Economists in general, but not in the theory of international trade) came to believe that the best policy for this country was not undiluted Free Trade, but to turn her Empire into a 'colonial Zollverein' (Robbins, *Robert Torrens*, p 228). Even McCulloch, sometimes thought to be an extreme and uncompromising advocate of Free Trade in fact took a pragmatic line (O'Brien, *J R McCulloch*, p 223).

Chapter 3: Who killed Laissez-Faire?

1. Asquith went up to Oxford in 1870. He later wrote that 'between 1870 and 1880, Green was undoubtedly the greatest personal force in the real life of Oxford'. Asquith said that he owed a good deal to Green's influence, but that he was not one of his worshippers (*Memories and Reflections*, p 19).

2. The message was passed on by Edward Caird according to Beveridge (*Power and Influence*, p 9). Beveridge's biographer sees him as influenced by the liberal idealism of Green, while subject to many other influences (Harris, *William Beveridge*, pp 2, 312, 472).

3. Carlyle, *Critical and Miscellaneous Essays*, 5, p 370.

4. Smith maintained that Britain derived 'nothing but loss' from colonies (*Wealth of Nations*, 2, p 116); but, assuming that an empire of sorts would persist, with characteristic practicality, he proceeded to indicate a form of political union that would enable it to work more satisfactorily (Ibid., pp 121–124). Bentham was ambivalent about empire, and J S Mill came to favour it (Winch, *Classical Political Economy and Colonies*, pp 23–38, 135, 143, 154–59).

5. White, *Political Thought of Coleridge*, pp 11, 16; Kitson Clark, *Churchmen and the Condition of England*, pp 295–97; White, *Conservative Tradition*, p 222.

6. Burke, *Works*, 2, p 348; Ibid., 5, pp 107–9; White ed., *Conservative Tradition*, pp 82–4; Boyle ed., *Tory Democrat*, pp 27–31.

7. Smith, *Disraelian Conservatism and Social Reform*, p 321.

8. For example, Boothby, Macmillan and others, *Industry and the State* (1927); and Macmillan, *The Middle Way* (1938).

9. For instance, Richter, *Politics of Conscience*, p 13.

10. Laski, *Studies in Law and Politics*, pp 131–32; Hobhouse, *Liberalism*, p 219 (q.v. Richter, p 267).

11. Richter, *Politics of Conscience*, p 267.

12. Green, *Works*, 2, pp 416, 450, 455.

13. Ibid., pp 514–15.

14. Ibid., pp 515–16.

15. Ibid., pp 345–46.

16. Ibid., pp 314–15; 3, p 371; 2, p 314; 3, pp 370–71.

17. Ibid., p 372.

18. Ibid., pp 374, 385–86, 375.

19. Ibid., pp 373–74, 461, 457–58, 460, 461.

20. Ibid., 2, pp 531–32.

21. Grampp, *Manchester School*, pp 1–4.

22. The interpreter concerned being Richter, *Politics of Conscience*, pp 290–91.

23. Read, *Cobden and Bright*, pp 214, 210–13, 209, 181–83, 215–16, 218, 216.

24. The challenger again being Richter, *Politics of Conscience*, pp 293, 329, 212; Hobhouse, *Metaphysical Theory of the State*, p 78; Hobhouse, *Elements of Social Justice*, p 43; Hobhouse, *Liberalism*, p 165.

25. Green, *Works*, 2, p 535.

26. Richter, *Politics of Conscience*, p 293. For all Richter's determination to undermine earlier views about Green, one can still draw from Richter's own work indications that Green's contribution to a changing view of the role of the State was by no means minimal. Richter said that 'in Green's day the negative definitions of freedom' had 'the effect of making it difficult to justify even moderate proposals for social and economic amelioration. The problem was how to incorporate within the same theory a criterion for State action which applied equally well to the protection of individual freedoms and the claim for a more equitable distribution of social opportunities. A balance was wanted: Green thought that it could be best attained by the notion that freedom consisted of the right of every individual to make the most of those powers admitted to be worth realizing by the moral consensus of the community.' Against conservative theories of man's nature and history, Richter wrote that 'Green set out a theory of progress, the speed of which would be determined by man's will' (Ibid., pp 224–25). Richter himself said that Green 'challenged liberal orthodoxies and introduced some novel propositions for public consideration: the possibility that an increase in government activity (in education, for example) might add to the liberty of individuals rather than diminish it' (Ibid., p 223).

27. Green, *Works*, 2, p 336.

28. Toynbee, *Lectures on the Industrial Revolution*, pp 219–20.

29. As is confirmed by, for example, J F C Harrison, 'A New View of Mr Owen' in Pollard and Salt eds., *Robert Owen*, pp 1–12.

30. As the title of his book indicated, Kendall, *The Revolutionary Movement in Britain 1900–1921*, thought that such a movement existed. He saw the establishment of the Communist Party as splitting and thus weakening this movement.

31. Marx and Engels, *Communist Manifesto*, pp 143, 152–53; R Miliband, 'Marx and the State', *Socialist Register*, 2 (1965), p 293; Graubard, *British Labour and the Russian Revolution*, p 292.

32. Marx and Engels, *Communist Manifesto*, pp 155–56; Raven, *Christian Socialism*, pp 340–60; Christensen, *Origin and History of Christian Socialism*, pp 271–79; Jones, *Christian Social Revival*, pp 25–6, 48–9, 446–47.

33. Terrill, *Tawney and his Times*, pp 252, 253, 251, 210–11.

34. Cole ed., *Webbs and their Work*, pp 8, 11.

35. Shaw ed., *Fabian Essays in Socialism*, pp 46–53, 200, 98, 61.

36. Cole, *Story of Fabian Socialism*, pp 46, 95–108, 87; Wiener, *Between Two Worlds*, pp 57–8; Pelling, *Short History of Labour Party*, p 16.

37. Cole ed., *Webbs and their Work*, p 114.

38. Eckstein, *English Health Service*, pp 103, 105. Eckstein gave as an example the attitudes present in Shaw's *The Doctor's Dilemma*.

39. Webbs, *State and the Doctor*, pp 148–50.

40. J M Winter, 'Arthur Henderson, the Russian Revolution, and the Reconstruction of the Labour Party', *Historical Journal*, 15 (1972), pp 753–73; Cole, *Story of Fabian Socialism*, p 167.

41. Labour Party, *Labour and the New Social Order*, pp 3–4.

42. Ibid., pp 4–5.

43. Ibid., pp 11–18.

44. Ibid., pp 19–20.

45. McKibbin, *Evolution of Labour Party*, pp 91–106.

46. Glass, *The Responsible Society*, pp 60–1.

47. Cole, *Story of Fabian Socialism*, p 175.

48. Webbs, *Constitution for the Socialist Commonwealth of Great Britain*, pp 318–56.

49. The Webbs' conversion to Soviet Communism is well described in Letwin, *Pursuit of Certainty*, pp 373–76.

Chapter 4: The Keynesian Revolution

1. Keynes, *Essays in Persuasion*, p 337; Jevons, *Theory of Political Economy*, pp 275–77; Schumpeter, *History of Economic Analysis*, pp 830, 833; Jevons, *Theory of Political Economy*, p 51; T W Hutchison, 'The "Marginal Revolution" and the Decline and Fall of English Classical Political Economy' in Black, Coats, and Goodwin eds., *Marginal Revolution in Economics*, pp 185, 201. Marshall has been fairly described as boldly proclaiming the essential validity of the Malthusian theory of population (Blaug, *Economic Theory in Retrospect*, p 408).

2. Hla Myint once described Marshall's famous analogy of the upper and lower blade of the scissors to illustrate supply and demand as 'the crowning symbol of the Neo-Classical approach' (*Theories of Welfare Economics*, p 132). Another candidate could be Marshall's use of the price of tea to explain consumer's surplus (*Principles*, pp 103–7).

3. Shackle, *Years of High Theory*, p 289.

4. Marshall, *Principles*, pp 395–410, 352, 284.

5. Robbins, *Essay on Nature and Significance of Economic Science*, p 24; Marshall, *Principles*, p 35; J M Keynes, 'Alfred Marshall 1842–1924' in Pigou ed., *Memorials of Alfred Marshall*, pp 37–8.

6. Ibid., p 16; Marshall, *Principles*, p 176; Marshall, 'Where to House the London Poor' in Pigou ed., *Memorials*, p 142; Marshall, 'Letters'

242   THE GROWTH OF GOVERNMENT

in Pigou ed., *Memorials,* p 462; Marshall, 'The Equitable Distribution of Taxation' in Pigou ed., *Memorials,* pp 348, 349, 352, 348.

7. Marshall, 'Social Possibilities of Economic Chivalry' in Pigou ed., *Memorials,* p 334; Marshall, *Industry and Trade,* pp vii–viii; Marshall, *Official Papers,* p 244; Marshall, *Industry and Trade,* pp 663–64.

8. E A G Robinson, 'Arthur Cecil Pigou' in D L Sills ed., *International Encyclopaedia of the Social Sciences,* 12, p 91; A C Pigou, 'In Memoriam: Alfred Marshall' in Pigou ed., *Memorials,* p 85; K Bharadwaj, 'Marshall on Pigou's *Wealth and Welfare', Economica,* N.S., 39 (1972), pp 32–46.

9. Pigou, *Wealth and Welfare,* p 488; Pigou, *Economics of Welfare,* p 485.

10. Hugh Dalton once suggested of Pigou that 'intellectually he derived from Sidgwick as much as from Marshall' (*Call Back Yesterday,* p 58). Marshall said of Sidgwick, 'I was fashioned by him. He was, so to speak, my spiritual father and mother' (J M Keynes, 'Alfred Marshall 1842–1924' in Pigou ed., *Memorials,* p 7).

11. E A G Robinson, 'Arthur Cecil Pigou', *International Encyclopaedia,* 12, p 92; Pigou, *Economics in Practice,* pp 120–21, 118–20, 116.

12. Ibid., pp 123–24; Pigou, *Economic Science in Relation to Practice,* pp 27–8; Hutchison, *Review of Economic Doctrines,* pp 416–17; Pigou, *Wealth and Welfare,* pp 485–86.

13. Pigou, *Economic Science in Relation to Practice,* p 23; Pigou, *Wealth and Welfare,* p 7; K J Hancock, 'Unemployment and the Economists in the 1920s', *Economica,* N.S., 27 (1960), pp 307–8, 313; A L Wright, 'The Genesis of the Multiplier Theory', *Oxford Economic Papers,* N.S., 7 (1956), pp 184–85; Pigou, *Theory of Unemployment,* p 5.

14. Sir J R Hicks, 'Dennis Holme Robertson 1890–1963', *Proceedings of the British Academy,* 50 (1964), p 306.

15. Hutchison, *Review of Economic Doctrines,* p 417. Hawtrey's views were expounded in his book *Good and Bad Trade,* pp 259–60.

16. As made by, for example, Baumol, *Welfare Economics and the Theory of the State,* p 165.

17. Marshall, *Industry and Trade,* pp 736, 672; K Bharadwaj, 'Marshall on Pigou's *Wealth and Welfare', Economica,* N.S. 39 (1972), pp 38–9, 45–6; Marshall, 'Fragments' in Pigou ed., *Memorials,* p 363; Pigou, *Socialism versus Capitalism,* pp 86–7; Pigou, *Economics in Practice,* p 127; Pigou, *Alfred Marshall and Current Thought,* pp 62–63; Pigou, *Socialism versus Capitalism,* pp 137–38.

18. For example, by Jha, *The Age of Marshall,* p ix; Blaug, *Economic Theory in Retrospect,* p 307; P R Brahmananda, 'A C Pigou (1877–1959)' in Reckenwald ed., *Political Economy,* p 365; D G Champernowne, 'Arthur Cecil Pigou', *Journal of the Royal Statistical Society* (1959) series A, 122, p 264.

19. Sir J R Hicks, 'Dennis Holme Robertson 1890–1963', *Proceedings of the British Academy,* 50 (1964), p 306; A C Pigou, 'Presidential Address', *Economic Journal,* 49 (1939), pp 220–21; P A Samuelson, 'D H Robertson (1890–1963)', *Quarterly Journal of Economics,* 77 (1963), pp 520–21.

20. As described by Pigou, 'Presidential Address', *Economic Journal,* 49 (1939), pp 219–20.

21. Shackle, *Years of High Theory,* pp 5–7.

22. Robinson, *Economics of Imperfect Competition,* pp v, 307.

23. Keynes, *General Theory,* p 381; Keynes, *Tract on Monetary Reform,* p 80; Keynes, *General Theory,* p 381.

24. For instance, see the remarks in Harrod, *Life of Keynes,* p 117.

25. Robinson, *Economic Philosophy,* p 79; Keynes, *General Theory,* p vii; A C Pigou, 'Mr J M Keynes's General Theory of Employment, Interest and Money', *Economica,* N.S., 3 (1936), p 115; Keynes, *General Theory,* p v; Robinson, *Economic Philosophy,* pp 79–80.

26. Keynes, *General Theory,* pp v, 3; J R Hicks, 'Mr Keynes and the "Classics"; a Suggested Interpretation', *Econometrica,* 5 (1937), p 147; H G Johnson, 'The General Theory after Twenty Five Years', *American Economic Review. Papers and Proceedings of the 73rd Annual Meeting of the American Economic Association* (1961), p 2; Robinson, *Economic Philosophy,* p 76; Keynes, *General Theory,* p vi.

27. H G Johnson, op. cit., p 2.

28. Keynes, *General Theory,* pp 19–20; J R Schlesinger, 'After Twenty Years: the *General Theory', Quarterly Journal of Economics,* 70 (1956), pp 583, 600; Hutchison, *Review of Economic Doctrines,* pp 422, 403; Shackle, *Years of High Theory,* p 196.

29. Although the multiplier remains more than an 'inexhausibly versatile mechanical toy' as described by Johnson, *Economics and Society,* p 70.

30. Blaug, *Economic Theory in Retrospect,* p 654.

31. R F Harrod, 'Retrospect on Keynes' in Lekachman ed., *Keynes's General Theory,* p 140; R F Harrod, 'Mr Keynes and Traditional Theory', *Econometrica,* 5 (1937), p 85; Schumpeter, *History of Economic Analysis,* p 1171; Keynes, *General Theory,* pp 264–65, 245, 378.

32. Ibid., pp 372, 375, 373–74; Harrod, *Life of Keynes,* p 462; Keynes, *Essays in Persuasion,* p 324; Lekachman, *Age of Keynes,* pp 241–42; Keynes, *General Theory,* p 377.

33. Keynes, *End of Laissez-Faire,* pp 52–3, 39–40; Keynes, *Essays in Persuasion,* p 336; Keynes, *End of Laissez-Faire,* pp 41–3; Keynes, *Essays in Persuasion,* pp 337–38; Keynes, *General Theory,* pp 33–4.

34. Ibid., pp 379, 378, 379, 380, 378.

35. Harrod, *Life of Keynes,* pp 469–70; A C Pigou, 'The Economist' in Sheppard *et al, John Maynard Keynes,* pp 21–2; R F Harrod, 'Retrospect on Keynes' in Lekachman ed., *Keynes's General Theory,* p 140; J R Hicks, 'Mr Keynes and the "Classics"; a Suggested Interpretation', *Econometrica,* 5 (1937), p 155; A P Lerner, 'Keynesian Economics in the Sixties' in Lekachman ed., *Keynes's General Theory,* p 228.

36. To say this is not to associate myself with monetarism as at present preached. If Keynes's work in the *Tract on Monetary Reform* and the *Treatise* were integrated with the *General Theory* the results might well be valuable.

37. Keynes, *Treatise on Money,* 2, pp 388–408; Harrod, *Life of Keynes,*

pp 411–13, 525–85; R N Gardner, 'Bretton Woods' in M Keynes ed., *Essays on Keynes*, pp 202–15; Lord Kahn, 'Historical Origins of the International Monetary Fund' in Thirlwall ed., *Keynes and International Monetary Relations*, pp 2–35.

38. S E Harris, 'Introduction: the Issues' in Harris ed., *New Economics*, p 5.

39. Keynes, *End of Laissez-Faire*, pp 46–7; Keynes, *General Theory*, p 378.

40. Harrod, *Life of Keynes*, p 641. Keynes—not the most consistent of men—did admit that he might later change his mind.

41. Ibid., pp 493, 535. Keynes had advocated, and costed, family allowances, in his *How to Pay for the War*. He also played a direct part in helping Beveridge with his Plan (Harris, *William Beveridge*, pp 408–12, 422–3).

Chapter 5: The Eighteenth Century Inheritance

1. Keynes, *General Theory*, pp 333–53. Keynes particularly had in mind what he called 'Heckscher's great work on *Mercantilism*', the first edition of which had been published in Britain in 1935.

2. The changes of the 1530s, with Thomas Cromwell as their author, have been described by G R Elton as *The Tudor Revolution in Government*. Elton took account of the controversy this aroused in *England under the Tudors*, pp 479–85. The main debate on the subject took place in *Past and Present* (1963–65), nos. 25, 26, 29, 31, 32.

3. Aylmer, *King's Servants*, pp 437–38.

4. G R Elton, 'An Early Tudor Poor Law', *Economic History Review*, 2nd series, 6 (1953–54), p 55.

5. On Jordan's estimate, in no year prior to 1660 was more than 7 per cent of the money spent on the care of the poor derived from taxation (*Philanthropy in England*, p 140). The precision of that estimate may be doubted, but what cannot be is that, apart from kith and kin, the main burden of social responsibility in pre-industrial England was borne by private charity. The development of the Poor Law in the sixteenth century was accompanied by a roughly parallel development of the law of charitable trusts. In both 1597–98 and 1601, the statute codifying and extending the legal meaning of charitable trusts was passed in the same year as the Poor Law. They were as closely linked in the eyes of the legislature as they seem to have been in the thinking of the community at large (Ibid., pp 77, 108).

6. Thomas Cromwell may have formed something like a planning staff (G R Elton, 'State Planning in Early Tudor England', *Economic History Review*, 2nd series, 13, 1960–61, p 434); but what effect, if any, its plans actually had is difficult to determine. The Elizabethan Privy Council seems to have had some success in influencing the spirit and form of English foreign trade, but to have had little impact on the domestic economy (V Ponko jnr., 'The Privy Council and the Spirit of

Elizabethan Economic Management 1558–1603', *Transactions of the American Philosophical Society*, N.S., 58, 1968, pt 4, p 43). It seems fair to say of all Tudor governments what was once said of Elizabethan government, that the administrative resources available, like those of finance, were extremely limited, and outstripped by their political aims and responsibilities (Hurstfield, *Queen's Wards*, p 336). The absence of a paid bureaucracy in the provinces was one of the major reasons— together with the lack of a substantial standing army—why the Stuart monarchs were unable to emulate their continental European rivals in imposing favoured policies (Kenyon, *Stuart Constitution*, pp 1–2). Even by contemporary standards, the general administrative structure was small in relation to the professed economic and social policies. It was certainly small, for instance, compared with the French system. In the 1630s, paid Crown servants in England and Wales totalled only about 3000–4000. A similar number of officials helped to govern one French province, Normandy (Aylmer, *King's Servants*, p 440). The Civil War and the Interregnum left surprisingly little mark on the English adminis- trative structure. The Restoration did witness more lasting changes, and ones which seem as important as those of Tudor times. Nevertheless, the main effect of the post-Restoration changes was to shore up the existing administrative arrangements, leaving England a country with a limited governmental presence.

7. J Carter, 'The Revolution and the Constitution' in Holmes ed., *Britain after the Glorious Revolution*, pp 39–56; W R Fryer, 'King George III: His Political Character and Conduct 1760–1784: a New Whig Interpretation', *Renaissance and Modern Studies*, 5 (1962), pp 68– 99. The best historiography of the George III controversy, together with the most interesting interpretation, is that of Butterfield, *George III and the Historians*. The history of the Prime Minister in the period down to 1832 has been well described as being like that of the Cheshire Cat (Pares, *George III and the Politicians*, p 176).

8. Williams, *Eighteenth Century Constitution*, p 76; Namier, *Personal- ities and Powers*, pp 21–9; J Brooke, 'Party in the Eighteenth Century' in Natan ed., *Silver Renaissance*, p 34; B W Hill, 'Executive Monarchy and the Challenge of Parties 1689–1832: two Concepts of Government and two Historiographical Interpretations', *Historical Journal*, 13 (1970), pp 379–401.

9. Kemp, *King and Commons*, pp 104–5; A S Foord, 'The Waning of "the Influence of the Crown"', *English Historical Review*, 62, (1947) pp 484–507; I R Christie, 'Economical Reform and the "Influence of the Crown"', *Cambridge Historical Journal*, 12 (1956), pp 144–54; E A Reitan, 'The Civil List in Eighteenth Century British Politics: Parlia- mentary Supremacy versus the Independence of the Crown', *Historical Journal*, 9 (1966), pp 318–37.

10. D L Keir, 'Economical Reform 1779–1787', *Law Quarterly Review*, 50 (1934), pp 373, 385; Cohen, *Growth of Civil Service*, Cass, p 69; Raphael, *Pensions and Public Servants*, p 136.

11. Critchley, *Conquest of Violence*, pp 48–50.

12. Holdsworth, *History of English Law*, 1, pp 285–98; Hart, *British Police*, pp 22–5; Critchley, *History of Police*, pp 1–28; Marshall, *Police and Government*, pp 21–5; Webbs, *English Local Government*, 6, pp 1–17.

13. Pool, *Navy Board Contracts*, pp 111–41; J M Haas, 'The Royal Dockyards: the Earliest Visitations and Reform 1749–1779', *Historical Journal* (1970), p 191.

14. Gordon, *War Office*, pp 39–43; O Gee, 'The British War Office in the Later Years of the American War of Independence', *Journal of Modern History*, 26 (1954), pp 123–43.

15. Knowles, *Economic Development of British Empire*, p 9; Harlow, *Founding of Second British Empire*, 2, p 786; *Cambridge History of British Empire*, 2, p v.

16. Woodruff, *Men who ruled India*, 1, p. 198.

17. C P Lucas, 'Introduction' in *Cambridge History of British Empire*, 1, p 6; C M Andrews, 'The Government of the Empire 1660–1763', Ibid., pp 413–14; D B Horn, 'The Board of Trade and Consular Reports 1696–1782', *English Historical Review*, 54 (1939), pp 476–80; V Harlow, 'The New Imperial System 1783–1815' in *Cambridge History of British Empire*, 2, pp 142–45; R B Pugh, 'The Colonial Office 1801–1925', Ibid., 3, p 711.

18. Sir A Strutt, 'The Home Office: An introduction to its Early History', *Public Administration*, 39 (1961), p 119; Thomson, *Secretaries of State*, 3–4, 32, 34–7, 39–47, 51–2, 68–75, 77–82, 90–4, 105, 126; Thomson, *Constitutional History*, pp 438–39.

19. Horn, *British Diplomatic Service*, p 1; Thomson, *Secretaries of State*, pp 158–61.

20. Roseveare, *Treasury*, p 86; Binney, *British Public Finance*, pp 244–54; Roseveare, *Treasury*, pp 120–24; D M Clark, 'The Office of Secretary to the Treasury in the Eighteenth Century', *American Historical Review*, 42 (1936–37), p 44.

21. Roseveare, *Treasury*, pp 94, 126; Hoon, *Organization of English Customs*, pp 290–91; W R Ward, 'The Office for Taxes 1665–1798', *Bulletin of the Institute of Historical Research*, 25 (1952), pp 204–9.

22. Ashton, *Economic History of England*, pp 113–14; F Cruizot, 'England and France in the Eighteenth Century: a Comparative Analysis of Two Economic Growths' in Hartwell ed., *Causes of the Industrial Revolution*, pp 144, 155–57; Williams, *British Commercial Policy*, pp 424–27; R Davis, 'The Rise of Protection in England 1689–1786', *Economic History Review*, 2nd series, 19 (1966), pp 306–17; Ehrman, *Younger Pitt*, p 483; W O Henderson, 'The Anglo-French Commercial Treaty of 1786', *Economic History Review*, 2nd series, 10 (1957–58), pp 104–12. It may be that if a distinction is made between induced patterns of growth (ones in which the State consciously allocates productive factors in a specified direction) and autonomous ones, the policies of almost all governments before 1914 should be regarded as permitting an autonomous process of growth (B F Hoselitz, 'Patterns of Economic Growth', *Canadian Journal of Economics and Political Science*, 21, 1956, p 425). This seems to be true even of Japan (D S Landes, 'Japan and Europe: Contrasts

in Industrialization' in Lockwood ed., *State and Economic Enterprise in Japan*, pp 105–6).

23. R Mitchison, 'The Making of the Old Scottish Poor Law', *Past and Present*, no 63 (1974), pp 58–93, and also the papers by R A Cage and Mitchison in no 69 (1975), pp 113–21; M Blaug, 'The Myth of the Old Poor Law and the Making of the New', *Journal of Economic History*, 23 (1963), pp 151–84, and 'The Poor Law Report Re-examined', Ibid., 24 (1964), pp 229–45; J S Taylor, 'The Mythology of the Old Poor Law', Ibid., 29 (1969), pp 292–97; Eden, *State of the Poor*, 1, pp 486–87 (q.v. Owen, *English Philanthropy*, p 100). Blaug and Taylor both seem to overrate the comprehensiveness and uniformity of the Old Poor Law.

24. Ellis, *Post Office*, pp viii, 124–25; R Mitchison, 'The Old Board of Agriculture 1793–1822', *English Historical Review*, 74 (1959), pp 41–69.

25. Webbs, *English Local Government*, 4, pp 353–55, 235–36.

26. M Neuman, 'Speenhamland in Berkshire' in Martin ed., *Comparative Development in Social Welfare*, pp 89, 91, 107–9; M Neuman, 'A Suggestion regarding the Origins of the Speenhamland Plan', *English Historical Review*, 84 (1969), p 322.

27. Best, *Temporal Pillars*, pp 11–34; Roseveare, *Treasury*, p 84; S E Finer, 'Patronage and the Public Service', *Public Administration*, 30 (1952), p 322; Horn, *British Diplomatic Service*, pp 12–41.

Chapter 6: The Machinery and Functions of Nineteenth Century Government 1815–1914

1. J Veverka, *The Growth of Government Expenditure in the United Kingdom in the Nineteenth Century*, University of Edinburgh Doctoral Thesis, 1962, pp 111–14. By 1900, public authorities were disposing of approximately the same amount of resources available to the whole community at the beginning of the century. In 1900, the national income was almost ten times the 1790 level while the population increased less than three times.

2. Hanham, *Reformed Electoral System*, p 35; N Blewett, 'The Franchise in the United Kingdom 1885–1918', *Past and Present*, no 32 (1965), pp 27–56; Gash, *Politics in Age of Peel*, pp 17–18; G Himmelfarb, 'Politics and Ideology: the Reform Act of 1867' in her *Victorian Minds*, pp 333–92.

3. Mackintosh, *British Cabinet*, pp 111–28, 222–45; Gash, *Politics in Age of Peel*, p xiii; Gash, *Sir Robert Peel*, pp 707, 710.

4. S E Finer, 'The Individual Responsibility of Ministers', *Public Administration*, 34 (1956), pp 377–96; P Fraser, 'The Growth of Ministerial Control in the Nineteenth Century House of Commons', *English Historical Review*, 75 (1960), pp 444–63; V Cromwell, 'The Losing of the Initiative by the House of Commons 1780–1914', *Transactions of the Royal Historical Society*, 5th series, 18 (1968), pp 1–23.

5. *Papers relating to the Reorganization of the Civil Service* (1855), p 92.

6. Fry, *Statesmen in Disguise*, pp 33–83. Murray first entered the Foreign Office. Fisher's comments are in his *Written Statement to the Royal Commission on the Civil Service* (1930), para 3.

7. E Hughes, 'Sir James Stephen and the Anonymity of the Civil Servant', *Public Administration*, 36 (1958), pp 28–36; F M G Willson, 'Ministries and Boards: Some Aspects of Administrative Development since 1832', Ibid., 33 (1955), pp 52–6.

8. Hanham, *Nineteenth Century Constitution*, pp 401–5.

9. J Hart, 'Reform of the Borough Police 1835–1856', *English Historical Review*, 70 (1955), pp 425–27; Hart *British Police*, pp 28–9, 31–2, 34; J Hart, 'The County and Borough Act 1956', *Public Administration*, 34 (1956) pp 405–17; H Parris, 'The Home Office and the Provincial Police in England and Wales 1856–1870', *Public Law* (1961), pp 230–55.

10. Seeley, *Expansion of England*, p 8; J S Galbraith, 'Myths of the "Little England" Era', *American Historical Review*, 67 (1962), pp 34–48; Knorr, *British Colonial Theories*, Cass, pp 246–47; Woodruff, *Men who ruled India*, 1, p 200.

11. Fieldhouse, *Colonial Empires*, pp 246, 248; Mill, *Representative Government*, p 377; Lucas ed., *Lord Durham's Report*, 2, pp 281–82; Graham, *Concise History of British Empire*, p 263; R A Huttenback, 'Indians in South Africa 1860–1914: the British Imperial Philosophy on Trial', *English Historical Review*, 81 (1968), pp 273–91.

12. H H Dodwell, 'The Development of Sovereignty in British India' in *Cambridge History of British Empire*, 4, p 593; W Foster, 'The India Board (1784–1858)', *Transactions of the Royal Historical Society*, 3rd series, 11 (1917), pp 61–85; Foster, *East India House*, pp 195–204, 207, 209, 213–14, 218–24; Harrod, *Life of Keynes*, p 122. Harrod added: 'This was no doubt a Keynesian exaggeration'.

13. Anderson, *Administrative Technique in Public Services*, p 6; Wheeler-Bennett, *John Anderson*, pp 16–19; Fiddes, *Dominions and Colonial Offices*, pp 9–10; Young, *Colonial Office*, p 3; MacDonagh, *Pattern of Government Growth;* O O G M MacDonagh, 'Emigration and the State 1833–55'; an Essay in Administrative History', *Transactions of the Royal Historical Society*, 5th series, 5 (1955), pp 133–59; and his 'Delegated Legislation and Administrative Discretions in the 1850s: a Particular Study', *Victorian Studies*, 2 (1958–59), pp 29–44; R C Snelling and T J Barron, 'The Colonial Office and its Permanent Officials 1801–1914' in Sutherland ed., *Studies in Nineteenth Century Government*, pp 139–66; J A Cross, *The Dominions Department of the Colonial Office: Origins and Early Years 1905–14*, University of London Doctoral Thesis, 1965; Heussler, *Yesterday's Rulers*, pp 3–5; Jeffries, *Colonial Empire and Civil Service*, p 6. The Colonial Office tended for most of the century to be staffed by people with no personal experience of the colonies. Sir Robert Herbert was a distinguished exception when Permanent Under Secretary (J R M Butler, 'Imperial Questions in British Politics 1868–1880', *Cambridge History of British Empire*, 3, p 32).

14. Sir O A R Murray, 'The Admiralty—I' *The Mariner's Mirror*, 23 (1937), pp 17, 28–9; Salter, *Memoirs of a Public Servant*, pp 34–50;

W Ashworth, 'Economic Aspects of Late Victorian Naval Administration', *Economic History Review*, 2nd series, 22 (1969), pp 491–505.

15. Anderson, *Liberal State at War*, pp 67–8; Hamer, *British Army*, pp ix, 8; Gordon, *War Office*, pp 51–5; A V Tucker, 'Army and Society in England 1870–1900: A Reassessment of the Cardwell Reforms', *Journal of British Studies*, 2 (1963), pp 110–41.

16. Johnson, *Defence by Committee*, pp 11–123; Hamer, *British Army*, pp 223–63; Gooch, *Plans of War*, pp 52–130, 299–330.

17. Howard, *Britain and Casus Belli*, p 163; Howard, *Splendid Isolation*, pp 96–7; O Furley, 'The Humanitarian Impact' in Bartlett ed., *Britain Pre-Eminent*, pp 128–51.

18. V Cromwell and Z Steiner, 'The Foreign Office before 1914: A Study in Resistance' in Sutherland ed., *Studies in Nineteenth Century Government*, pp 167–94; Jones, *Nineteenth Century Foreign Office*, pp 111–35, 144–45; Tilley and Gaselee, *Foreign Office*, p 124; Z Steiner, 'Last Years of the Old Foreign Office 1898–1905', *Historical Journal*, 6 (1963), pp 59–90.

19. S T Bindoff, 'The Unreformed Diplomatic Service 1812–60', *Transactions of the Royal Historical Society*, 4th series, 18 (1935), pp 143–72; Jones, *Nineteenth Century Foreign Office*, pp 136–42.

20. Yet one notes that Stratford de Redcliffe did not believe this (A Cecil, 'The Foreign Office' in *Cambridge History of British Empire*, 3, p 598).

21. Steiner, *Foreign Office and Foreign Policy*, pp 21–2.

22. Roseveare, *Treasury*, pp 138–42.

23. *Royal Commission on the Civil Establishments* (1888), *Minutes of Evidence of the Second Report*, questions 10,623, 10,705 and 10,709.

24. M Wright, 'Treasury Control 1854–1914' in Sutherland ed., *Studies in Nineteenth Century Government*, pp 195–226.

25. M Jack, 'The Purchase of the British Government's Shares in the British Petroleum Company 1912–1914', *Past and Present*, no 39 (1968), pp 139–68; Churchill, *World Crisis*, 1, pp 134–35, 172. Churchill gave his reasons for the venture in the relevant debate in 1914 (63 H.C. Deb 5s, c. 1131–53).

26. Robinson, *British Post Office*, p 221; Kieve, *Electric Telegraph*, pp 119–75; A Hazlewood, 'The Origin of the State Telephone Service in Britain', *Oxford Economic Papers*, N.S., 5 (1953), pp 13–25; R Nottage, 'The Post Office: A pioneer of Big Business', *Public Administration*, 37 (1959), pp 55–64.

27. Finer, *Municipal Trading*, pp 36–7; Chaloner, *People and Industries*, p 128; M E Falkus, 'The British Gas Industry before 1850', *Economic History Review*, 2nd series, 20 (1967), pp 494–508; Clapham, *Economic History of Modern Britain*, 3, pp 440, 443.

28. Habakkuk, *Industrial Organization*, pp 4–5; Clapham, *Economic History of Modern Britain*, 1, pp 202–3, 205; 2, pp 151, 301; 3, pp 213, 302; P L Payne, 'The Emergence of the Large Scale Company in Great Britain 1870–1914', *Economic History Review*, 2nd series, 20 (1967),

pp 519–42; Macrosty, *Trust Movement in British Industry*, p 345; Hunt, *Development of Business Corporation*, pp 94, 134–36.

29. The view is that of Prouty, *Transformation of Board of Trade*, pp 1–12. Prouty did not seem to appreciate that Free Trade was an act of *laissez-faire*.

30. Llewellyn Smith, *Board of Trade*, pp 147–224.

31. Llewellyn Smith, *Board of Trade*, pp 90–146, 174–80; Cleveland-Stevens, *English Railways*, p 117; Dyos and Aldcroft, *British Transport*, p 134; Parris, *Government and Railways*, pp 28, 220–21.

32. A L Dakyns, 'The Water Supply of English Towns in 1846', *Manchester School*, 2 (1931), pp 18–26; Chantler, *British Gas Industry*, p 86; Ballin, *Organization of Electricity Supply*, pp 4–15; W A Robson, 'The Public Utility Services' in Laski, Jennings and Robson eds., *Century of Municipal Progress*, pp 299–331.

33. V L Allen, 'The Origins of Industrial Conciliation and Arbitration', *International Review of Social History*, 9 (1964), pp 237–54; J H Porter, 'Wage Bargaining under Conciliation Agreements 1860–1914', *Economic History Review*, 2nd series, 23 (1970), pp 460–75; Phelps Brown, *Growth of Industrial Relations*, p 203; Allen, *Trade Unions and Government*, pp 121–23.

34. R Davidson, 'Llewellyn Smith, the Labour Department and Government Growth 1886–1909' in Sutherland ed., *Studies in Nineteenth Century Government*, pp 227–62; Harris, *William Beveridge*, pp 108–97; Beveridge, *Power and Influence*, pp 66–75; R Churchill, *Winston Churchill*, 2, pp 281–9, 296–315; B B Gilbert, 'Winston Churchill versus the Webbs: the Origins of British Unemployment Insurance', *American Historical Review*, 71 (1966), pp 846–62.

35. Platt, *Finance, Trade and Politics*, pp 371–81.

36. Ibid., pp 381–87.

37. Djang, *Factory Inspection*, pp 26–66; B Martin, 'Leonard Horner: a Portrait of an Inspector of Factories', *International Review of Social History*, 14 (1969), pp 412–43; O MacDonagh, 'Coal Mines Regulation: the First Decade 1842–1852' in Robson ed., *Ideas and Institutions*, pp 58–86; R K Webb, 'A Whig Inspector', *Journal of Modern History*, 27 (1955), pp 352–64; and also Tremenheere's own story, *I was There*.

38. Orwin and Whetham, *History of British Agriculture*, pp 178–202.

39. Kier Hardie, for example, was opposed to unemployment insurance and labour exchanges. The Labour Movement was divided over unemployment insurance (Gilbert, *Evolution of National Insurance*, p 256; Brown *Labour and Unemployment*, pp 129, 144–59).

40. Webbs, *English Local Government*, 8, p 1; Finer, *Chadwick*, p 88.

41. Ibid., pp 96–207; (Majority) *Report of the Royal Commission on the Poor Laws and Relief of Distress* (Cd. 4499, 1909), part 4, chapter 1.

42. Webbs, *English Local Government*, 8, pp 81–22, 224–26, 242.

43. D Fraser, 'Introduction' and A Paterson, 'The Poor Law in Nineteenth Century Scotland', in Fraser ed., *New Poor Law in Nineteenth Century*, pp 16–17, 171–93.

44. Brockington, *Public Health in Nineteenth Century*, pp 1–135;

Finer, *Chadwick*, pp 209–487; Lewis, *Chadwick*, pp 319–75; R Lambert, 'Central and Local Relations in Mid-Victorian England: the Local Government Act Office 1858–71', *Victorian Studies*, 6 (1962–63), pp 121–150.

45. Lambert, *Sir John Simon*, pp 606–7; Simon, *English Sanitary Institutions*, pp 299–300; Redlich and Hirst, *English Local Government*, pp 155, 159–60.

46. Simon, *English Sanitary Institutions*, pp 353–432; W A Ross, 'Local Government Board and After: Retrospect', *Public Administration*, 34 (1956), pp 17–18.

47. Milne, *Scottish Office*, p 213.

48. Gosden, *Development of Educational Administration*, pp 1–99.

49. Morant's contribution remains controversial. The absence of a scholarly biography and the advocates of Michael Sadler's claims help to ensure that. Hostilities are ably surveyed by D N Chester, 'Robert Morant and Michael Sadler', *Public Administration*, 28 (1950), pp 109–16.

50. Milne, *Scottish Office*, p 214.

51. Bunbury ed., *Lloyd George's Ambulance Wagon*, pp 63–4, 82–90; Gilbert, *Evolution of National Insurance*, pp 289–447.

52. The reluctance with which the Government gave a promise of support in the Baring Crisis of 1890 (Clapham, *Bank of England*, 2, pp 330–35) was an indication of the extent to which it thought that the banking system was for the Bank of England to independently manage. The interpretation of the Gold Standard is reflective of de Cecco, *Money and Empire*, and W N Scammell, 'The Working of the Gold Standard', *Yorkshire Bulletin of Economic and Social Research*, 17 (1965–66), pp 32–4.

53. As regards trade this is not to say that Britain was above the acts of neo-colonialism of the kind that took place in China (Fairbank, Reischauer and Craig, *East Asia*, pp 177, 340, 714) and Turkey (Ward and Rustow eds., *Modernization in Japan and Turkey*, pp 153–54, 457–58). The notion that Britain had an 'informal Empire' (which dates from Fay, *Imperial Economy*, p 46) is of limited utility except when itself treated informally as a reminder, if such is needed, that British economic activity was not even mainly confined in the nineteenth century to those areas which were formally hers. Britain did practise Free Trade within her own Empire, which made that unique among empires.

54. M Flinn, 'Introduction' in Stewart and Jenkins, *Medical and Legal Aspects of Sanitary Reform*, pp 8–9; Gauldie, *Cruel Habitations*, pp 302, 305. Even such an active local authority as Glasgow provided accommodation for no more than 1 per cent of its population in 1914 (S D Chapman, 'Introduction' in Chapman ed., *History of Working Class Housing*, pp 11–12).

55. T W Fowle, *The Poor Law*, p 142 (q.v. Webbs, *English Local Government*, 8, p 100); *Poor Law Commissioners' Report of 1834* (Cmd. 2728, 1909), p 263; N McCord, 'The Poor Law and Philanthropy' in Fraser ed., *New Poor Law in Nineteenth Century*, p 100; Henderson, *Lancashire Cotton Famine*, p 68; Owen, *English Philanthropy*, p 213.

56. Schaffer, *The Administrative Factor*, Frank Cass, p 3.

57. Hanham, *Nineteenth Century Constitution*, p 376; Redlich and Hirst, *History of Local Government*, pp 116–38, 179–221; J P D Dunbabin, 'The Politics of the Establishment of County Councils', *Historical Journal*, 6 (1963), pp 226–52, and 'The Expectations of the New County Councils and their Realization', Ibid., 8 (1965), pp 353–79.

58. Smellie, *History of Local Government*, pp 27–8; E P Hennock, 'Finance and Politics in Urban Local Government in England 1835–1900', *Historical Journal*, 6 (1963), pp 224–25; (Majority) *Report of the Royal Commission on the Poor Laws and Relief of Distress* (Cd. 4499, 1909), Part 4, Chapter 1, paras 8, 41.

59. H J Hanham, 'The Creation of the Scottish Office', *Juridical Review*, N.S., 10 (1965), pp 205–44.

60. Parris, *Constitutional Bureaucracy*, pp 22–4, 27, 49; H T Manning 'Who ran the British Empire 1830–1850?', *Journal of British Studies*, 5 (1965), pp 88–121 (and also Knaplund's biography and Galbraith, *Reluctant Empire*); Finer, *Chadwick*, p 143; Brown, *Board of Trade*, pp 208–13.

61. Dale, *Higher Civil Service*, pp 96–7, 212–15. See also the remarks on Morant on p 153.

62. M Abramovitz and V Eliasberg, 'The Trend of Public Employment in Great Britain and the United States', *American Economic Review, Papers and Proceedings*, 43 (1953), pp 205–12.

Chapter 7: The Machinery and Functions of Twentieth Century Government 1914–1939

1. Johnson, *Land Fit for Heroes*, p 299.

2. Daalder, *Cabinet Reform*, pp 49–50; Hankey, *Supreme Command*, pp 582–91; Roskill, *Hankey*, 1, pp 337–46, 353–54.

3. The Conservatives, of course, were well placed to win in 1918 anyway. They had fought the patriotic fight, but, unlike in 1939, they had not led the country into war. In 1945, the Conservatives were overdue for an electoral defeat. In 1918, they were overdue for a victory. The actual result was complex (R Douglas, 'A Classification of Members of Parliament elected in 1918', *Bulletin of Historical Research*, 47, 1974, pp 74–94). The expansion of the electorate has been neglected as an explanation of the demise of the Liberals (H G C Matthew, R I McKibbin, J A Kay, 'The Franchise Factor in the Rise of the Labour Party', *English Historical Review*, 91, 1976, pp 723–52). The evidence that the advent of Labour was inevitable remains inconclusive.

4. Vansittart, *Mist Procession*, p 444.

5. For example, Baldwin's remark in a neglected part of his famous 'appalling frankness' speech in 1936 (317 H.C. Deb. 5s. c. 1143).

6. Laski, *Parliamentary Government*, pp 93–110.

7. Ibid., pp 317–19; Cole ed., *Beatrice Webb's Diaries 1924–32*, p 9; Ministry of Reconstruction, *Report of the* (Haldane) *Machinery of Government Committee*, Cd. 9320 (1918), part 1, paras 1–2; Cole ed.,

Beatrice Webb's Diaries 1912–24, pp 97–8, 137–8; Haldane Report, part 1, paras 55–6, 7, 9, 6; W J M Mackenzie, 'The Structure of Central Administration' in Campion *et al, British Government since 1918,* pp 59–60.

8. F Stack, 'Civil Service Associations and the Whitley Report of 1917', *Political Quarterly,* 40 (1969), pp 283–95; the contribution of the Reorganization Committee is assessed by Fry, *Statesmen in Disguise,* p 40; *Tomlin Report* (Cmd. 3909, 1931), paras 229–34.

9. For Trevelyan's remarks see Fry, *Statesmen in Disguise,* pp 49, 56–7. The cult of the generalist was derived from Macaulay. For Fisher's 'musical chairs' comment see *Tomlin evidence,* question 18,556.

10. This is, of course, part of the famous thesis of Dangerfield, *Strange Death of Liberal England.*

11. Renshaw, *General Strike,* pp 128–33; Wheeler-Bennett, *John Anderson,* pp 83–117.

12. Critchley, *History of Police,* pp 203–9; Critchley, *Conquest of Violence,* pp 194–97. The trend towards legislation is evident from the table in Brownlie, *Law Relating to Public Order,* pp xiii–xviii.

13. *Whitaker's Almanack* (1921), pp 480, 483; Graham, *Concise History of British Empire,* pp 263–67; Mansergh, *Commonwealth Experience,* pp 269–94.

14. Amery, *My Political Life,* 2, pp 335–70; Woodruff, *Men who ruled India,* 2, pp 271–72, 348–61; G C Abbott, 'A Re-examination of the 1929 Colonial Development Act', *Economic History Review,* 2nd series, 24 (1971), pp 68–81.

15. Lloyd George, *War Memoirs,* 1, pp 242–44; Morgan, *Lloyd George,* p 53.

16. Derry, *Radical Tradition,* p 387; F Lloyd George, *Years that are Past,* pp 86–7.

17. The tale was told with special relish by Taylor, *English History 1914–45,* pp 84–5.

18. Jones, *Lloyd George,* p. 112.

19. Snow, *Variety of Men,* pp 97–8; Churchill, *Second World War,* 1, pp 57–8; Middlemas and Barnes, *Baldwin,* pp 781–83; Rhodes James, *Memoirs of a Conservative,* pp 405–6; Roskill, *Hankey,* 3, p 207, argued that Inskip's reputation for ineptitude was unfair. Such a revised estimate may be needed. The notion that Baldwin was the prime mover for rearmament rather than Neville Chamberlain remains to be further substantiated.

20. This is not to say that Britain was unprepared. The Regular Army was 'small but of high quality' (Liddell Hart, *History of the Second World War,* p 18). The Expeditionary Force was 'the first occasion on which a wholly mechanised army was despatched overseas' (Ellis, *War in France and Flanders,* p 9).

21. Feiling, *Neville Chamberlain,* pp 253–54; Middlemas and Barnes, *Baldwin,* p 840; 339 H.C. Deb. 5s. c. 359–60.

22. A Cecil, 'The Foreign Office' in *Cambridge History of British Foreign Policy,* 3, p 619; C Larner, 'The Amalgamation of the Diplomatic

Service with the Foreign Office', *Journal of Contemporary History*, 7 (1972) part 1, pp 107–26; Z Steiner and M Dockrill, 'The Foreign Office Reforms 1919–21', *Historical Journal*, 16 (1974), pp 131–56.

23. There is an assessment of Fisher in Fry, *Statesmen in Disguise*, pp 52–5. Fisher was given to imperialistic behaviour as Head of the Civil Service (such as when, in 1922, he tried to annex the Cabinet Secretariat to the Treasury: Roskill, *Hankey*, 2, pp 309–20). The Foreign Office, used to independence, resented such behaviour. Nevertheless, my subsequent researches indicate that Fisher's views on rearmament and Appeasement were fairly represented in his article, 'The Beginnings of Civil Defence', *Public Administration*, 26 (1948), pp 212–13.

24. Sir H P Hamilton, 'Sir Warren Fisher and the Public Service', *Public Administration*, 29 (1951), pp 3–38.

25. *Sixteenth Report of the Select Committee on National Expenditure* (1941–42), Section 4, para 56; Hicks, *Finance of British Government*, p 28.

26. Harrod, *Life of Keynes*, pp 421–23; Daalder, *Cabinet Reform*, pp 206–7, 209, 238. The Bank of England's role is authoritatively described in the standard history by Sayers. The controversies surrounding that role are well brought out in Hugh Gaitskell's remarkds on the Bank Rate and on Czech gold in the nationalization debate in 1945 (415 H.C. Deb. 5s. c. 85–6).

27. Churchill, *Great Contemporaries*, p 229; Amery, *My Political Life*, 2, p 502; Skidelsky, *Politicians and the Slump*, pp 101–4, 188–89; Mosley, *My Life*, pp 231–34.

28. Ince, *Ministry of Labour*, pp 35–40; R Lowe, 'The Ministry of Labour 1916–1924: A Graveyard of Social Reform?', *Public Administration*, 52 (1974), pp 415–38; E Briggs and A J Deacon, 'The Creation of the Unemployment Assistance Board', *Policy and Politics*, 2 (1973–74), pp 43–62.

29. Llewellyn Smith, *Board of Trade*, pp 82, 85, 156, 277; T M Varcoe, 'Scientists, Government and Organized Research in Great Britain: the Early History of the D.S.I.R.', *Minerva*, 8 (1970), pp 192–216; Jenkins, *Ministry of Transport*, p 35; P Byrd, 'Regional and Functional Specialization in the British Consular Service', *Journal of Contemporary History*, 7 (1972), part 1, pp 127–45.

30. Winnifrith, *Ministry of Agriculture*, pp 25–6; Giddings, *Marketing Boards and Ministers*, pp 6–8.

31. Indeed, the Post Office was subject to a great deal of criticism, which led to the Bridgeman Committee of Inquiry (Cmd. 4149, 1932). The Post Office lumbered on.

32. Gordon, *Public Corporation in Britain*, pp 84–92.

33. Middlemas and Barnes, *Baldwin*, pp 393–94; 193 H.C. Deb. 5s. c. 1713, 1794, 1871; Gordon, *Public Corporation in Britain*, pp 98–9.

34. Ibid., p 113; 295 H.C. Deb. 5s. c. 1947–48.

35. 250 H.C. Deb. 5s. c. 66–7; *The Times,* January 16th 1926; Hanson ed., *Nationalization*, pp 12, 82, 83; Liberal Party, *Britain's Industrial Future*, p 77; 250 H.C. Deb. 5s. c. 55–7, 59; 349 H.C. Deb. 5s. c. 1831.

The Conservative position on nationalization had its confusions: for example, the remarks of the Attorney General in 1926 when he saw the creation of the Central Electricity Board as frustrating nationalization (193 H.C. Deb. 5s. c. 1947–48).

36. H R G Greaves, 'Post-War Machinery of Government. 7—Public Boards and Corporations', *Political Quarterly*, 16 (1945), pp 70–1; and Morrison's remarks in 250 H.C. Deb. 5s. c. 67.

37. Gosden, *Development of Educational Administration*, pp 108–12; Johnson, *Homes Fit for Heroes*, pp 80, 81, 84–5, 96, 116, 136, 151–2, 175–76, 184–86, 231, 239–40, 286, 288–9, 338, 340, 342, 353, 418.

38. Feiling, *Neville Chamberlain*, pp 126–48; B Keith-Lucas, 'Poplarism', *Public Law* (1962), pp 52–80; G W Jones, 'Herbert Morrison and Poplarism', Ibid., (1973), pp 11–31.

39. Chester and Willson, *Organization of Central Government*, pp 26, 249–63; H V Wiseman, 'Parliament and the University Grants Committee', *Public Administration*, 34 (1956), pp 75–92.

40. The slogan 'back to 1914' seems to have been coined in August 1918 by Lord Inchcape (31 H.L. Ded. 5s. c. 373).

41. Morgan, *Studies in British Financial Policy*, pp 59–66, 375; Pigou, *Aspects of British Economic History*, p 126.

42. Mitchell, *British Historical Statistics*, p 249; Shirras and Rostas, *Burden of British Taxation*, p xi; Peacock and Wiseman, *Growth of Public Expenditure*, p 164.

43. A E Booth and S Glynn, 'Unemployment in the Inter-War Period: A Multiple Problem', *Journal of Contemporary History*, 10 (1975), pp 611–36; J A Dowie, 'Growth in the Inter-War Period: Some More Arithmetic', *Economic History Review*, 2nd series, 21 (1968), pp 93–112; and Richardson, *Economic Recovery in Britain*.

44. The State was forced into the arena of industrial relations by the strike wave that persisted through the war, and was not really to abate until the failure of the General Strike in 1926. Once this was settled, and the Trade Disputes Act of the following year passed, government relapsed into a less participatory role. For an example see G W McDonald and H F Gospel, 'The Mond-Turner Talks 1927–1933: A Study of Industrial Co-operation', *Historical Journal*, 16 (1973), pp 807–29.

45. Scott, *Vickers*, pp 163–68. Although the Bank of England had participated in earlier 'rationalization' exercises in the iron and steel, cotton textiles and armaments industries, its general involvement in what was seen as industrial reconstruction seems to have been fairly limited before 1930 when, with other banks, it formed the Bankers' Industrial Development Company (Clay, *Lord Norman*, pp 318–59).

46. K J Hancock, 'The Reduction of Unemployment as a Problem of Public Policy 1920–29', *Economic History Review*, 2nd series, 15 (1962–63), pp 328–43. The government departments' reply to the Yellow Book was contained in Cmd. 3331 (1928).

47. Daalder, *Cabinet Reform in Britain*, pp 204–7; Sir R Hopkins, 'Introductory Note' in Chester ed., *Lessons of British War Economy*, p 3; and Howson and Winch, *Economic Advisory Council*. The view that

Snowden, and, hence, the MacDonald Government pursued a 'policy of negation' (Skidelsky, *Politicians and the Slump*, p 388) is disputed by R McKibbin, 'The Economic Policy of the Second Labour Government 1929–1931', *Past and Present*, no 68 (1975), pp 95–123.

48. Feiling, *Neville Chamberlain*, p 229.

49. Spender, *Great Britain, Empire and Commonwealth*, pp 797–812; Sir B Blackett, 'The Era of Planning' in Taylor ed., *Great Events in History*, pp 855–920.

50. In the inter-war period, over a quarter of the houses built in England and Wales (Bowley, *Housing and the State*, p 271) and about two-thirds of those built in Scotland (Department of Health for Scotland, *Annual Report for 1938*, Cmd. 5969, 1939, p 177) were constructed by the local authorities who had previously built as well as owned virtually none.

51. P.E.P., *British Social Services*, p 139. The term was first officially used in the 'Drage Return' of expenditure in 1920 (Ibid., p 36).

52. MacAdam, *The New Philanthropy*, p 18.

53. When Churchill outlined the 1925 scheme in his Budget Speech, he revealed that the Exchequer contribution was designed to equal the estimated annual fall in the cost of war pensions in the coming decade. Thus, during this period there could be no increase in total Exchequer pensions expenditure. In fact, the annual Exchequer contribution was estimated at rather less than the annual war pensions expenditure. Thus, over the ten year period annual pensions expenditure was expected to fall by £9 millions per annum (P M Williams, *The Development of Old Age Pensions Policy in Great Britain 1878–1925*, University of London Doctoral Thesis, 1970, p 444). A contemporary Civil Servant was later to suggest that the Conservatives need not have worried about the Labour Party trumping their ace, because that Party was divided over the contributory principle, with Snowden in favour of it (Walley, *Social Security*, p 60). What the Conservatives feared seems to have been a non-contributory pension financed by a capital levy (Gilbert, *British Social Policy*, p 235).

54. Walley, *Social Security*, pp 41, 48, 53, 58–60, 62–63.

Chapter 8: The Machinery and Functions of Twentieth Century Government from 1939

1. Titmuss, *Problems of Social Policy*, p 506; *Social Insurance and Allied Services* (Cmd. 6404, 1942), paras 19, 30, 31; B.I.P.O., *Beveridge Report and the Public*, pp 10–11; Harris, *William Beveridge*, pp 378–451; Beveridge, *Power and Influence*, p 330. A secret Conservative Party Report on the Beveridge Plan, completed in January 1943, was certainly hostile to Beveridge. It was said by its Chairman to represent the views of 90 per cent of Conservative MPs. What many Conservatives objected to was the redistributive nature of the scheme, involving continuing high rates of taxation. A majority of the Committee concerned favoured

family allowances and for all children (H Kopsch, *The Approach of the Conservative Party to Social Policy during World War II*, University of London Doctoral Thesis, 1970, pp 90–209, 392–96). Nevertheless, in the Conservative Party, the Leader decides policy. The Coalition Government eventually made the commitments. It can be noted that the Churchill Caretaker Government introduced a Bill to carry out the agreed proposals for industrial injuries insurance. A contemporary Civil Servant has since written that he has heard it said that Churchill had done this at the request of Bevin as an indication that the Conservatives would implement the Coalition's social insurance plans if re-elected (Walley, *Social Security*, p 85).

2. Sayers, *Financial Policy*, p 95; Hancock and Gowing, *British War Economy*, p 542; *Employment Policy* (Cmd. 6527, 1944), pp 4–5, 18–19, 28; T Balogh, 'The International Aspect' in Worswick and Ady eds., *British Economy 1945–50*, p 499.

3. Ibid., pp 477–88; P D Henderson, 'Britain's International Position', Ibid., p 65; Dalton, *High Tide and After*, pp 73–5; Dow, *Management of the British Economy*, p 18.

4. Blank, *Industry and Government*, p 30; P J D Wiles, 'Pre-War and Wartime Controls' in Worswick and Ady eds., *British Economy 1945–50*, p 158; Bullock, *Ernest Bevin*, 1, p 654; Ibid., 2, pp 3–5.

5. Anderson, *Machinery of Government*, p 31; *The Reorganization of Central Government* (Cmd. 4506, 1970), pp 13–14; *Report of the Public Inquiry ordered by the Minister of Agriculture into the disposal of land at Crichel Down* (Cmd. 9176, 1954); G K Fry, 'Thoughts on the Present State of the Convention of Ministerial Responsibility', *Parliamentary Affairs*, 23 (1969–70), pp 10–20.

6. *The Parliamentary Commissioner for Administration* (Cmnd. 2767, 1965); G K Fry, 'The Sachsenhausen Concentration Camp Case and the Convention of Ministerial Responsibility', *Public Law* (1970), pp 336–57; *The Civil Service. Report of the* (Fulton) *Committee 1966–68* (Cmd. 3638, 1968); G K Fry, 'Some Weaknesses in the Fulton Report on the British Civil Service', *Political Studies*, 17 (1969), pp 484–94.

7. Chester and Willson, *Organization of Central Government*, p 356; *Final Report of the* (Willink) *Royal Commission on the Police* (Cmd. 1728, 1962); *Report of the* (Beeching) *Royal Commission on Assizes and Quarter Sessions* (Cmd. 4153, 1969).

8. Furse, *Aucuparius*, pp 267–309; Heussler, *Yesterday's Rulers*, pp 192, 202; J A Cross, 'The Beginning and End of the Commonwealth Office', *Public Administration*, 47 (1969), pp 113–19.

9. *Central Organization for Defence* (Cmd. 2097, 1963); Howard, *Central Organization for Defence; Government Organization for Defence Procurement and Civil Aerospace* (Cmnd. 4641, 1970).

10. *Proposals for the Reform of the Foreign Service* (Cmd. 6420, 1943); F T A Ashton-Gwatkin, 'Reform of the Foreign Service', *Public Administration*, 21 (1943), pp 82–4; *Report of the* (Plowden) *Committee on Representational Services Overseas* (Cmnd. 2276, 1964); *Report of the* (Duncan) *Review Committee on Overseas Representation* (Cmnd. 4107,

1969); C Larner, 'The Organization and Structure of the Foreign and Commonwealth Office' in Boardman and Groom eds., *Management of External Relations,* pp 31–71. Lord Avon assured me in 1969 that the Fisher experience was not a factor in the 1943 reform proposals.

11. Bridges, *Treasury,* pp 169–79.

12. D N Chester, 'The Treasury, 1956', *Public Administration,* 35, (1957), pp 15–23; D N Chester, 'The Treasury, 1962', Ibid., 40 (1962), pp 419–26; *Control of Public Expenditure,* Cmnd. 1432 (1961); D N Chester *et al,* 'The Plowden Report', *Public Administration,* 41 (1963), pp 3–50; Heclo and Wildavsky, *Private Government of Public Money; Cash Limits on Public Expenditure* (Cmnd. 6440, 1976); C Pollitt, 'The Public Expenditure Survey 1961–72' and M Wright, 'Public Expenditure in Britain: The Crisis of Control', *Public Administration,* 55 (1977), pp 127–69.

13. Dow, *Management of British Economy,* pp 13–14, 27; Chester ed., *Lessons of British War Economy;* D N Chester, 'Machinery of Government and Planning' in Worswick and Ady eds., *British Economy 1945–50,* pp 336–64.

14. Daalder, *Cabinet Reform,* pp 224–25; Butler, *Art of the Possible,* pp 154–82; H Phelps Brown, 'The National Economic Development Organization', *Public Administration,* 41 (1963), pp 239–46; Brittan, *Steering the Economy,* pp 187–290; J Knapp and K Lomax, 'Britain's Growth Performance: The Enigma of the 1950s', *Lloyd's Bank Review,* no 74 (1964), pp 1–24.

15. Sir E Roll *et al,* 'The Machinery for Economic Planning', *Public Administration,* 44 (1966), pp 1–72; Brittan, *Steering the Economy,* pp 291–415.

16. Grove, *Government and Industry,* pp 85–8; Wilson, *Labour Government 1964–70,* pp 8–9; M E Beesley and G M White, 'The Industrial Reorganization Corporation: A Study in Choice of Public Management', *Public Administration,* 51 (1973), pp 61–89; *The Reorganization of Central Government* (Cmnd. 4506, 1970), pp 7–9.

17. Grove, *Government and Industry,* pp 88–9, 200–16, 361–81; Wilson, *Labour Government 1964–70,* pp 521–22; *The Reorganization of Central Government* (Cmnd. 4506, 1970), p 8.

18. Chester, *Nationalization of British Industry,* p 20.

19. Dalton, *High Tide and After,* pp 32–50.

20. Shinwell, *Conflict Without Malice,* p 172.

21. 423 H.C. Deb. 5s. c. 46–8; 418 H.C. Deb. 5s. c. 798, 969; D N Chester, 'The Nationalized Industries', *Three Banks Review* (1952), p 43.

22. Robson ed., *Problems of Nationalized Industry,* p 310; Robson, *Nationalized Industry and Public Ownership,* p 145; D N Chester, 'The Nationalized Industries', *Three Banks Review* (1952), p 42.

23. D N Chester, 'Note on the Price Policy indicated by the Nationalization Acts', *Oxford Economic Papers,* N.S., 2 (1950), pp 67–74.

24. Hanson, *Parliament and Public Ownership,* pp 217–18; H A Clegg, 'The Fleck Report', *Public Administration,* 33 (1955), pp 269–75; *Report*

of the (Herbert) *Committee of Inquiry into the Electricity Supply Industry,* Cmnd. 9672 (1956), paras. 372–73; *First Report from the Select Committee on Nationalized Industries* (1967–68), para. 282; *The Financial and Economic Obligations of the Nationalized Industries* (Cmnd. 1337, 1961); *Nationalized Industries. A Review of Economic and Financial Objectives* (Cmnd. 3437, 1967).

25. *Reorganization of the Post Office* (Cmnd. 3233, 1967).

26. *Interim Report of a Court of Inquiry into a Dispute between the British Transport Commission and the National Union of Railwaymen* (Cmnd. 9352, 1955), para. 10.

27. Dalton, *High Tide and After,* p 358.

28. For a characteristic review see U Cormack, 'The Seebohm Committee Report—A Great State Paper', *Social and Economic Administration,* 3 (1969), pp 52–61.

29. *The Reorganization of Central Government* (Cmnd, 4506, 1970), pp 10–11.

30. Hall, Land, Parker and Webb, *Change, Choice and Conflict in Social Policy,* pp 410–71.

31. Terrill, *Tawney and his Times,* p 230.

32. J Viner, 'Mr Keynes on the Causes of Unemployment', *Quarterly Journal of Economics,* 51 (1936–37), p 149.

33. *Economic Trends,* no 268 (February 1976), p 120. The figure is for mid-1974.

34. C Sandford and A Robinson, 'Public Spending. A Decade of Unprecedented Peacetime Growth', *The Banker,* 125 (1975), pp 1241–55. The decade concerned is 1964–74 at the end of which—depending on the definition used—public expenditure represented either 49·3 per cent, 52·5 per cent or 56·2 per cent of the Gross National Product.

35. The State's losses in 'traditional' functions have been considerable. The Empire has been lost. Defence responsibilities are shared with NATO, and mainly met by the USA. Foreign policy is circumscribed by this alliance, and Britain's generally diminished economic importance. Internally, foreign ownership limits economic sovereignty as does membership of the European Economic Community. There is also Celtic nationalism which may not stop at devolution.

Select Bibliography

I General

Dicey, A V, *Lectures on the Relation between Law and Public Opinion in England during the Nineteenth Century,* 2nd edn. (1914)
Friedman, W, *Law in a Changing Society* (1959)
Galbraith, J K, *The New Industrial State,* 2nd edn. (1972)
Halévy, E, *A History of the English People in the Nineteenth Century,* 6 vols, 2nd edn. (1949–52: trans. E I Watkin and D A Barker)
Hayek, F A, *The Road to Serfdom* (1944)
Hayek, F A, *The Constitution of Liberty* (1960)
Myrdal, G, *Beyond the Welfare State* (1960)
Oakeshott, M J, *Political Education* (1951)
Polanyi, K, *The Origins of Our Time. The Great Transformation* (1945)
Popper, Sir K R, *The Poverty of Historicism,* 3rd edn. (1969)
Popper, Sir K R, *The Open Society and its Enemies,* 2 vols, 5th edn. (1966–74)
Schumpeter, J A, *Capitalism, Socialism and Democracy,* 5th edn. (1952)

II Changing Ideas about the role of Government since 1780

(i) *Texts*

Bentham, J, *Works,* 11 vols. (ed. J Bowring, 1838–43)
Bentham, J, *A Fragment on Government and An Introduction to the Principles of Morals and Legislation* (ed. W Harrison, 1948)
Bentham, J, *Economic Writings,* 3 vols. (ed. W Stark, 1952–54)
Bosanquet, B, *The Philosophical Theory of the State,* 3rd edn. (1920)
Burke, E, *Works,* 6 vols. (1883 edn.)
Cairnes, J E, *Essays in Political Economy. Theoretical and Applied* (1873)
Green, T H, *Works,* 3 vols. (ed. R L Nettleship, 1906)
Hume, D, *A Treatise on Human Nature* (ed. L A Selby-Bigge, 1888)
Hume, D, *Enquiries Concerning the Human Understanding and Concerning the Principles of Morals* (ed. L A Selby-Bigge, 1902)
Hume, D, *Writings on Economics* (ed. E Rotwein, 1955)
Jevons, W S, *The Theory of Political Economy,* 3rd edn. (1888)
Keynes, J M, *A Treatise on Money,* 2 vols. (1930)
Keynes, J M, *The General Theory of Employment, Interest and Money* (1936)
McCulloch, J R, *The Principles of Political Economy,* 2nd edn. (1843)
Malthus, T R, *An Essay on the Principle of Population* (1789 edn., ed. A Flew, 1970; 1826 edn., ed. G T Bettany, 1890)

Malthus, T R, *The Principles of Political Economy* (1836)
Marshall, A, *Industry and Trade*, 2nd edn. (1920)
Marshall, A, *Principles of Economics*, 8th edn. (1920: 1949 reprinting)
Marshall, A, *Money, Credit and Commerce* (1923)
Marx, K, *Capital*, 3 vols. (1906–33: trans. S Moore and E Aveling, and E Untermann)
Marx, K and Engels, F, *Manifesto of the Communist Party* (ed. H J Laski, 1948)
Mill, J, *An Essay on Government* (1824)
Mill, J, *Selected Economic Writings* (ed. D Winch, 1966)
Mill, J S, *Utilitarianism. On Liberty. Considerations on Representative Government* (ed. A D Lindsay, 1910)
Mill, J S, *Principles of Political Economy with Some of their Applications to Social Philosophy* (ed. W J Ashley, 1909)
Pigou, A C, *Wealth and Welfare* (1912)
Pigou, A C, *The Theory of Unemployment* (1933) (now Cass)
Pigou, A C, *The Economics of Welfare*, 4th edn. (1952)
Ricardo, D, *Works and Correspondence* (ed. P Sraffa, 1951–55)
Ritchie, D G, *Principles of State Interference* (1891)
Robinson, J, *The Economics of Imperfect Competition* (1933)
Senior, N W, *Industrial Efficiency and Social Efficiency* (ed. S L Levy, 1929)
Shaw, G B, ed., *Fabian Essays in Socialism* (1889)
Smith, A, *An Inquiry into the Nature and Causes of the Wealth of Nations*, 2 vols. (ed. E Cannan, 1904)
Smith, A, *The Theory of Moral Sentiments* (ed. D Stewart, 1869)
Smith, A, *Lectures on Justice, Police, Revenue and Arms* (ed. E Cannan, 1896)
Tawney, R H, *The Acquisitive Society* (1921)
Tawney, R H, *Equality*, 4th edn. (1952)

(ii) *Interpretative and Other Works*

Barker, E, *Political Thought in England 1848–1914* (1928)
Barker, (Sir) E, *Principles of Political and Social Theory* (1953)
Baumol, W J, *Welfare Economics and the Theory of the State* (1952)
Berlin, I, *Karl Marx. His Life and Environment*, 2nd edn. (1948)
Black, R D C, *Economic Thought and the Irish Question 1817–1870* (1960)
Black, R D C, Coates, A W, and Goodwin, C D W, eds., *The Marginal Revolution in Economics. Interpretation and Evaluation* (1973)
Blake, R, *Disraeli* (1966)
Blaug, M, *Ricardian Economics. A Historical Study* (1958)
Blaug, M, *Economic Theory in Retrospect*, 2nd edn. (1968)
Bowley, M, *Nassau Senior and Classical Economics* (1937)
Bowley, M, *Studies in the History of Economic Theory before 1870* (1973)
Boyle, Sir E, *Tory Democrat. Two Famous Disraeli Speeches* (1950)
Bryson, G E, *Man and Society. The Scottish Inquiry of the Eighteenth Century* (1945)

Bullock, A, and Shock, M, eds., *The Liberal Tradition. From Fox to Keynes* (1956)

Campbell, T D, *Adam Smith's Science of Morals* (1971)

Carlyle, T, *Critical and Miscellaneous Essays,* 6 vols. (1869)

Carpenter, L P, *G D H Cole. An Intellectual Biography* (1973)

Christensen, T, *Origin and History of Christian Socialism* (1962)

Clark, J M, *et al, Adam Smith 1776–1926* (1928)

Coats, A W, ed., *The Classical Economists and Economic Policy* (1971)

Cole, M, ed., *The Webbs and their Work* (1949)

Cole, M, *The Story of Fabian Socialism* (1961)

Corry, B A, *Money, Savings and Investment in English Economics 1800–1850* (1962)

Cowling, M, *Mill and Liberalism* (1963)

Cropsey, J, *Polity and Economy. An Interpretation of the Principles of Adam Smith* (1957)

Deane, H A, *The Political Ideas of Harold J Laski* (1955)

Disraeli, B, *Sybil or the Two Nations* (1845)

Disraeli, B, *Coningsby* (1853)

Everett, C W, *Jeremy Bentham* (1966)

Feuer, L, ed., *Marx and Engels. Basic Writings on Politics and Philosophy* (1969)

Freemantle, A, *This Little Band of Prophets. The British Fabians* (1959)

Friedman, M, *Essays in Positive Economics* (1953)

Friedman, M, *Price Theory. A Provisional Text* (1962) (now Cass)

Friedman, M, *The Optimum Quantity of Money and Other Essays* (1969)

Friedman, M, *The Counter-Revolution in Monetary Theory* (1970)

Glass, D V, ed., *Introduction to Malthus* (Frank Cass 1953)

Glass, S T, *The Responsible Society. The Ideas of Guild Socialism* (1966)

Grampp, W D, *The Manchester School of Economics* (1960)

Grampp, W D, *Economic Liberalism,* 2 vols. (1965)

Graubard, S R, *British Labour and the Russian Revolution 1917–1924* (1956)

Halévy, E, *The Growth of Philosophic Radicalism* (1952)

Harris, J F, *William Beveridge. A Biography* (1977)

Harris, S E, ed., *The New Economics. Keynes's Influence on Theory and Public Policy* (1947)

Harrison, J F C, *Robert Owen and the Owenites in Britain and America* (1969)

Harrod, R F, *The Life of John Maynard Keynes* (1951)

Hazlitt, H, ed., *The Critics of Keynesian Economics* (1960)

Heilbroner, R L, and Streeten, P, *The Great Economists. Their Lives and their Conceptions of the World* (1955)

Hicks, Sir J R, *The Crisis in Keynesian Economics* (1974)

Hla Myint, U, *Theories of Welfare Economics* (1948)

Hobhouse, L T, *Democracy and Reaction* (1904)

Hobhouse, L T, *Liberalism* (1911)

Hobhouse, L T, *Social Evolution and Political Theory* (1911)

Hobhouse, L T, *The Metaphysical Theory of the State. A Critique* (1918)

Hobhouse, L T, *The Elements of Social Justice* (1922)

Hobson, J A, *The Evolution of Modern Capitalism,* 2nd edn. (1906)

Hobson, J A, *The Crisis of Liberalism. New Issues of Democracy* (1909)

Hobson, J A, *The Economics of Unemployment,* 2nd edn. (1931)

Hobson, J A, *From Capitalism to Socialism* (1932)

Hobson, J A, *Imperialism. A Study,* 3rd edn. (1938)

Hobson, J A, and Ginsberg, M, *L T Hobhouse. His Life and Work* (1931)

Hollander, S, *The Economics of Adam Smith* (1973)

Hoselitz, B F, ed., *Theories of Economic Growth* (1960)

Houghton, W E, *The Victorian Frame of Mind 1830–1870* (1957)

Hutchison, T W, *A Review of Economic Doctrines 1870–1929* (1953)

Hutchison, T W, *'Positive' Economics and Policy Objectives* (1964)

Hutchison, T W, *Keynes vesus the 'Keynesians'* (1977)

Johnson, H G, *Money, Trade and Economic Growth* (1962)

Johnson, H G, *Essays in Monetary Economics* (1967)

Johnson, H G, *Inflation and the Monetarist Controversy* (1972)

Johnson, H G, *On Economics and Society* (1975)

Jones, P D'A, *The Christian Socialist Revival 1877–1914* (1968)

Kendall, W, *The Revolutionary Movement in Britain 1900–21* (1969)

Kerr, C, *Marshall, Marx and Modern Times. The Multi-Dimensional Society* (1969)

Keynes, J M, *The Economic Consequences of the Peace* (1919)

Keynes, J M, *A Revision of the Treaty* (1922)

Keynes, J M, *A Tract on Monetary Reform* (1923)

Keynes, J M, *A Short View of Russia* (1925)

Keynes, J M, *The Economic Consequences of Mr Churchill* (1925)

Keynes, J M, *The End of Laissez-Faire* (1926)

Keynes, J M, *Essays in Persuasion* (1931)

Keynes, J M, *Essays in Biography* (1933)

Keynes, J M, *The Means to Prosperity* (1933)

Keynes, J M, *How to Pay for the War* (1940)

Keynes, M, ed., *Essays on John Maynard Keynes* (1975)

Klein, L R, *The Keynesian Revolution,* 2nd edn. (1968)

Kurihara, K K, ed., *Post-Keynesian Economics* (1955)

Laski, H J, *Studies in Law and Politics* (1932)

Laski, H J, *The State in Theory and Practice* (1935)

Laski, H J, *The Rise of European Liberalism. An Essay in Interpretation* (1936)

Laski, H J, *The Decline of Liberalism* (1940)

Leijonhufvud, A, *On Keynesian Economics and the Economics of Keynes* (1968)

Lekachman, R, ed., *Keynes and the Classics* (1964)

Lekachman, R, ed., *Keynes's General Theory. Reports of Three Decades* (1964)

Lekachman, R, *The Age of Keynes* (1967)

Letwin, S R, *The Pursuit of Certainty. David Hume. Jeremy Bentham. John Stuart Mill. Beatrice Webb* (1965)

Letwin, W, *The Origins of Scientific Economics. English Economic Thought 1660–1776* (1963)

Levy, S L, *Nassau W Senior 1790–1864. Critical Essayist, Classical Economist and Adviser to Governments* (1970)

Little, I M D, *A Critique of Welfare Economics,* 2nd edn. (1957)

McBriar, A M, *Fabian Socialism and English Politics 1884–1918* (1962)

McCleary, G F, *The Malthusian Population Theory* (1953)

MacCunn, J, *Six Radical Thinkers* (1910)

MacFie, A L, *The Individual in Society. Papers on Adam Smith* (1967)

MacGregor, D H, *Economic Thought and Policy* (1949)

Mack, M P, *Jeremy Bentham. An Odyssey of Ideas 1748–1792* (1962)

McKibbin, R, *The Evolution of the Labour Party 1910–1924* (1974)

McLellan, D, *Marxism before Marx* (1970)

Manning, D J, *The Mind of Jeremy Bentham* (1968)

Marcet, J, *Conversations on Political Economy* (1836)

Martineau, H, *Illustrations on Political Economy,* 9 vols. (1832–42)

Martineau, H, *A History of the Thirty Years Peace A.D. 1816–1846,* 4 vols. (1877–78)

Meek, R L, *The Economics of Physiocracy* (1962)

Mill, J S, *Autobiography* (1873)

Milne, A J M, *The Social Philosophy of English Idealism* (1962)

Milner, A, *Arnold Toynbee. A Reminiscence.* (1895)

Moggridge, D E, ed., *Keynes: Aspects of the Man and his Work* (1974)

Myrdal, G, *The Political Element in the Development of Economic Theory* (1953)

Napoleoni, C, *Economic Thought in the Twentieth Century* (1972)

Nath, S K, *A Reappraisal of Welfare Economics* (1969)

O'Brien, D P, *J R McCulloch. A Study in Classical Economics* (1970)

O'Brien, D P, *The Classical Economists* (1975)

Pelling, H, ed., *The Challenge of Socialism* (1954)

Pigou, A C, ed., *Memorials of Alfred Marshall* (1925)

Pigou, A C, *Economics in Practice. Six Lectures on Current Issues* (1935)

Pigou, A C, *Socialism versus Capitalism* (1937)

Pigou, A C, *Keynes's General Theory. A Retrospective View* (1950)

Pigou, A C, *Alfred Marshall and Current Thought* (1953)

Plamenatz, J P, *The English Utilitarians,* 2nd edn. (1958)

Pollard, S, and Salt, J, eds., *Robert Owen. Prophet of the Poor* (1971)

Rae, J, *Life of Adam Smith* (1895)

Raven, C E, *Christian Socialism 1848–1854* (1920) (now Cass)

Read, D, *Cobden and Bright. A Victorian Political Partnership* (1967)

Richter, M, *The Politics of Conscience. T H Green and His Age* (1964)

Robbins, L C, *Essay on the Nature and Significance of Economic Science* (1932)

Robbins, L C, *The Great Depression* (1934)

Robbins, L C, *The Theory of Economic Policy in English Classical Political Economy* (1952)

Robbins, L C, *Robert Torrens and the Evolution of Classical Economics* (1958)

Robbins, L C (Lord), *The Theory of Economic Development in the History of Economic Thought* (1968)

Robbins, L C (Lord), *The Evolution of Modern Economic Theory and Other Papers in the History of Economic Thought* (1970)

Robbins, L C, (Lord), *Autobiography of an Economist* (1971)

Robertson, D H, *A Study of Industrial Fluctuation* (1915)

Robertson, D H, *Money* (1922)

Robertson, D H, *The Control of Industry* (1923)

Robertson, D H, *Banking Policy and the Price Level* (1926)

Robertson, D H, *Economic Fragments* (1931)

Robertson, D H, *Essays in Monetary Theory* (1940)

Robertson, D H, *Utility and All That and Other Essays* (1952)

Robertson, D H, *Economic Commentaries* (1956)

Robertson, D H, *Lectures on Economic Principles,* 3 vols. (1957–59)

Robertson, D H, *Growth, Wages, Money* (1961)

Robinson, J, *The Economics of Imperfect Competition* (1933)

Robinson, J, *Economic Philosophy* (1962)

Robinson, J, ed., *After Keynes* (1973)

Robson, J M, *The Improvement of Mankind. The Social and Political Thought of John Stuart Mill* (1968)

Roll, Sir E, *A History of Economic Thought* (1973)

Ryan, A, *The Philosophy of John Stuart Mill* (1970)

Sait, E M, ed., *Masters of Political Thought,* 3 vols. (1942–1959)

Samuels, W J, *The Classical Theory of Economic Policy* (1966)

Schumpeter, J A, *History of Economic Analysis* (1954)

Schwarz, P, *The New Political Economy of J S Mill* (1972)

Scott, W R, *Adam Smith as Student and Professor* (1937)

Shackle, G L S, *The Years of High Theory. Invention and Tradition in Economic Thought* (1967)

Sheppard, J T *et al, John Maynard Keynes 1883–1946* (1949)

Shoup, C, *Ricardo on Taxation* (1960)

Sidgwick, A, and Sidgwick, E M, *Henry Sidgwick. A Memoir* (1906)

Skinner, A S, and Wilson, T, *Essays on Adam Smith* (1975)

Smith, K, *The Malthusian Controversy* (1951)

Smith, P, *Disraelian Conservatism and Social Reform* (1967)

Sowell, T, *Say's Law. An Historical Analysis* (1972)

Sowell, T, *Classical Economics Reconsidered* (1974)

Spencer, H, *The Man versus the State* (1909)

Stephen, Sir L, *The English Utilitarians,* 3 vols. (1900)

Taussig, F W, *Wages and Capital. An Examination of the Wages Fund Doctrine* (1896)

Terrill, R, *R H Tawney and his Times. Socialism as Fellowship* (1974)

Thirlwall, A P, ed., *Keynes and International Monetary Relations* (1976)

Toynbee, A, *Lectures on the Industrial Revolution of the 18th Century in England. Popular Addresses, Notes and other Fragments* (1902)

Vickers, D, *Studies in the Theory of Money 1690–1776* (1959)

Viner, J, *Studies in the Theory of International Trade* (1937)

Viner, J, *The Long View and the Short* (1958)

Wallas, G, *Human Nature in Politics* (1908)

Wallas, G, *The Great Society* (1914)

Wallas, G, *Men and Ideas* (1940)

Watson, G, *The English Ideology. Studies in the Language of Victorian Politics* (1973)

Webb, B, *My Apprenticeship* (1926)

Webb, B, *Our Partnership* (1948)

Webb, R K, *Harriet Martineau. A Radical Victorian* (1960)

Webb, S, *Socialism in England* (1890)

Webb, S, *Twentieth Century Politics. A Policy of National Efficiency* (1906)

Webb, S, and Webb, B, *A Constitution for the Socialist Commonwealth of Great Britain* (1920)

Webb, S, and Webb, B, *The Decay of Capitalist Civilization* (1923)

Webb, S, and Webb, B, *Soviet Communism. A New Civilization?* (1935)

White, R J, ed., *The Political Thought of Samuel Taylor Coleridge* (1938)

White, R J, ed., *The Conservative Tradition,* 2nd edn. (1964)

Wiener, M J, *Between Two Worlds. The Political Thought of Graham Wallas* (1971)

Willey, B, *The Seventeenth Century Background* (1934)

Willey, B, *The Eighteenth Century Background* (1940)

Willey, B, *Nineteenth Century Studies. Coleridge to Matthew Arnold* (1949)

Willey, B, *Samuel Taylor Coleridge* (1972)

Winch, D, *Classical Political Economy and Colonies* (1965)

Wolin, S S, *Politics and Vision. Continuity and Innovation in Western Political Thought* (1961)

III The Development of the Machinery and Functions of Government since 1780

Abramovitz, M and Eliasberg, V F, *The Growth of Public Employment in Great Britain* (1957)

Addison, P, *The Road to 1945. British Politics and the Second World War* (1975)

Aitken, H J, ed., *The State and Economic Growth* (1959)

Aldcroft, D H, and Fearon, P, eds., *Economic Growth in Twentieth Century Britain* (1969)

Allen, B M, *Sir Robert Morant. A Great Public Servant* (1934)

Allen, V L, *Trade Unions and the Government* (1960)

Anderson, Sir J, *The Machinery of Government* (1946)

Anderson, Sir J, *Administrative Technique in the Public Service* (1949)

Anderson, O, *A Liberal State at War. English Politics and Economics during the Crimean War* (1967)

Ashton, T S, *An Economic History of Britain. The Eighteenth Century* (1955)

Aylmer, G E, *The State's Servants. The Civil Service of the English Republic 1649–1660* (1973)

Aylmer, G E, *The King's Servants. The Civil Servants of Charles I 1625–1642,* 2nd edn. (1974)

Ballin, H H, *The Organization of the Electricity Supply in Great Britain* (1946)

Barnes, D G, *A History of the English Corn Laws 1660–1846* (1930)

Barnett, C, *Britain and Her Army 1509–1970. A Military, Political and Social Survey* (1970)

Barnett, C, *The Collapse of British Power* (1972)

Bartlett, C J ed., *Britain Pre-eminent. Studies of British World Influence in the Nineteenth Century* (1969)

Baugh, D A, *British Naval Administration in the Age of Walpole* (1965)

Baxter, S B, *The Development of the Treasury 1660–1702* (1957)

Beckingsale, B W, *Burghley. Tudor Statesman 1520–1598* (1967)

Bell, H C F, *Lord Palmerston,* 2 vols (1936) (now Cass)

Beloff, M, *New Dimensions in Foreign Policy. A Study in British Administrative Experience* (1961)

Benians, E A, Butler, J R M, Mansergh, P N S, and Walker, E A, eds., *The Cambridge History of the British Empire,* 9 vols (1929–59)

Bennett, Sir J A Wheeler-, *John Anderson. Lord Waverley* (1962)

Best, G F A, *Temporal Pillars. Queen Anne's Bounty, the Ecclesiastical Commissioners and the Church of England* (1964)

Beveridge, J, *Beveridge and his Plan* (1954)

Beveridge, Sir W H, *Insurance for All and for Everything* (1924)

Beveridge, Sir W H, *The Past and Present of Unemployment Insurance* (1930)

Beveridge, Sir W H, *Unemployment. A Problem of Industry,* 2nd ed (1930)

Beveridge, Sir W H, *The Pillars of Security* (1943)

Beveridge, Sir W H, *Full Employment in a Free Society* (1944)

Beveridge, Sir W H, *Why I am a Liberal* (1945)

Beveridge, Lord, *Voluntary Action* (1948)

Beveridge, Lord, *Power and Influence* (1953)

Beveridge, Lord, and Wells, A F, *The Evidence for Voluntary Action* (1949)

Bigge, Sir L A Selby-, *The Board of Education* (1927)

Binney, J E D, *British Public Finance and Administration 1774–92* (1958)

Blank, S, *Industry and Government in Britain. The Federation of British Industries in Politics 1945–65* (1973)

Boardman, R, and Groom, A J R eds., *The Management of Britain's External Relations* (1973)

Bodelsen, C A, *Studies in Mid-Victorian Imperialism* (1960)

Booth, C, ed., *Life and Labour of the People in London,* 17 vols (1892–1902)

Bourne, K, *Britain and the Balance of Power in North America 1815–1908* (1967)

Bowley, M, *Housing and the State 1919–1944* (1945)

Brand, J L, *Doctors and the State* (1965)

Bridges, Lord, *The Treasury,* 2nd edn (1966)

Briggs, A, *Social Thought and Social Action. A Study of the Work of Seebohm Rowntree 1871–1954* (1961)

Brittan, S, *Steering the Economy. The Role of the Treasury* (1970)

Brockington, C F, *Public Health in the Nineteenth Century* (1965)

Brown, B H, *The Tariff Reform Movement in Great Britain 1881–1895* (1943)

Brown, L, *The Board of Trade and the Free Trade Movement 1830–1842* (1958)

Brown, R G S, *The Changing National Health Service* (1973)

Brown, R G S, *The Management of Welfare. A Study of British Social Service Administration* (1975)

Brownlie, I, *The Law relating to Public Order* (1968)

Bunbury, Sir H L ed., *Lloyd George's Ambulance Wagon. Being the Memoirs of William J Braithwaite 1911–1912* (1957)

Burn, D L, *The Age of Equipoise. A Study of the Mid-Victorian Generation* (1964)

Butler, Lord, *The Art of the Possible* (1971)

Cameron, R E ed., *Banking and Economic Development. Some Lessons of History* (1972)

Campion, Lord *et al, British Government since 1918* (1950)

Cell, J W, *British Colonial Administration in the Mid-Nineteenth Century. The Policy Making Process* (1970)

Chaloner, W H, *People and Industries* (Frank Cass, 1963)

Chambers, J D, and Mingay, G E, *The Agricultural Revolution 1750–1880* (1968)

Chester, D N ed., *Lessons of the British War Economy* (1951)

Chester, D N, *Central and Local Government. Financial and Administrative Relations* (1951)

Chester, Sir, D N, *The Nationalization of British Industry 1945–51* (1975)

Chester, D N, and Willson, F M G, *The Organization of British Central Government 1914–64,* 2nd edn. (1968)

Churchill, W S, *Great Contemporaries* (1949)

Churchill, W S, *The Second World War,* 6 vols (1948–54)

Clapham, J H, *An Economic History of Modern Britain,* 3 vols (1926–38)

Clapham, Sir J H, *The Bank of England. A History,* 2 vols (1944)

Clark, D M, *The Rise of the British Treasury. Colonial Administration in the Eighteenth Century* (1960)

Clark, G S R Kitson, *The Making of Victorian England* (1962)

Clark, G S R Kitson, *An Expanding Society. Britain 1830–1900* (1967)

Clark, G S R Kitson, *Churchmen and the Condition of England 1832–1885* (1973)

Clarkson, L A, *The Pre-Industrial Economy in England 1500–1750* (1971)

Clay, Sir H, *Lord Norman* (1957)

Clough, S B, *France. A History of National Economics 1789–1939* (1964)

Coleman, D C ed., *Revisions in Mercantilism* (1969)

Cramond, R D, *Housing Policy in Scotland 1919–1964. A Study in State Assistance* (1966)

Critchley, T A, *A History of Police in England and Wales 900–1966* (1967)

Critchley, T A, *The Conquest of Violence. Order and Liberty in Britain* (1970)

Crombie, Sir J, *Her Majesty's Customs and Excise* (1962)

Crosland, C A R, *The Future of Socialism* (1956)

Daalder, H, *Cabinet Reform in Britain 1914–1963* (1964)

Dale, H E, *The Higher Civil Service in Great Britain* (1941)

Dalton, Lord, *Memoirs,* 3 vols (1953–62)

Dangerfield, G, *The Strange Death of Liberal England 1910–1914* (1935)

Deane, P, and Cole, W A, *British Economic Growth 1688–1959* (1962)

De Cecco, M, *Money and Empire. The International Gold Standard 1890–1914* (1974)

Dickson, F M G, *The Financial Revolution in England. A Study in the Development of Public Credit 1688–1756* (1967)

Djang, T K, *Factory Inspection in Great Britain* (1942)

Donnison, D V, *The Government of Housing* (1967)

Donnison, D V, *et al, Social Policy and Administration Revisited. Studies in the Development of Social Services at the Local Level* (1975)

Dow, J C R, *The Management of the British Economy 1945–60* (1964)

Eckstein, H, *The English Health Service* (1958)

Edsall, N C, *The Anti-Poor Law Movement 1834–44* (1971)

Ellis, K, *The Post Office in the Eighteenth Century. A Study in Administrative History* (1958)

Elton, G R, *The Tudor Revolution in Government. Administrative Changes in the Reign of Henry VIII* (1953)

Elton, G R, ed., *The Tudor Constitution. Documents and Commentary* (1960)

Elton, G R, *Henry VIII. An Essay in Revision* (1962)

Elton, G R, *Policy and Police. The Enforcement of the Reformation in the Age of Thomas Cromwell* (1972)

Elton, G R, *Reform and Renewal. Thomas Cromwell and the Common Weal* (1973)

Elton, G R, *Studies in Tudor and Stuart Politics and Government,* 2 vols (1974)

Elton, G R, *England under the Tudors,* 2nd edn (1974)

Evans, F M G, *The Principal Secretary of State. A Survey of the Office from 1558 to 1660* (1923)

Feiling, K, *The Life of Neville Chamberlain* (1946)

Ferguson, S, and Fitzgerald, H, *Studies in the Social Services* (1954)

Ferguson, T, *The Dawn of Scottish Social Welfare* (1948)

Ferguson, T, *Scottish Social Welfare 1864–1914* (1958)

Fiddes, Sir G V, *The Dominions and Colonial Offices* (1926)

Fieldhouse, D K, *The Colonial Empires. A Comparative Survey from the Eighteenth Century* (1965)

Fieldhouse, D K, *Economics and Empire 1830–1914* (1973)

Finer, H, *Municipal Trading* (1941)

Finer, S E, *The Life and Times of Sir Edwin Chadwick* (1952)

Foot, M M, *Aneurin Bevan. A Biography,* 2 vols (1962–73)

Foster, W, *The East India House. Its History and Associations* (1924)

Fraser, D ed., *The New Poor Law in the Nineteenth Century* (1976)

Fry, G K, *Statesmen in Disguise. The Changing Role of the Administrative Class of the British Home Civil Service 1853–1966* (1969)

Fuller, J F C, *The Conduct of War 1789–1961* (1961)

Furse, Sir R, *Aucuparious. Recollections of a Recruiting Officer* (1962)

Galbraith, J S, *Reluctant Empire. British Policy on the South African Frontier 1834–1854* (1963)

Gash, N, *Politics in the Age of Peel. A Study in the Techniques of Parliamentary Representation* (1953)

Gash, N, *Mr Secretary Peel. The Life of Sir Robert Peel to 1830* (1961)

Gash, N, *Sir Robert Peel. The Life of Sir Robert Peel after 1830* (1972)

Gauldie, E, *Cruel Habitations. A History of Working Class Housing 1780–1918* (1974)

Gerschenkron, A, *Economic Backwardness in Historical Perspective* (1962)

Giddings, P J, *Marketing Boards and Ministers* (1974)

Gilbert, B B, *The Evolution of National Insurance in Great Britain* (1966)

Gilbert, B B, *British Social Policy 1914–1939* (1970)

Gooch, J, *The Plans for War. The General Staff and British Military Strategy 1900–1916* (1974)

Gordon, H, *The War Office* (1935)

Gordon, L, *The Public Corporation in Great Britain* (1938)

Gosden, P H J H, *The Friendly Societies in England 1815–1875* (1961)

Gosden, P H J H, *The Development of Educational Administration in England and Wales* (1966)

Grenville, J A S, *Lord Salisbury and Foreign Policy. The Close of the Nineteenth Century* (1964)

Hague, D C, Mackenzie, W J M, and Barker, A, *Public Policy and Private Interests* (1975)

Hall, H L, *The Colonial Office. A History* (1937)

Hall, P, Land, H, Parker, R, and Webb, A, *Change, Choice and Conflict in Social Policy* (1975)

Hamer, W S, *The British Army. Civil-Military Relations 1885–1905* (1970)

Hancock, W K, *Survey of British Commonwealth Affairs,* 2 vols (1937–42)

Hancock, W K, and Gowing, M M, *British War Economy* (1949)

Hanham, H J, *Elections and Party Management. Politics in the time of Disraeli and Gladstone* (1959)

Hanham, H J, *The Reformed Electoral System in Great Britain 1832–1914* (1968)

Hanham, H J, *The Nineteenth Century Constitution 1815–1914. Documents and Commentary* (1969)

Hanson, A H, *Parliament and Public Ownership* (1961)

Hanson, A H ed., *Nationalization. A Book of Readings* (1963)

Harlow, V T, *The Founding of the Second British Empire 1763–1793,* 2 vols (1952–64)

Harris, J F, *Unemployment and Politics 1886–1914* (1972)

Harris, J S, *British Government Inspection. The Local Services and the Central Departments* (1955)

Harris, N, *Competition and the Corporate State. British Conservatives, the State and Industry 1945–1964* (1972)

Hart, J M, *The British Police* (1951)

Hartwell, R M ed., *Causes of the Industrial Revolution in England* (1967)

Hawke, G R, *Railways and Economic Growth in England and Wales 1840–1870* (1970)

Heckscher, E F, *Mercantilism*, 2nd edn, 2 vols (1955)

Heclo, H, and Wildavsky, A B, *The Private Government of Public Money* (1974)

Henderson, W O, *The State and the Industrial Revolution in Prussia 1748–1870* (1958)

Henderson, W O, *The Industrial Revolution on the Continent. Germany, France, Russia 1800–1914* (1961) (now Cass)

Hepworth, N P, *The Finance of Local Government*, 2nd edn (1971)

Heussler, R, *Yesterday's Rulers. The Making of the British Colonial Service* (1963)

Hibbs, J, *The History of British Bus Services* (1968)

Hicks, Sir J R, *A Theory of Economic History* (1969)

Hicks, U K, *The Finance of British Government 1920–1936* (1938)

Hicks, U K, *British Public Finances. Their Structure and Development 1880–1952* (1954)

Hodgkinson, R G, *The Origins of the National Health Service. The Medical Services of the New Poor Law 1834–1871* (1967)

Holdsworth, Sir W S, *A History of English Law*, 17 vols (1936 –72)

Holmes, G S, *British Politics in the Age of Anne* (1967)

Holmes, G S ed., *Britain after the Glorious Revolution 1689–1714* (1969)

Honigsbaum, F, *The Struggle for the Ministry of Health 1914–1919* (1970)

Hoon, E E, *The Organization of the English Customs System 1696–1786* (1968)

Horn, D B, *The British Diplomatic Service 1689–1789* (1961)

Howard, C, *Splendid Isolation* (1967)

Howard, C, *Britain and the Casus Belli 1822–1902* (1974)

Howard, M ed., *Soldiers and Governments. Nine Studies in Civil-Military Relations* (1957)

Howard, M, *Studies in War and Peace* (1970)

Howard, M, *The Continental Commitment. The Dilemma of British Defence Policy in the Era of two World Wars* (1972)

Howson, S, and Winch, D, *The Economic Advisory Council 1930–1939* (1977)

Hughes, E, *Studies in Administration and Finance 1558–1825* (1934)

Humphreys, B V, *Clerical Unions in the Civil Service* (1958)

Hunt, B C, *The Development of the Business Corporation in England 1800–1867* (1936)

Hurstfield, J, *The Queen's Wards* (1958) (now Cass)

Hutchins, B L, and Harrison, A, *A History of Factory Legislation* (1903)

Hutchinson, Sir H, *Tariff Making and Industrial Reconstruction. An Account of the work of the Import Duties Advisory Committee 1932–39* (1965)

Imlah. A H, *Economic Elements in the Pax Britannica. Studies in British Foreign Trade in the Nineteenth Century* (1958)

Ince, Sir G, *The Ministry of Labour and National Service* (1960)

Jackson, R M, *The Machinery of Local Government*, 2nd edn (1965)

Jackson, R M, *The Machinery of Justice in England,* 6th edn (1972)

James, A ed., *The Bases of International Order* (1973)

Jeffries, C, *The Colonial Empire and its Civil Service* (1938)

Jeffries, Sir C, *Whitehall and the Colonial Service. An Administrative Memoir 1939–1956* (1972)

Jenkins, Sir G, *The Ministry of Transport and Civil Aviation* (1959)

Johnson, F A, *Defence by Committee. The British Committee of Imperial Defence 1885–1959* (1960)

Johnson, P B, *Land Fit for Heroes. The Planning of British Reconstruction 1916–1919* (1968)

Johnston, Sir A, *The Inland Revenue* (1962)

Jones, G Stedman, *Outcast London. A Study in the Relationship between Classes in Victorian Society* (1971)

Jones, J H, *Josiah Stamp. Public Servant* (1964)

Jones, K, *A History of the Mental Health Services* (1972)

Jones, R, *The Nineteenth Century Foreign Office* (1971)

Jordan, W K, *Philanthropy in England 1480–1660* (1959)

Keith, A B, *Constitutional History of the First British Empire* (1930)

Kemp, B, *King and Commons 1660–1832* (1959)

Kenyon, J P ed., *The Stuart Constitution 1603–1688. Documents and Commentary* (1966)

Kerridge, E, *The Agricultural Revolution* (1967)

Kieve, J, *The Electric Telegraph. A Social and Economic History* (1973)

Kindleberger, C P, *Economic Growth in France and Britain 1851–1950* (1964)

Kindleberger, C P, *The World in Depression 1929–1939* (1973)

King, Sir G S, *The Ministry of Pensions and National Insurance* (1958)

Kingsley, J D, *Representative Bureaucracy. An Interpretation of the British Civil Service* (1944)

Knaplund, P, *James Stephen and the British Colonial System 1813–1847* (1953)

Knowles, L C A, *The Economic Development of the British Overseas Empire,* 3 vols (1924–36)

Koebner, R, *Empire* (1961)

Koebner, R and Schmidt H D, *Imperialism. The Story and Significance of a Political Word 1840–1960* (1964)

Kubicek, R V, *The Administration of Imperialism. Joseph Chamberlain at the Colonial Office* (1969)

Lambert, R, *Sir John Simon 1816–1904 and English Social Administration* (1903)

Landes, D S, *The Unbound Prometheus. Technological Change and Industrial Development in Western Europe from 1750 to the Present* (1969)

Lee, J M, *Reviewing the Machinery of Government 1942–1952. An Essay on the Anderson Committee and its Successors* (1977)

Lewis, R A, *Edwin Chadwick and the Public Health Movement 1832–1854* (1952)

Lipson, E, *A Planned Economy or Free Enterprise. The Lessons of History* (1944)

Lockwood, W W ed., *The State and Economic Enterprise in Japan. Essays in the Political Economy of Growth* (1965)

Longmate, N, *King Cholera. The Biography of a Disease* (1966)

Lowndes, G A N, *The Silent Social Revolution. An Account of the Expansion of Public Education in England and Wales 1895–1965* (1969)

Lucas, A F, *Industrial Reconstruction and the Control of Competition. The British Experiments* (1937)

MacAdam, E, *The New Philanthropy* (1934)

MacDonagh, O O G M, *A Pattern of Government Growth 1800–60. The Passenger Acts and Their Enforcement* (1961)

McDowell, R B, *The Irish Administration 1801–1914* (1964)

McGuire, E B, *The British Tariff System*, 2nd edn (1951)

Mackintosh, J P, *The British Cabinet*, 3rd edn (1977)

Macleod, R M, *Treasury Control and Social Administration* (1968)

Macrosty, H W, *The Trust Movement in British Industry. A Study of Business Organization* (1907)

Mansergh, N, *The Irish Question 1840–1921* (1965)

Mansergh, N, *The Commonwealth Experience* (1969)

Marder, A J, *The Anatomy of British Sea Power. A History of British Naval Policy in the Pre-Dreadnought Era 1880–1905* (1964) (now Cass)

Marder, A J, *From the Dreadnought to Scapa Flow. The Royal Navy in the Fisher Era 1904–1919*, 5 vols (1961–70)

Marshall, G, *Police and Government. The Status and Accountability of the English Constable* (1965)

Martin, G, *The Durham Report and British Policy. A Critical Essay* (1972)

Martin, L W, *British Defence Policy. The Long Recessional* (1969)

Midwinter, E C, *Social Administration in Lancashire 1830–1860* (1969)

Millett, J D, *The Unemployment Assistance Board. A Case Study in Administrative Autonomy* (1940)

Millward, A S, and Saul, S B, *The Economic Development of Continental Europe* (1973)

Mitchell, B R, *Abstract of British Historical Statistics* (1967)

Mitchell, J, *Crisis in Britain 1951* (1963)

Mitchell, J, *Groundwork to Economic Planning* (1966)

Mitchell, J, *The National Board for Prices and Incomes* (1972)

Moggridge, D E, *British Monetary Policy 1924–1931. The Norman Conquest of $4.86* (1972)

Moir, E, *The Justice of the Peace* (1964)

Morgan, E V, *The Theory and Practice of Central Banking 1797–1913* (1943)

Morgan, E V, *Studies in British Financial Policy 1914–25* (1952)

Mountfield, S, *Western Gateway. A History of the Mersey Docks and Harbour Board* (1965)

Mowat, C L, *The Charity Organization Society 1869–1913* (1961)

Namier, Sir L, *Personalities and Powers* (1955)

Natan, A ed., *Silver Renaissance. Essays in Eighteenth Century English History* (1961)

Nevin, E, *The Mechanism of Cheap Money. A Study of British Monetary Policy 1931–1939* (1955)

Newsam, Sir F, *The Home Office* (1954)

Nicolson, H, *Diplomacy,* 3rd edn (1963)

Orwin, C S, and Whetham, E H, *History of British Agriculture 1846–1914* (1964)

Owen, D, *English Philanthropy 1660–1960* (1965)

Oxley, G W, *Poor Relief in England and Wales 1601–1834* (1974)

Parris, H, *Government and the Railways in Nineteenth Century Britain* (1965)

Parris, H, *Constitutional Bureaucracy. The Development of British Central Administration since the Eighteenth Century* (1969)

Peacock, A T, and Robertson, D J eds., *Public Expenditure. Appraisal and Control* (1963)

Peacock, A T, and Wiseman, J, *The Growth of Public Expenditure in the United Kingdom,* 2nd edn (1967)

Pigou, A C, *Aspects of British Economic History 1918–1925* (1947) (now Cass)

Platt, D C M, *Finance, Trade, and Politics in British Foreign Policy 1815–1914* (1968)

Polanyi, G, *Comparative Returns from Investment in Nationalized Industries* (1968)

Polanyi, G, *Contrasts in Nationalized Transport since 1947* (1968)

Political and Economic Planning, *Report on the British Health Services* (1937)

Political and Economic Planning, *Report on the British Social Services* (1937)

Postan, M M, *British War Production* (1952)

Poynter, J R, *Society and Pauperism. English Ideas on Poor Relief 1795–1834* (1969)

Prouty, R, *The Transformation of the Board of Trade 1830–1855* (1957)

Pryke, R, *Public Enterprise in Practice. The British Experience of Nationalization over Two Decades* (1971)

Raphael, M, *Pensions and Public Servants. A Study of the Origins of the British System* (1964)

Rathbone, E, *The Disinherited Family* (1924)

Redlich, J, and Hirst, F W, *The History of Local Government in England* 2nd edn (1970)

Richards, P G, *The Reformed Local Government System,* 2nd edn (1975)

Richardson, H W, *Economic Recovery in Britain 1931–9* (1967)

Roberts, C, *The Growth of Responsible Government in Stuart England* (1968)

Roberts, D, *Victorian Origins of the British Welfare State* (1960)

Robinson, H, *The British Post Office. A History* (1948)

Robinson, R, Gallagher, J, and Denny, A, *Africa and the Victorians. The Official Mind of Imperialism* (1963)

Robson, W A ed., *Public Enterprise. Developments in Social Ownership and Control in Great Britain* (1937)

Robson, W A ed., *The British Civil Servant* (1937)
Robson, W A, *The Government and Misgovernment of London*, 2nd edn (1948)
Robson, W A, *The Development of Local Government*, 2nd edn (1948)
Robson, W A, *Justice and Administrative Law*, 3rd edn (1951)
Robson, W A, *Nationalized Industry and Public Ownership*, 2nd edn (1962)
Rosencrance, R N, *Defense of the Realm. British Strategy in the Nuclear Epoch* (1968)
Roseveare, H, *The Treasury. The Evolution of a British Institution* (1969)
Roseveare, H, *The Treasury 1660–1870. The Foundations of Control* (1973)
Roskill, S, *Hankey. Man of Secrets*, 3 vols (1970–74)
Rowntree, B S, *Poverty. A Study of Town Life* (1901)
Rowntree, B S, *Poverty and Progress. A Second Social Survey of York* (1941)
Rowntree, B S, and Lavers, G R, *Poverty and the Welfare State. A Third Social Survey of York* (1951)
Sabine, B E V, *A History of Income Tax* (1965)
Sayers, R S, *Financial Policy 1939–45* (1956)
Sayers, R S, *Central Banking after Bagehot* (1957)
Sayers, R S, *The Bank of England 1891–1944*, 3 vols (1976)
Scotland, J, *The History of Scottish Education*, 2 vols (1969)
Searle, G R, *The Quest for National Efficiency. A Study in British Politics and Political Thought 1899–1914* (1971)
Self, P, and Storing, H, *The State and the Farmer* (1962)
Semmel, B, *Imperialism and Social Reform. English Social-Imperial Thought 1895–1914* (1960)
Semmel, B, *The Rise of Free Trade Imperialism* (1970)
Shehab, F, *Progressive Taxation* (1953)
Shonfield, A, *Modern Capitalism. The Changing Balance of Public and Private Power* (1965)
Simey, T S, *Principles of Social Administration* (1937)
Simey, T S, and M B, *Charles Booth. Social Scientist* (1960)
Skidelsky, R, *Politicians and the Slump. The Labour Government of 1929–1931* (1967)
Smellie, K B, *A Hundred Years of English Government*, 2nd edn (1950)
Smith, Sir H Llewellyn, *The Board of Trade* (1928)
Snow, C P, *Variety of Men* (1967)
Snyder, W P, *The Politics of British Defence Policy 1945–1962* (1964)
Spoor, A, *White Collar Unionism. Sixty Years of NALGO* (1967)
Steiner, Z, *The Foreign Office and Foreign Policy 1898–1914* (1969)
Strang, Lord, *The Foreign Office* (1955)
Strang, Lord, *The Diplomatic Career* (1962)
Supple, B E, *The State and the Industrial Revolution* (1971)
Sutherland, G ed., *Studies in the Growth of Nineteenth Century Government* (1972)
Sutherland, G, *Policy Making in Elementary Education 1870–1895* (1973)
Tarn, J N, *Five Per Cent Philanthropy. An Account of Housing in Urban Areas 1840–1914* (1973)

Thomson, M A, *The Secretaries of State 1681–1782* (1932) (now Cass)

Thomson, M A, *A Constitutional History of England 1642–1801* (1938)

Thornton, A P, *The Imperial Idea and its Enemies* (1959)

Titmuss, R M, *Problems of Social Policy* (1950)

Titmuss, R M, *Income Distribution and Social Change* (1962)

Titmuss, R M, *Essays on 'The Welfare State'* (1963)

Titmuss, R M, *Commitment to Welfare* (1968)

Titmuss, R M, *The Gift Relationship. From Human Blood to Social Policy* (1970)

Troup, Sir E, *The Home Office,* 2nd edn (1926)

Varcoe, I M, *Organizing for Science in Britain. A Case Study* (1974)

Vernon, R V, and Mansergh N, ed., *Advisory Bodies. A Study of their Uses to Central Government 1919–1939* (1940)

Ward, Sir A W, and Gooch, G P, eds., *The Cambridge History of British Foreign Policy 1783–1919,* 3 vols (1922–23)

Webb, S and B, *English Local Government,* 11 vols (Cass, 1963 edn)

Williams, E N ed., *The Eighteenth Century Constitution 1688–1815. Documents and Commentary* (1960)

Wilson, J H, *The Labour Government 1964–70* (1971)

Winch, D, *Economics and Policy. A Historical Study* (1969)

Winnifrith, Sir A J D, *The Ministry of Agriculture, Fisheries and Food* (1962)

Woodruff, P, *The Men Who Ruled India,* 2 vols (1954)

Worswick, G D N, and Ady, P H, eds., *The British Economy 1945–1950* (1952)

Worswick, G D N, and Ady, P H, eds., *The British Economy in the 1950s* (1962)

Wright, M, *Treasury Control of the Civil Service 1855–1874* (1969)

Young, D M, *The Colonial Office in the Early Nineteenth Century* (1961)

Young, G M, *Victorian England. Portrait of an Age* (1937)

Zimmern, A, *The Third British Empire* (1926)

Index

Abdication, 1936, 165, 166, 174
Addington, 102
agriculture: Act, 1947, 203;
Marketing Acts, 1931 *and* 1933,
186; 19th C., 140–1; post-war,
222–3
America: anti-imperialism, 211–12;
Britain's relations with, 125, 214;
fear of Soviet Communism, 203;
Lend-Lease, 202; Marshall Aid,
203, 218; New Deal, 196; role,
World War I, 179
Amery, Leopold, 174, 175, 184
Anderson, John, 121, 161, 172–3;
on collective responsibility, 207;
and General Strike, 172
Anglo-French Commercial Treaty,
1786, 103; 1860, 138
Anglo-Iranian Oil Dispute, 1951,
203
Anglo-Japanese Alliance, 1902, 124
Anglo-Persian Oil Co, 151
Ashley, Wilfred, 187
Ashton-Gwatkin, Frank, 214
Asquith, Herbert H., 1, 41, 62, 152,
165–6, 172
Attlee, Clement, 206
Authority, 69, 79, 83, 88

Bacon, Francis, 95
Baldwin, Stanley, 166–7, 172, 179,
181; and defence research, 178;
and foreign policy, 167; and
public corporations, 187–9
Balfour, Arthur, 149
Balfour Declaration, 1926, 174
Bank Charter Act, 1844, 24, 153
Bank of England: importance inter-
war, 183; nationalization, 218,
223
banking system: Bank Rate, 183;
19th C., 153; Ricardo and, 23–4;
Smith and, 13

Bentham, Jeremy, 10, 15–22, 29,
37: and administration of justice,
115; on centralization, 35; changing views, 15–16; *Constitutional
Code*, 16, 19–20; on defence, 17;
on Free Trade, 21; on increase of
wealth, 16–17, 21; and *laissez-
faire*, 16, 22; radicalism, 20–1;
on representative democracy, 20;
on role of government, 15–22; on
social welfare, 16, 17–19;
socialism and, 41; on statistics,
20; on taxation, 20–1; utilitarianism, 16, 20, 40
Bevan, Aneurin: on housing, 228;
and National Health Service,
228
Beveridge, Sir William, 1, 42, 137
Beveridge Report 1942, 1, 88, 198,
200–1; Conservative Party and,
201; implementation, 201, 206;
Labour Party and, 201, 206
Bevin, Ernest, 184; in Cabinet, 204;
at Foreign Office, 214–15
Bitter Cry of Outcast London, The,
57
Blackstone, Sir William, 92
Bland, Hubert, 59
Board of Trade: changing functions, 132; and employment, 136–
7; and Foreign Office, 132, 138,
185; and industrial relations,
136–8; and industrial reconstruction, 185; inter-war changes,
185–6; Labour Party and, 221;
post-war functions, 220–1; and
private industry, 133; and public
utilities, 134–6; and transport,
133, 138, 185
Boer War, 62, 120, 122, 123–4, 143
Booth, Charles, 57, 143
Bosanquet, Bernard, 52, 54
Braithwaite, W. B., 151

forms, 122, 123; Churchill and, 212; Committee of Imperial Defence, 124; conscription, 179, 212; government employment in, 162; government function, 1, 4, 92; Haldane reforms, 124; Hore-Belisha reforms, 179; Imperial General Staff, 124; Lloyd George and, 175–8; Macmillan and, 213; Ministry of, 213; Ministry of Munitions, 175–6, 178; nuclear, 212–13; and public expenditure, 3, 96, 128–9; rearmament, 178–9; Smith and, 12–13; Suez, 212–13, 214, 215;
White Paper, 1935, 178; 1957, 212;
World War I, 171, 175–7; *see also* War Departments

de Gaulle, Charles, 205

democracy: democratic socialism, 168; liberal, 29, 233; Mill on, 32–3; parliamentary, 92, 110; representative, 20, 33, 61, 111; trade unions and, 67; Webbs on, 64

Depressions, 132, 163, 184, 194–5; Pigou on, 192

Dicey, A. V., 16

Diplomatic Service, 124, 126, 139; Eden reforms, 214; merger with Foreign Office, 180; Plowden Report, 1964, 215

Disraeli, Benjamin, 43; and extension of Conservative support, 112; nationalism, 124

Durham, Lord, *Report on the Affairs of British North America*, 119–20

dynamic economics, 83, 87

East India Co, 97, 99, 103, 120, 139

economic theory, change in basis, 78–9

Economical Reform, 91, 96, 98, 108; Burke and, 94; Pitt and, 94, 102

Economist, The, 36

Eden, Anthony, Foreign Service reforms, 214–15

Eden, Sir Frederick, 104

education:
Act, 1870, 52, 149; 1902, 149–50; 1944, 201;
Board of, 149; Charity Commissioners and, 149; Classical Economists and, 37; Educational Reform, 94; Green on, 46, 49–50; Marshall on, 71; Mill on, 30; 19th C., 148–50; post-war responsibility, 229; Privy Council Committee, 149; Scotland, 150; Senior on, 28; Smith on, 14; 'voluntary principle', 103–4; Webb on, 61

effective demand, 22–3

egalitarianism: Tawney, 58; Webb, 64

electricity industry, 187–9; Central Electricity Board, 187–9; Electricity (Supply) Act, 1926, 188, 210; Herbert Report, 226–7

employment: Acts of Parliament concerning, 137, 152; Board of Trade and, 136–7; equilibrium and, 82; exchanges, 150, 222; full, definition, 231; Keynes and, 76, 79–80, 82–3, 86–7; Managed Economy Welfare State and, 201–2; post-war responsibility, 222; Ricardian ('Treasury') theory, 22, 39, 70, 74–5, 79; saving and, 23; theory, beginnings, 83

Engels, Friedrich, 56–7; *Communist Manifesto*, 55–6

equilibrium, economic, and employment, 82

Esher Committee, 1904, 124

Europe, commitment, to, 209; European Economic Community, 214

Excise Bill, 1802, 101

expediency, Senior on, 27

World War I, 62, 63, 116, 120, 128, 141; America's role, 179; Armistice, 1918, 164; causes, 124; economic controls, 163–4; effect on Liberal Party, 166; effect on taxation and expenditure, 192; lasting repercussions, 171; Lloyd George and, 175–7; Versailles Settlement, 79, 171

World War II, 2, 78; declaration, 180; effect on economy, 202, 217; effect on social welfare reform, 198, 200; Empire support, 174; lack of preparation, 179

Yellow Book, 1928, 76, 189, 195